D0962359

Empire of the Fund

Birdthistle, William A.,
Empire of the fund :
the way we save now /
[2016]
33305240709901
sa   03/13/18

Empire of the Fund

The Way We Save Now

WILLIAM A. BIRDTHISTLE

OXFORD
UNIVERSITY PRESS

OXFORD
UNIVERSITY PRESS

Oxford University Press is a department of the University of Oxford. It furthers
the University's objective of excellence in research, scholarship, and education
by publishing worldwide. Oxford is a registered trade mark of Oxford University
Press in the UK and certain other countries.

Published in the United States of America by Oxford University Press
198 Madison Avenue, New York, NY 10016, United States of America.

© Oxford University Press 2016

All rights reserved. No part of this publication may be reproduced, stored in
a retrieval system, or transmitted, in any form or by any means, without the
prior permission in writing of Oxford University Press, or as expressly permitted
by law, by license, or under terms agreed with the appropriate reproduction
rights organization. Inquiries concerning reproduction outside the scope of the
above should be sent to the Rights Department, Oxford University Press, at the
address above.

You must not circulate this work in any other form
and you must impose this same condition on any acquirer.

Library of Congress Cataloging-in-Publication Data
Names: Birdthistle, William A., author.
Title: Empire of the fund : the way we save now / William A. Birdthistle.
Description: New York, NY : Oxford University Press, 2016. |
Includes bibliographical references and index.
Identifiers: LCCN 2016007563 | ISBN 9780199398560 (hardback)
Subjects: LCSH: Mutual funds—United States—History. |
Saving and investment—United States—History. | BISAC: BUSINESS & ECONOMICS /
Investments & Securities. | BUSINESS & ECONOMICS / Personal Finance / General. |
LAW / Business & Financial.
Classification: LCC HG4930 .B47 2016 | DDC 332.63/27—dc23
LC record available at http://lccn.loc.gov/2016007563

5 7 9 8 6 4
Printed by Edwards Brothers Malloy, United States of America

For Alison.

To Elspeth, Isolde, and Alana.

CONTENTS

PART III   ALTERNATIVE REMEDIES

PART IV   CURES

ACKNOWLEDGMENTS

I thank my colleagues and friends for their extremely helpful comments, especially Lori Andrews, Kathy Baker, Jack Bogle, Larry Cunningham, John Demers, Tamar Frankel, John Kastl, David LaCroix, David Lat, John L., John Morley, B. Carruthers McNamara, Frank Partnoy, John Rekenthaler, and Christopher Schmidt. Many students provided valuable research assistance, particularly Priya Gopalakrishnan, Gordon Klein, Matthew McElwee, Ashley Montalbano, and Jessica Ryou.

I thank Faber and Faber Limited for kind permission to quote the lines from Philip Larkin's poem, "Toads."

I greatly appreciate Scott Parris, Cathryn Vaulman, and Oxford University Press for their support of this project, Carole Berglie for her skillful editing, and Eunice Moyle for her stylish design.

I am most grateful for Alison, Elspeth, Isolde, and Alana.

Introduction

Nearly 80 million baby boomers will file for retirement benefits over
the next 20 years—an average of 10,000 per day.
— Social Security Administration,
Annual Performance Plan for Fiscal Year 2012

Over the past 30 years, America has embarked on a grand experiment—perhaps the richest and riskiest in our financial history—to change the way we save money. The hypothesis of our experiment is that millions of ordinary, untrained, and busy citizens can successfully manage trillions of dollars in a financial system dominated by wealthy, skilled, and powerful investment firms—firms that on many occasions have treated investors shabbily. As ten thousand baby boomers retire from the workforce each day and look to survive for almost two decades largely on the mutual funds in their personal accounts, we will soon learn whether our massive experiment has been a success. And if not, we will also soon discover just how enormous the costs of failure will be.

Just a single generation ago, large numbers of Americans enjoyed the protection of a pension offered by their employer. The typical pension guaranteed its beneficiaries a steady stream of payments from their retirement until their death. Together with the benefits of Social Security, pensions provided secure retirements to millions of working Americans.[1] The golden age of the pension, however, is effectively over. And it may at best have been merely gilded, for not once in the past thirty-five years did more than 40 percent of American workers ever participate in such a plan.[2]

Today, the benefits of Social Security and pensions look alarmingly inadequate. The average monthly benefit for retirees from Social Security is now $1,335, or just over $16,000 per year.[3] Pensions, meanwhile, have rapidly disappeared from our economic ecosystem: public pensions are underfunded by trillions of dollars,[4] and the number of U.S. private-sector workers covered solely by pensions has fallen to an all-time low of 3 percent.[5] Americans in the future will have to support themselves far more on the success or failure of their personal investment accounts.

We as a nation have chosen to entrust our savings not to large pools overseen by professional asset managers but instead to the smaller, individual accounts of almost 90 million investing amateurs. In the argot of the investment world, Americans are losing *defined benefit plans*, such as pensions, and are being directed into *defined contribution plans*, such as 401(k)s.

The rise of these individual accounts has, in turn, funneled massive amounts of retirement savings—more than $6.9 trillion—into one of the most popular investment options in personal accounts: the mutual fund. American investments have built an empire of 8,000 funds holding more than $16 trillion.[6]

The way we save now may enable some Americans to earn comfortable returns in the years ahead, but is also likely to leave many others disappointed. Though mutual funds and 401(k) plans may feel familiar to many of us, in fact they present a number of challenges and dangers to lay investors.

The primary consequences of our new approach, for instance, are that ordinary Americans now find themselves responsible for deciding whether to enroll in an investment account, what amount of each paycheck to contribute to that account, and how to invest those savings successfully for up to forty years of a career and for decades more in retirement. As Thomas Friedman observes, "It is a 401(k) world": "Government will do less for you. Companies will do less for you."[7]

Though the rhetoric of individual choice may appeal greatly to the American psyche, this change also brings personal liability for getting any of these difficult decisions wrong. And we *are* getting them wrong: approximately one-third of U.S. households currently have no retirement savings at all.[8] Of the remaining two-thirds, those who have accumulated nest eggs have enthusiastically vouchsafed them to the mutual fund. So if there are any problems in that particular basket, American investors will find themselves extremely exposed to those vulnerabilities.

As we will see, funds do suffer from a number of problems. By illustrating the structural vulnerabilities in mutual funds, the perverse incentives of fund managers, and the litany of scandals that have bedeviled the investment industry, this book attempts to forewarn and forearm Americans. To negotiate our new investing paradigm successfully, Americans will need a greater understanding of mutual funds, more transparency from the financial firms that manage them, and stronger enforcement by prosecutors of the regulations that govern funds.

This book also proposes an alternative way for Americans to invest their savings, one that is less expensive and more scrupulously managed than the mutual funds in which individuals can participate today. By pooling the bargaining strength of millions of investors into a powerful savings plan, Americans could enjoy the benefits of both individual control and economic security.

The Demise of the Pension

Unrest in the Midwest

February is no time to wander outside in Wisconsin. Certainly not without a compelling reason or the warmth of a grilled brat. In February 2011, the average high temperature in the state capital, Madison, was only 29.6 degrees Fahrenheit.[9] The Green Bay Packers won the Super Bowl in Texas that month,[10] but the last tailgate at Lambeau Field—prior to a satisfying home win over the Chicago Bears[11]—had been weeks before, on January 2. In any normal winter, citizens of the Badger State should have been tucked up inside, savoring their ability to play football, craft delicious dairy products,[12] and behave sensibly.

Instead, tens of thousands of them—over a hundred thousand by some estimates—were outside in the cold. Not just for a quick dash to replenish the frozen custard and cheese curds. But for hours. Then for days. Then for weeks and months. When these massive and persistent crowds of Wisconsinites did step back indoors, they did so most dramatically by forcing their way into the rotunda of the State Capitol, where they interrupted lawmakers with drumbeats and chants. Even, if reports are to be believed, with the utterance of an epithet or two.[13]

For a few tumultuous months, these un-midwestern displays by the citizens of Wisconsin captivated the front pages of newspapers across the United States. Yet they were surpassed by the enormities of the state itself. Indeed, by officials in each branch of the Wisconsin government: executive, legislative, and judicial. The newly elected governor, just a few months into his term, prompted these massive demonstrations by announcing his controversial plan to limit employee benefits.[14] Fourteen state senators who opposed the plan evaded capture by the Wisconsin State Patrol and fled to an undisclosed location in Illinois—in an attempt to prevent a quorum for a vote on the governor's bill.[15] When the bill nevertheless became law, a challenge to its legality made its way to the Wisconsin Supreme Court, where tempers amongst the justices frayed to the point that one accused another of putting her in a chokehold.[16]

Americans today are much more familiar with the Wisconsin governor who triggered this astonishing chain of events, now that he has survived a recall election, won reelection, and run for president of the United States. He is, of course, Scott Walker.[17]

But what could possibly have been in his plan that so exercised the good people of America's Dairyland? Some provisions of Governor Walker's bill enraged public employees for obvious reasons, such as requiring them to contribute far more to their pensions and curtailing their ability to bargain collectively. But the law, formally titled 2011 Wisconsin Act 10, also included another idea, one less prominent but with a greater potential impact on the citizens of Wisconsin. Section 9115 of the bill required a study of the effect of "establishing a defined contribution plan as an option for participating employees."[18]

Whatever such an academical exercise might entail, it certainly doesn't sound very important or threatening, does it? In fact, the proposal hinted at the beginning of the end of public pensions in Wisconsin and their eventual replacement by defined-contribution accounts. This substitution is one that private companies in the United States widely adopted to improve their balance sheets in the 1990s.[19] And state and municipal governments throughout our country might hope it will do the same for their budgets some day.

Illinois Isn't Burning, Yet

Perhaps the most combustible government in the union is another midwestern state, just one to the south of Wisconsin. The risks of ignition in Illinois arise from its poor credit rating, unfunded pension liability, and insoluble political paralysis. Illinois's credit rating and pension liability are the worst in the nation; its political problems might be, too, if such things could be quantified.[20]

The Standard & Poor's rating of Illinois's credit is A-, which might be cause for self-congratulation on a high-school report card, but is an abysmal score in the world of credit ratings. Six grades below the best possible rating (AAA, which fifteen states hold), Illinois's A- is lower than every other state's rating.[21]

The unfunded pension liability in Illinois is now more than $111,000,000,000 (that is, $111 billion). This caravan of zeros represents the void separating the amount that Illinois has promised to pay its retirees and the amount it has actually set aside to honor those promises. For scale, consider that Illinois collects about $40 billion in annual revenues.[22]

Though political paralysis is a difficult phenomenon to measure, the dysfunction in Illinois is evident even to a casual observer. Not only from the state's impressive lineage of incarcerated governors but, in this financial crisis, also from the inability of politicians to negotiate any sort of workable solution. A recent legislative effort to fix the gaping budgetary hole was struck down as unconstitutional by the state's supreme court, to little surprise.[23]

That people in the Land of Lincoln are not yet marching on Springfield and gatecrashing the capitol might be due only to the failure of politicians to prescribe medicine strong enough for Illinois's ailment. Still, public finances are now in such a dire condition, worsened through years of malign neglect, that when legislators do eventually get around to proposing a serious solution, large groups of Illinoisans will be upset. The most serious, if not the most popular, solution in Illinois is likely to be the same idea as set forth in Governor Walker's law: to shift new state employees out of a pension and into a defined contribution plan.[24]

Illinois and Wisconsin are far from alone in suffering these budgetary woes. The Pew Charitable Trusts reports that the majority of American states are delinquent with their pensions.[25] Indeed, the aggregate unfunded gap in state pensions is now well more than 1 trillion dollars.[26] Even by the louche standards of our nation's recent financial debacles, this number is gigantic.

For those Americans who still have them, such as public employees in Wisconsin and Illinois, pensions remain vitally important. But we should be careful not to overstate the historical importance of pensions. And at no time did pensions swaddle the land in a security blanket. In 1975, even before the introduction of 401(k) plans, fewer than 40 million Americans participated in pensions, and all pension plans combined held less than $200 billion. Only 21 percent of private-sector employees at the time received any money from them, and their median annual income was less than $5,000 in today's dollars. Pensions were not then a financial panacea for the United States and will not be anytime soon.

On the contrary, pensions are dwindling quickly. In America's public sector, the pension is very ill; in the private sector, it is effectively dead.

The Rise of the Fund

In place of the pension has arisen the individual savings account and, more specifically, the investment fund. Let us first examine the difference between pensions and individual investments, and then consider why we have shifted from one to the other.

Pensions versus Individual Accounts

A pension is, metaphorically, something like a bus: a functional if unglamorous conveyance driven by a professional to carry us as passengers on our trip to future financial security. Individual accounts, by metaphoric comparison, are more like cars: zippier vehicles that we drive ourselves to whatever destination we hope to reach with our savings. And for those investors who do drive their own cars, perhaps the most wildly popular road on which to travel is the mutual fund. Our experience with mutual funds, however, provides sobering evidence that these roads can be dangerous to travel.[27]

Though we have seen fierce opposition in places like Madison, employees across the United States have for the most part quietly accepted individual accounts. Recall that those protestors in Wisconsin ultimately lost their battle when Governor Walker and his legislative allies successfully enacted their new law.[28]

Indeed, the adoption of individual accounts appears to be proceeding as comprehensively as did our adoption of automobiles a century ago. We Americans, it turns out, tend to like driving our own cars. Paternalistic advice that a bus or a train might be safer isn't terribly compelling; indeed, it may seem unappealingly European. Like automobiles, our new innovation of individual accounts can, when used prudently, bring many potential benefits. And mutual funds, too, are important and useful financial pathways for guiding people to save for their future, their health care, and the education of their children. The mutual fund is now the central investment tool that Americans use to save, in both retirement and all other personal accounts.

But, one might wonder, are not financial professionals involved in both pensions and mutual funds? And, if so, are not the risks of the two modes of saving comparable? Yes, managers do indeed participate in both systems, but, no, the risks are not comparable. The timing and manner of professional involvement differ critically and lead to very different outcomes. Automotive experts help to create both buses and cars, but a professional drives the bus, while you drive the car.

In a pension plan, employees have no involvement whatsoever in how monies are invested. In an individual account, on the other hand, each employee chooses the specific mutual fund, if any, in which to invest. Managers of a pension fund act under a duty to generate streams of payments to people who are no longer working. Managers of a mutual fund pursue far narrower objectives. Investors in their funds, after all, may be senior citizens saving for retirement or hedge funds executing a short-term trading tactic. With over 8,000 U.S. mutual funds in the market, the investment approach of any given fund is often narrow, specialized, and aggressive.[29]

To use an alternative metaphor, pension managers and mutual fund advisers are both chefs of a sort. But pension managers create entire meals to provide nutrition, while fund advisers sell individual dishes to satisfy taste. If investors eat their complete pension breakfast, they are likely to benefit from a nutritious, if modest, meal. If investors pick and choose individual foods, they can easily hurt themselves by binging on obscene amounts of truffled omelets. Mutual fund investors can and regularly do lose substantial amounts through fees and poor performance; pensioners get no more, and rarely any less, than what they have been promised.

Pensions, again, are known more technically as defined benefit plans and, though hopelessly technocratic, that dollop of jargon does capture their essence: in a pension, the benefit one receives is defined in advance. That is, the payout an employee will receive at retirement is established long before that person ever becomes a pensioner.

Typically, the amount of the benefit is set forth as a formula for determining an annuity—that is, a regular stream of payments the employer will pay to the employee from the moment she retires until the day she dies. A basic formula would be a certain percentage of the employee's final salary, multiplied by years worked. Pensions, of course, can differ widely and offer more or less generous benefits. A more generous pension might increase the monthly amounts through annual cost-of-living adjustments or, upon the death of the pensioner, continue to be paid to the pensioner's surviving spouse for the remainder of that person's life.[30]

Another common pension perquisite has inadvertently evolved into one of the most generous: healthcare coverage. As part of a standard pension plan, the retiring employee typically remains covered by the employer's health insurance following retirement and for the rest of the pensioner's life.[31]

An employer responsible for making monthly pension payments to its army of pensioners is confronted with a mathematical challenge. How can the employer amass enough money to pay all those indefinite obligations that will come due decades into the future? One way to tackle this problem in a pension is, in some form, to set aside regular contributions and to save those sums while the employee is an active member of the employer's workforce. As useful as that pile of money might be, it will rarely be sufficient to cover an unknown stream of pension payments years into the future. But, of course, the savings alone are not intended to support the pension payouts. Employers do not simply stash these contributions in a coffee can under the bed. Instead, they place the sums in a pension fund and hire professional money managers to invest the savings over the course of decades, in an effort to build a corpus of investment returns that will augment the original contributions. Indeed, in a successfully managed pension, those investment returns, compounded over decades, might vastly outweigh the amount of the original contributions.

If employers rely on these contributions to fund pensions and hire experts to increase those sums, why have they soured so much on these plans? The problem for employers arises when their pension plans have not saved or appreciated sufficiently to cover their obligations. And, in recent history, problems have arisen not so much with the savings and investment returns flowing in but, rather, with the amounts due to flow out. Pension obligations have ballooned well beyond what employers predicted decades ago. And the essence of a pension is that employers are contractually responsible for covering any and all shortfalls between what their pension promised and what the pension fund may actually have accumulated.

Why have obligations increased so unexpectedly? For two primary reasons. First, Americans have developed the tenacious habit of living longer. In the past quarter-century, the life expectancy of Americans has increased by almost a decade.[32] From an employer's perspective, that increase represents ten more years of obligatory pension payments. Jane Austen long ago instructed us on the health-giving powers of an annuity, when her Fanny Dashwood, in *Sense and Sensibility*, bemoaned the idea of giving one to her father-in-law's widow, Mrs. Dashwood:

> But if you observe, people always live for ever when there is an annuity to be paid them; and she is very stout and healthy, and hardly forty. An

annuity is a very serious business; it comes over and over every year, and there is no getting rid of it.[33]

Of course, since the founding of the Republic, Americans have been increasing their life expectancy, and any decent actuarial predictions made twenty-five years ago should have foreseen many of those extra years of pension payments. They did, but their math was still off.

What the actuaries did not predict was the second reason that pension obligations have swollen so much: healthcare costs in the United States have spiked in recent years.[34] Since many pension benefits included healthcare coverage, employers have also been responsible for those unexpected increases in health insurance premiums. And not only have healthcare costs risen rapidly in general, those costs are most acute at the end of a person's life, when we devour a huge percentage of our lifetime healthcare services. That extra decade of life expectancy has come to us not, alas, in our dashing twenties but in our seventies and eighties, when we're consuming buffets of prescription medications, hip replacements, and life-prolonging treatments.

Employers surprised by—and financially responsible for—these unexpectedly expanding obligations have felt themselves shackled to a corpse and have sought to rid themselves of their pension plans.[35] For existing pensioners or employees whose pension benefits have already vested, an employer may not easily renege on pension payments. That is, an employer cannot simply announce that it has changed its mind and no longer wishes to make any more pension payments; that path would be littered with lawsuits for breach of contract. Instead, a particularly determined employer might attempt to discharge its pension obligations through bankruptcy, and many have done so. In the private sector, pensions are disappearing like a sumptuous stand of tropical rainforest. In the public sector, pensions remain prevalent, but even municipal bankruptcies are on the rise, and lawsuits are proliferating as states and municipalities attempt to obviate their pension obligations.

America's Embrace of Individual Savings Accounts

The public employees of Wisconsin, Illinois, and many other states may be fighting to keep their pension plans, but they appear to be losing the struggle. Employers both private and public are prevailing in their efforts to shunt their employees into individual accounts, primarily as a means of shifting the costs and risks of future payouts from employers to employees.

These days, in the private—and perhaps soon the public—sector, employers rarely promise newly hired employees a pension. Instead, they offer a different savings plan: a defined contribution plan. That technical term includes 401(k) plans, 403(b) plans, 529 plans, and individual retirement accounts. What is defined in this new species of plan is no longer the *benefit*, as it was in a classic pension plan. Rather, these plans define only the *contribution*, which is the amount paid in. That is, the employer disavows any responsibility for what the plan is capable of—or answerable for—paying out in the future.[36]

In practice, a certain percentage of each employee's paycheck is set aside, before taxes are deducted, and contributed to the defined contribution plan. Sometimes, but not always, the employer chooses to contribute an additional amount into the employee's plan with each paycheck. An employer's decision to contribute any matching sums will turn on the same array of factors as influence all employers' offers to their employees: in the market for labor, how much do they need to sweeten their package of salary and benefits to attract talent?

Once an employee elects to enroll in one of these accounts, the employee—not a firm of investment professionals—determines how much of each paycheck to set aside (up to certain federal maximums) and in what particular investments to allocate those sums. As in pension plans, the overarching goal is that the corpus of contributions, augmented with decades of investment returns, will eventually amount to a valuable nest egg that can support the employee when she is no longer actively employed and earning. To accomplish that goal, most investors with individual accounts direct their savings into mutual funds.

Funds May Not Be as Familiar as They Seem

Though mutual funds may seem ubiquitous and familiar to many Americans, they can carry hidden dangers. Let us return to our automotive analogy for a vivid warning.

Karl Benz, widely acknowledged as the inventor of the modern automobile, designed his first engine in 1878.[37] Section 401(k) of the Internal Revenue Code, widely acknowledged as the source of the individual tax-advantaged retirement account, first appeared in the Revenue Act of 1978.[38] We are now almost forty years into our experience with the 401(k). At about this stage of our embrace of the automobile, in 1915, approximately 6,800 people died in motor vehicle accidents.[39] As Americans tightened their embrace of automobiles in the subsequent decades, annual deaths swelled to the tens of thousands before reaching a grisly peak of more than 54,000 in 1972.[40]

Now consider the financial crisis of 2008. During that unpleasantness, we saw the value of mutual funds plummet, slashing as much as 40 percent from the savings of investors on the very cusp of their retirement.[41] Our national zeal for individual accounts might very well inflict significant costs on Americans in the years to come. As individuals, obviously, but also as a nation.

What Don't We Know About Mutual Funds?

Mutual funds are widely considered to be simple tools used by school teachers and plumbers as a safe means to preserve their life savings. When scandals afflicted other aspects of our financial industry, these funds appeared to be the rare investment resistant to fiscal intemperance. Indeed, observers hailed their portfolio managers and boards of trustees as models for corporate America.[42] Mutual funds, alas, do have plenty of their own secrets.

Many of these skeletons tumbled out in a dramatic press conference in September 2003.[43] The attorney general of New York State surprised watchers that day by naming four large mutual fund firms as perpetrators of "a fundamental violation of the rights of shareholders."[44] Bank of America, Janus, Strong Financial, and Bank One had collaborated with a hedge fund named Canary Capital Partners, alleged the attorney general in his complaint, to swindle fund investors using a pair of schemes known as late trading and market timing.[45]

The head of Canary was a fellow by the name of Edward Stern, most famous prior to this unpleasantness as the son of Leonard Stern, the billionaire magnate whose name graces the business school of New York University. Stern the younger did not follow his father's path by making a fortune selling dog food and copies of the *Village Voice*; instead, he went panning for gold in the quiet waters of mutual funds.[46]

Stern persuaded this quartet of mutual fund firms and other intermediaries to grant him permission to do the legally impermissible. With Bank of America, for instance, Stern bargained for the ability to place late trades in mutual funds until 6:30 P.M. New York time. Entering a mutual fund trade any time after 4:00 P.M. Eastern Time and receiving that day's price, however, is a violation of federal securities law. As the New York State attorney general characterized the practice, "late trading can be analogized to betting today on yesterday's horse races."[47] The winnings from Canary's dead certs came out of gains that would otherwise have accrued to ordinary, law-abiding investors in the mutual funds. Bank of America, naturally, received compensation from Canary for extending this privilege.[48]

In Stern's other schemes, involving market timing, he won the complicity of investment firms to trade millions of dollars in and out of their funds on short notice. This style of rapid trading, which capitalizes on arbitrage opportunities, was expressly banned by the funds' legal documents. Funds publicly prohibit market timing because it diverts profits out of the accounts of the funds' long-term investors and into the hands of market timers. Indeed, fund firms like Bank of America even employed "timing police" to protect their funds from this sort of behavior. As with their late-trading arrangement, however, Canary simply paid Bank of America to keep those constables off the beat.[49]

Stern may have lacked his father's acumen and integrity, but he certainly shared his ambition. Stern *fils* and Bank of America were not content with the occasional order faxed over after market-moving news, nor a few hundred thousand dollars quickly bounced in and out of a fund. Instead, the bank gave Stern a "state-of-the-art electronic late-trading platform"[50] that allowed Canary to place late trades from its own computers directly into Bank of America's system without needing anyone's authorization. The bank also provided Canary with a credit line of approximately $300 million to finance this late trading and market timing. Only when Canary's practice of churning $9 million in and out of funds each day had sufficiently exasperated employees at Bank of America did they deploy their own timing police.[51]

The New York State attorney general with this gift for a narrative—and telegenic Repp ties, tailored suits, and scandals of his own to come—was of course Eliot Spitzer. His revelation on September 3, 2003, triggered a wave of investigations into all aspects of mutual funds. Lawyers and accountants scoured this multi-trillion-dollar industry to which 91 million individuals had entrusted their savings.[52]

Regulators, plaintiffs, and trustees soon alleged that many of the most trusted firms in the business had engaged in illicit practices beyond the original sins of market timing and late trading; for instance, failing to remit promised discounts;[53] selectively disclosing the holdings of fund portfolios to preferred clients;[54] failing to "fair value" the worth of assets under their management;[55] and, not surprisingly, destroying evidence of these abuses.[56]

Twenty of the country's oldest and most renowned fund complexes paid out unprecedented settlements to government regulators: Bank of America paid $375 million; Invesco Funds Group Inc. paid $325 million; and Bear, Stearns paid $250 million. Many more, including Alliance Capital Management, MFS, Citigroup, and AIG, also paid nine-digit settlements, for a total of almost $4 billion in penalties.[57]

But news coverage of these abuses in mutual funds soon gave way to the subprime mortgage scandals of our subsequent financial crisis.[58] And the public's appetite for mutual funds soured only for a short while. After a brief period of withdrawals, the number of fund investors rose to 96 million, and by 2006 their assets climbed above $10 trillion.[59]

So why should we continue to worry about the failings of one sleepy financial instrument amid the regular implosions of so many? As we shall see, problems with mutual funds are problems for millions of ordinary Americans.

How Does Our Experiment Appear to Be Proceeding So Far?

The Center for Retirement Research at Boston College reports that for those on the cusp of retirement—workers between the ages of fifty-five and sixty-four—the median balance in household 401(k) or IRA accounts is $111,000.[60] Perhaps such a six-figure sum appears opulent, but when we consider that it must support a retirement that could continue for decades, it is inadequate.

Today, the average American retires at sixty-one and dies at seventy-nine.[61] At our current rates of interest, inflation, and life expectancy, $111,000 would provide only about $7,300 in each year of a two-decade retirement. People with a balance that meager are about to confront an extremely lean retirement. Note also that more than one-fifth of the workers in this survey hold balances of less than $13,000. Amounts that small would not even provide the pittance of $1,000 each year.

The state of our experiment is alarming. In the cohort of 76 million retiring baby boomers,[62] many of whom are going to rely heavily on individual accounts, we can be sure that millions will fall short. When they do, large swaths of Americans will soon require substantial financial assistance from other sources.

We won't really discover the broader results of our experiment until these baby boomers have retired en masse and have attempted to support themselves on the balances of their accounts without additional income from regular salaries. The statistics on savings we have amassed so far suggest that we are likely to hear a great deal more about the inadequacy of individual savings accounts in the years to come.

So what happens if an individual employee mismanages this project and the monies in his retirement account turn out to be insufficient to cover the necessities of his retirement?

Recall that with a pension, the employer promises to draw upon the corporate or public revenues to cover any such shortfalls in the plan. Corporate employers make this promise via contracts, so they are legally enforceable for as long as the employer remains solvent. Public employers make their promises via contracts, state statutes, or even provisions in state constitutions, which can render them extremely difficult to break. Staring into their budget chasm, Illinois lawmakers have tried but failed to wriggle out of the state's constitutional provision mandating that pension benefits "shall not be diminished or impaired."[63]

Even in bankruptcy, pension payments may be continued to some extent by the Pension Benefit Guaranty Corporation (PBGC), a governmental agency charged with insuring pensions in much the way the Federal Deposit Insurance Corporation protects deposits in banks that go bust.[64] But with so many demands on its insurance of late, the PBGC is not a well institution. Like so many of its beneficiaries, the PBGC runs a worrisome deficit of its own: in 2015, its obligations exceeded its assets by more than $76 billion.[65]

Unlike a pensioner, the employee in a defined contribution plan is alone left with the consequences. If money in the employee's account runs short, the employee runs out. So the implicit promise of a defined contribution plan differs fundamentally from that of a defined benefit plan.

Perhaps, though, this difference is capitalist and meritocratic, and so is quintessentially American: more risk, certainly, but also greater possible reward.

Whether trillions of dollars of American life savings ought to be directed into investments with higher risks and rewards depends, in great part, on the personal and societal consequences of those risks' being realized.

Failure and Success

The Consequences of Failure in Our Experiment with Mutual Funds

If, indeed, mutual funds and individual accounts are vulnerable, heaping so much of our money upon them could be an extremely dangerous adventure in public policy.

One might argue that the risk of people losing their own money in individual accounts is offset by their greater possible rewards and, in any event, ought to be no concern of the rest of society. This libertarian strain of argument insists that government should have no interest in the success or failure of an individual's efforts to save for her own future. As with the perils of smoking—the argument might go—what business is it of ours if someone wishes to harm herself, whether it be with cigarettes or inept investing?

The answer might turn, as it did with smoking, on the second-hand and societal consequences of disastrous investing. As a country, we began to care far more about cigarettes when we learned of the harms that smoking inflicts on the lungs of others, as well as on the public health budgets of our commonwealth. The value of individual accounts will implicate similar policy considerations if maladroit investing on a vast scale damages our nation's fiscal health.

If Americans turn out to be largely inexpert at saving and our experiment does not succeed, great swaths of our fellow citizens could become destitute in their most vulnerable years. How likely is that eventuality? John C. Bogle, one of America's leading authorities on mutual fund investments, warns that our retirement system is "headed for a train wreck."[66] If he and many like-minded experts are correct, then as a nation we will face the choice of either ignoring the plight of those whose 401(k)s are bare or of providing very expensive support to the impoverished.[67] At a time of historic financial inequality, the state of our union surely will not benefit from more sources of economic dysfunction.

One cannot know, of course, how our future politicians and policymakers might solve such a problem, but the elderly have long been a very powerful voting constituency in our democracy. Little imagination is needed to suspect that if defined contribution plans turn out to be a widespread disaster, those suffering the most will vote for financial assistance. If millions of elderly Americans lose in the 401(k) sweepstakes and face crushing poverty in their later years, they are likely to push for all American taxpayers to share in the costs of our grand

misadventure. And, like our other post hoc financial bailouts, the consequences
are likely to be expensive, divisive, and broadly unsatisfying.

Success with Better Investors and Better Investments

Just like racing down the open road in our own cars, taking control of our finances
can be a compelling notion with intuitive American appeal. But with investing as
with driving, we can be injured through any combination of engineering flaws in
the cars or roads we use, of our own shortcomings as drivers, and of the peril of
others on the road. This book proposes a suite of tools—transparency, financial
literacy, and enforcement—to help investors avoid these dangers.

First, consider the structural vulnerabilities of mutual funds. Many investors
are unaware of the operations or economics of these funds. The financial houses
that run mutual funds, for instance, owe conflicting allegiances to two very different groups of people: their own shareholders and the fund investors whose money
they manage. To satisfy their own shareholders, fund managers must maximize
fees, yet every increase in fees drains money directly from the savings of fund
investors. Each year, the industry with this conflict of interest pockets nearly $100
billion of our savings.[68]

With greater transparency, investors would learn that fund firms make more
money by increasing the size of a fund, even if they do so only by bringing in
new investments without generating any positive returns for existing investors. In this system, therefore, marketing can triumph over prudent investment. Indeed, federal law permits fund advisers to use the money of current
investors—via infamous 12b-1 fees[69]—to advertise the fund to prospective
investors. Ultimately, every fund investor should be taken aback to learn that
this industry is one of the rare economic markets in which price and performance are inversely related.[70] That is, the more one pays for a mutual fund, the
more likely that fund is to produce lower investment returns. Imagine a world
in which the most expensive cars were the worst jalopies. Financial drag from
high fees causes this quirk of mutual funds and can profoundly erode our savings, particularly when compounded over decades. But greater transparency in
the ways of the mutual fund can help investors to protect themselves from these
structural impediments.

Second—and though we all hate to do it—let us reflect upon our own possible
shortcomings. We would all like to believe that, with a little motivation and some
self-help, we could win friends like Dale Carnegie and invest like Warren Buffett.
But empirical studies repeatedly demonstrate that laypersons lack the institutional resources and the financial expertise we need to succeed at this project of
investing large amounts by ourselves for years to come.[71]

The discomfiting reality is that the average individual does not abound in the
key requirements of successful investing: discipline, deferred gratification, and

math.[72] As humans, we tend not to be very sapient at forecasting our economic requirements decades into the future, at setting aside income today that we will need for the years ahead, and at calculating the investment options that will provide the best mix of risk and reward to increase our savings to sustain our future lives. As Richard Thaler notes, we simply don't enjoy many opportunities to get better at this project: "when it comes to saving for retirement, barring reincarnation we do that exactly once."[73] Indeed, those challenges are difficult even for the most powerful, wealthy, and experienced investors in our nation's economy.[74] Improving financial literacy, however, can help prepare investors to face these challenges.

Third, consider the risks from our counterparts' behaving badly. The history of Wall Street is blotted with tales of financial insiders who have deceived ordinary investors. Though the structure of funds allows firms to obtain large amounts of our savings legally, some professionals have proved creative at squeezing ever more pennies out of our accounts illegally. Investment banks like Bear, Stearns and Bank of America, hedge funds like Canary Capital, and fund advisers like Putnam, MFS, and Allianz among many others have paid many billions of dollars to settle claims of wrongdoing in an alarming array of unlawful schemes like late trading, market timing, unfair valuation, and more. Several of the chapters in this book will illustrate the diverse array of schemes by which experts in the fund industry have absconded with the savings of ordinary investors. Through greater enforcement of mutual fund investments, financial regulators could reduce the most problematic excesses in the industry.

To forestall those ominous outcomes, American investors need alternative— and better—solutions.

This book is an effort to teach investors how to use our new investing technology safely. How many lives might have been saved if our society had more quickly recognized the perils of speeding and drinking? Or the benefits of seatbelts, safety glass, and airbags? If investors today can—with a little driver's education—learn the structural vulnerabilities of investing on their own and the dangers to avoid in mutual funds, we stand a much greater chance of preserving our individual financial health and the nation's fiscal and democratic vitality in the years to come.

Of course, even the most sophisticated investors need better tools. No individual 401(k) investor, no matter how brilliant or wealthy, has the bargaining power to demand the best prices and most scrupulous behavior from a trillion-dollar investment industry. To ensure that Americans can make the most of our new world of individual accounts, we must create an inexpensive and well-run account for all Americans. As it happens, just such an option already exists in the Thrift Savings Plan for federal employees: a plan managed by one of America's leading investment firms for astonishingly low fees. Why does BlackRock run these investments so well and so inexpensively? Because the 4.5 million investors constitute a powerful buying club with more than $400 billion in assets. By opening this plan more broadly or creating similar pools, more Americans could prosper in our new investing paradigm.

This book provides an introductory lesson in how to navigate investment funds, and makes an argument for how individuals can work together to demand better investment tools. The sooner we improve the way we save now, the more surely we can safeguard our own financial destinies and our nation's fiscal strength.

PART I

ANATOMY OF A FUND

Because of the unique structure of this industry ... the forces of
arm's-length bargaining do not work ... in the same manner as they
do in other sectors of the American economy.

—U.S. Senate Report, *1970*

Though mutual funds now dominate the financial accounts of 55 million
households in this country, ordinary investors are largely unaware of their
complexity and peril.[1] To understand these ubiquitous instruments—and
to appreciate their hidden dangers—let us begin by exploring their anatomy. When we inquire into their purpose, structure, and economics, we
will answer the wherefore of mutual funds.

Many books on personal finance adopt an approach similar to diet
books: "Invest in nothing but the ten worst performing stocks . . . they can
only go up!" "Consume nothing but paprika and 7-Up . . . you'll cleanse the
toxins and weight away!" This book strives to be more like a simple medical
text: by learning how funds are put together and where the money flows,
you can inoculate yourself against a broad range of common investing mal-
adies. But the better metaphor may again be automotive.

If individual accounts like 401(k)s and IRAs are the midsize sedans of
American investment, then mutual funds are the charming old U.S. highways upon which they travel. A jaunt along Route 66 may not be as expe-
ditious as a sprint down an interstate, as exhilarating as a few laps of the
Indianapolis Speedway, or as glamorous as a joyride through Beverly Hills,
but it is a stolid and sensible way to get where one hopes to go. In finance,
high-frequency trading funds are faster than mutual funds, hedge funds are
more volatile, and private equity funds are often more lucrative. But those
exotic investment tools are also far more dangerous ways to invest. And
they are certainly no place for ordinary citizens to nurture their life savings.

Mutual funds are—and, in large part, ought to be—the overwhelmingly popular choice for most American families.[2]

As a nation, we currently save more than $16 trillion in these funds, entrusting them with everything from our future savings to our retirement nest eggs, to our children's tuition. Mutual funds now hold almost a quarter of all our household financial assets and 60 percent of all the money in our individual retirement accounts—and those percentages are both rising as mutual funds establish themselves as a standard default option for our investments. In short, when Americans find themselves with an extra dollar to save, the obvious destination for that investment is a mutual fund.[3]

Thus, to understand America's finances, and our own, we must understand mutual funds.

1

PURPOSE

As a tradesman in the City, too, he began to have an interest in the
Lord Mayor, and the Sheriffs, and in Public Companies; and felt
bound to read the quotations of the Funds every day, though he was
unable to make out, on any principle of navigation, what the figures
meant, and could have very well dispensed with the fractions.

—Charles Dickens, *Dombey and Son*

So, just what exactly is a mutual fund?

A mutual fund is a financial tool that gathers money from several different investors and uses the combined pool of assets to buy a portfolio of stocks, bonds, or other investments. If the portfolio is successful and generates financial gains, each of the investors in the fund will enjoy a proportional share of those positive returns. If, on the other hand, the portfolio declines, then the investors must share in the losses—as well as in the transactional costs incurred by working jointly through a mutual fund.

These funds travel under a variety of aliases. In the argot of Wall Street, they are known as "collective investment vehicles." *Collective* because they aggregate monies from a variety of individual investors and deploy them as a common fund, rather than as separate accounts. *Investment* because the goal of the enterprise is ultimately to risk the money on other profit-making ventures, not simply to provide security, as might be the case with a bank deposit. *Vehicles* because Wall Street loves its technocratic buzzwords, and "collective investment things" just doesn't sound impressive enough.

In the even-clunkier circumlocution of the federal securities regulations, mutual funds are "open-end investment companies."[4] *Open-end* because the fund's shares are redeemable to the fund itself, unlike closed-end funds and other publicly traded corporations whose finite number of shares are bought or sold on a stock exchange.[5] *Investment* because funds hold themselves out as being engaged primarily in the business of investing in securities, rather than making goods or providing services. *Companies* because mutual funds are, technically, distinct legal entities, not merely financial products offered by investment advisers.

The Origin of Mutual Funds in America

Notwithstanding all this newfangled and infelicitous jargon for mutual funds, the instruments themselves are not particularly new. The provenance of funds resembling the ones we have today dates back several hundred years—depending on how broadly one cares to draw the analogy—to investment schemes developed in the European merchant centers of Amsterdam and Brussels in the eighteenth and nineteenth centuries.

Later in the nineteenth century, investment trusts proliferated throughout Britain. Victorian literature of that period is rich with references to the "funds": Lady Bracknell, in Wilde's *Importance of Being Earnest*, learns that Cecily Cardew has "a hundred and thirty thousand pounds in the Funds" and of a sudden finds her "a most attractive young lady, now that I look at her." Becky Sharp, in Thackeray's *Vanity Fair*, resents "the great rich Miss Crawley," who "preferred the security of the funds" and enjoyed "seventy thousand pounds in the five per cents."[6] Charlotte Brontë's eponymous heroine Jane Eyre inherits 20,000 pounds upon the death of her uncle and is told that her "money is vested in the English funds."[7]

But these "funds" are false cognates and not our mutual funds. They are more likely consolidated annuities, known as the Consols, a type of perpetual bond first issued by the Bank of England in 1751. Our most likely equivalent would be Treasury bills backed by the full faith and credit of the United States, if such instruments offered a fixed return in perpetuity.

In the United States, the first generally recognized mutual fund opened for business on March 21, 1924. Edward G. Leffler, a Wisconsinite transplanted to Boston, organized this fund, called Massachusetts Investors Trust, with $50,000. Leffler also participated in the early stages of the second and third American mutual funds: the State Street Investment Corporation, formed on July 29, 1924; and Incorporated Investors, formed on November 23, 1925. All three of these initial funds had connections to the first families of Boston.[8] Indeed, the head of State Street Investment Corporation was one Paul Codman Cabot, of the Brahmin Codmans and Cabots.

> And this is good old Boston,
> The home of the bean and the cod,
> Where the Lowells talk only to Cabots,
> And the Cabots talk only to God.

When speaking with mortals, Cabot favorably distinguished "the reputation of the old Boston conservative trustee" from the "reputation of the slick Wall Street fellows who take the shirt off your back."[9] Today, Boston is still home to many of America's largest funds, and Massachusetts Investors Trust has grown to hold $7.6 billion.

The Dispensability of Mutual Funds

So, the mutual fund is not a terribly new idea, nor is it a particularly indispensable one. For anyone who wishes to invest in a diverse array of financial investments, at least two other options exist: self-help and pensions.

First, investors with sufficient wherewithal and leisure at their disposal could, as an alternative technique, simply assemble their own portfolios of investments. One need not combine forces with other shareholders or seek help from financial advisers to acquire a broad collection of stocks or bonds. One must, however, be willing to spend the time and money to research and pay for all those transactions. Mutual funds can certainly help to husband both those resources.

Second, anyone with a pension already participates in a collective pool of assorted investments. And pensions, when used as directed, are managed by professionals, backed by employers, and guaranteed by the Pension Benefit Guarantee Corporation. One wonders whether Philip Larkin would be quite so ironic about them today as he was when he wrote *Toads* in 1955 that he wished he were "courageous enough to shout *Stuff your pension!*":

> But I know, all too well, that's the stuff
> That dreams are made on.[10]

Pensions have, however, had the stuffing knocked out of them in recent decades. We have seen already how employers have a financial incentive to remove expanding pension obligations from their books, but how in practice have they managed to do so?

First, many private employers—and a few public ones—have simply stopped offering pension benefits to any new employees they hire. This change in policy immediately curtails future increases in pension obligations. And as existing employees with pension benefits shuffle on to new jobs or off their mortal coils, an employer's obligations will begin to dwindle. Some employers have also pursued a more drastic and immediate way to shed pension obligations.

They have declared bankruptcy. The airline, steel, and automobile industries, most notoriously, filed for bankruptcy en masse in part to escape their pension liabilities. Between 2002 and 2005, four of the nation's seven largest airlines persuaded bankruptcy courts to transfer their pension plans to the Pension Benefit Guaranty Corporation. United Airlines alone shed a plan it had underfunded by almost $10 billion.

In more recent years, municipal employers have also tiptoed toward that solution. Cities like Detroit, Michigan, and Stockton, California, have filed for bankruptcy and sought to avoid some of their pension obligations with modest success.[11] States such as Illinois have similarly mismanaged their way into crushing pension deficits. But states—as separate sovereigns in our federal republic—are not eligible to submit themselves to the jurisdiction of a U.S. bankruptcy court. For now, at least.

So, the flow of money into the pension tub has been stoppered, and the tub itself has been punctured. As a result, pensions in America are asymptoting toward irrelevance.

The Rise of Individual Investing

Individual savings accounts, on the other hand, are surging. And their growth has spurred the imperial expansion of the most popular investment choices in those accounts: mutual funds. As figure 1.1 shows, after more than half a century of apparent hibernation, mutual funds leapt off the x-axis beginning in the late nineteen-seventies.

A critical step in this savings revolution began with the perspicacity of a young tax expert by the name of Ted Benna. When the U.S. Congress added an abstruse subchapter (k) to section 401 of the Internal Revenue Code in 1978, Benna was the first to recognize and harness the possibilities of this new provision.

Congress added the new language in an effort to clarify uncertainty surrounding deferred compensation arrangements for corporate executives. In some

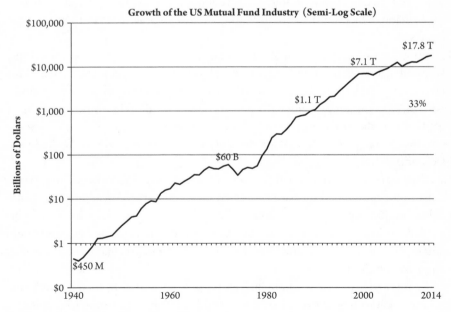

Figure 1.1 Growth of U.S. Mutual Fund Industry.

corporations, executives attempted to defer their compensation—and thus to defer the taxes owed on that compensation—into a retirement account. But these plans were, at the time, limited to a small number of senior executives, and the Joint Committee on Taxation predicted that this new "provision will have negligible effect upon budget receipts."[12] How wrong they were.

When Benna realized that employers could offer similar plans to all employees and could boost their appeal by supplying matching funds, he became the "father of the 401(k)."[13] In crafting the earliest 401(k) accounts, Benna created an instrument that enjoyed a variety of ostensible improvements over traditional pensions and almost immediate success.

First, a 401(k) plan is portable. Unlike savings in a pension, which can be lost if an employee changes employers before benefits vest, money in a 401(k) remains the property of its owner wherever she works. Second, the investments in a 401(k) plan are directed by the individual, who may have particular risk tolerances, investment goals, or preferred investing strategies that differ from the collective approach of a pension fund. This second attribute of 401(k)s, however, is the locus of serious contention and is far from universally embraced as a benefit. Certainly, some policymakers, academics, and investment firms celebrate the self-directed nature of individual accounts. Others warn of its potential danger.

And even those who do laud the features of 401(k)s can reasonably question whether accounts intended to shelter bonus compensation for executives are the appropriate arks to preserve trillions of dollars in life savings for all Americans.

Benna himself has concluded otherwise: "Hey, if I were starting over from scratch today with what we know, I'd blow up the existing structure and start over."[14]

Employers, however, have indisputably embraced defined contribution plans. And as those plans have swollen—they now hold almost $7 trillion—so, too, have mutual funds.

The Popularity of Mutual Funds

Mutual funds offer certain conveniences that clearly appeal to large swaths of America's investing public. Those conveniences, fueled by the rise of individual investing through defined-contribution plans and IRAs, have boosted mutual funds to the pinnacle of the U.S. savings hierarchy.

In the near-century since the formation of America's first mutual fund, the empire of funds in the United States has expanded to encompass a massive $16 trillion today. This striking growth, punctuated by an explosive doubling of investments in the past decade alone, places funds squarely at the heart of the way we save now. Indeed, institutions like mutual funds have come to dominate our stock markets. Whereas in the first half of the twentieth century, institutional investors such as funds owned only about 5 percent of the stock market, by the end of 2010 they owned 67 percent.[15]

Funds first needed about twenty years to cross the billion-dollar threshold in 1945, then another forty-five years to reach the trillion-dollar mark in 1990. But in the quarter-century since then, funds have on average added another trillion dollars about every twenty months. Some years have been truly remarkable: in the bullish twelve months between 2012 and 2013, funds added almost $2 trillion.[16]

Benefits of Mutual Funds

The investment industry ascribes much of our devotion to mutual funds to a trinity of benefits they promise to investors: instant diversification, professional money management, and easy redemption.

Instant Diversification

Just as exhortations of regular exercise and a prudent diet are to our corporeal well-being, the encouragement to diversify is to our fiscal health. That is a well-known, oft-ignored mantra, yet a sound one. Indeed, diversification was worth a Nobel Prize for Professor Harry Markowitz, the chief proponent of modern portfolio theory in the twentieth century. Markowitz's primary contribution to theoretical finance was his mathematical support for the proposition that diversification can imbue a portfolio of several investments with less risk than any of its constituent assets. Though many lay investors may be well aware of the general advice to diversify, the task of actually compiling a diverse portfolio on one's own, without professional assistance, is far from straightforward.

First, consider the price of simply purchasing the investments themselves. If one were to attempt to replicate the Dow Jones Industrial Average—perhaps the most widely cited barometer of the U.S. stock market's performance—one would need to acquire a portfolio of thirty different stocks. The cost of purchasing even a single share of each of those thirty stocks would amount to a total of more than $2,500.[17] For an individual investor of modest means, then, the expense of this crude, homegrown attempt at diversification might well be prohibitive. Broader indices measure a greater, and perhaps even more prudent, swath of the market's overall diversity. For example, the five hundred stocks of the Standard & Poor's 500 and the 3,698 stocks of the Wilshire 5000 Total Market Index are more diverse market portfolios. (The name of that Wilshire index is aspirational, as sometimes there are notably fewer than 5,000 publicly traded stocks in America.) Of course, replicating those broader indices would impose even more outlandish costs on an individual investor.

Next, consider the transactions costs involved in this exercise. Acquiring thirty different stocks would require placing thirty different trades with a brokerage firm. With the commission of $9.99 per trade that the online brokers E*Trade and TD Ameritrade charge, the transactions costs of assembling a Dow Jones portfolio would amount to $299.70.[18] Even with TradeKing's rock-bottom commissions of $4.95 per trade,[19] those costs would add up to almost $150. So, for a portfolio of the thirty Dow Jones stocks, brokerage commissions alone would add a burden of more than 11 percent on top of the price of the stocks themselves via E*Trade and TD Ameritrade and more than 5 percent via TradeKing. These costs do not, of course, include the additional commissions involved in selling the portfolio to recognize any potential gains. Nevertheless, they already inflict a profound— indeed, prohibitive—drag on this homemade portfolio's performance.

A mutual fund, by contrast, can provide its investors with instant diversification at a far lower price and with a far smaller percentage of additional transactions costs. Consider one of America's largest mutual funds, the Vanguard Total Stock Market Index Fund, which holds stock in more than 3,700 different companies and has a total value of approximately $350 billion.[20] A single share of that fund costs about $50. Granted, mutual funds like this one do at times—though not always—require an initial minimum investment of $1,000 or more, but additional investments into the fund can be had for as little as $50.[21] Note that even the budget TradeKing commissions for assembling a comparable portfolio of 3,700 stocks would, by themselves and irrespective of the price of the actual stocks, amount to more than $18,000. In 2013, the Vanguard Total Stock Market Index Fund paid $5,089,000 in brokerage commissions, which certainly is a large transaction cost, but one that constitutes less than two thousandths of a percent of the fund's overall value.[22]

How can Vanguard assemble such an expansive portfolio with so few transactions costs? First, by operating with very large economies of scale. Buying in bulk is often a good way to save, and that's as true for stock trades as it is for cereal and toilet paper at Costco. Second, by limiting the amount of turnover in the fund's portfolio. Once Vanguard has acquired those 3,700 stocks, it has no need to engage in many more transactions. The Vanguard portfolio manager might choose to rebalance the fund's holdings from time to time, but that task involves only tinkering around the edges, not rebuilding the entire portfolio each year.

Mutual funds are, in essence, the Las Vegas buffets of the financial world. For the price of an ordinary entrée, a broad-minded and adventurous diner can instead pay for a buffet and partake of dozens of different dishes in a single setting (albeit something of a garish and smoke-filled one). Buying those dozens of dishes individually would be far more expensive, of course, and might require trips to several different kinds of restaurants. A good buffet, then, can deliver instant diversification at lower proportional transactions costs (though perhaps with fewer nutritional benefits). By pooling investments from a large number of investors, a mutual fund is similarly able to acquire a far more diverse portfolio at far lower transactions costs than an ordinary individual investor could accomplish alone. An investor who acquires a small sliver of that fund is, in turn, able to share in all the fund's breadth of diversification and many of its lower transactions costs.

Professional Money Management

The mutual fund industry prominently suggests that Americans choose to invest in mutual funds, at least in part, to avail themselves of the investing judgment of professional money managers. The advice of experts can, of course, be wise counsel. As Dolly Longestaffe says of his own financial affairs in Anthony Trollope's *Way We Live Now*, "When a fellow is stupid himself, he ought to have a sharp fellow to look after his business."[23] Whether the judgment of fund advisers is worth paying much for, however, is an altogether different question.

And Longestaffe's friend, Lord Nidderdale, asks it: "Won't he rob you, old fellow?" Longestaffe's reply is perhaps a touch more sanguine than what most of us can afford: "Of course he will;—but he won't let any one else do it. One has to be plucked, but it's everything to have it done on a system. If he'll only let me have ten shillings out of every sovereign [twenty shillings] I think I can get along."[24] We will turn to fund economics and fees in subsequent chapters, but first a word more on the professional management one can obtain through mutual funds.

The universe of approximately 8,000 U.S. mutual funds is taxonomically divisible into two major categories: index funds, which attempt simply to replicate existing market indices (such as the Dow Jones Industrials or S&P 500); and actively managed funds, which attempt to outperform market benchmark indices (such as the Dow Jones or S&P 500).

In an index fund, the human portfolio managers who run the fund exercise a modicum of judgment initially in determining how best to track the index, how to weight individual components of the index, and perhaps even how to program a computer algorithm to execute ongoing investment decisions automatically. Yet, the ultimate goal in this type of fund is simply to replicate an external and independent phenomenon, therefore comparatively little human judgment is involved going forward. The professional judgment of the managers of an index fund does not, in consequence, typically represent a great deal of value, and the fees charged by the managers of those funds are relatively and unsurprisingly low.

In an actively managed fund, by contrast, the human portfolio managers in charge exercise far more particularized judgment. Humans directly pick the actual amount and timing of individual purchases and sales of specific investments in their effort to generate the best possible returns for the fund. Not surprisingly, in light of this surfeit of human involvement, fees charged by the managers of actively managed funds are comparatively higher.[25] The judgment and success of those active fund managers do not, however, appear to be worth very much.

Almost every serious study of the performance of actively managed funds has suggested that, over time, human portfolio managers are simply incapable of out-performing the market.[26] Indeed, another, more recent Nobel Laureate, Eugene Fama of the University of Chicago, examined the question whether active managers were lucky or skillful. Not much of either, evidently.[27]

Fama's study found that only a minuscule percentage of active managers demonstrated sufficient skill to cover the costs they charged. And, remember, fund investors face the challenge of identifying that miniscule percentage of advisers. Fama concluded that "research shows that it is impossible to pick people who can beat the market."[28]

So, while some investors may, indeed, invest in mutual funds to acquire the professional judgment of fund managers, that judgment may not be worth very much given that those humans are either doing very little (in an index fund) or doing very little successfully (in an actively managed fund).

Easy Redemption

A third common explanation for the popularity of mutual funds relates to the ease with which investors can pull their money out of them. Investors in mutual funds can, under all but the most extraordinary circumstances, redeem their fund shares on any given business day.[29] The fund industry commonly employs a settlement period of T+3, which means that a selling investor should receive ready cash from her sale by the third day following the date on which she placed her redemption order.[30] So, for an order placed on a Monday, the proceeds should arrive by Thursday, in the absence of intervening holidays or market calamities.

This ability to redeem mutual funds may appear no easier than the typical sale of publicly traded stocks and bonds. Indeed, it is not, as those securities often settle on the T+3 timeline also.[31] But the typical sale of publicly traded stocks and bonds may not be the most illuminating comparison. The sale of other, far more commonly held investments reveals the claims of mutual funds to greater advantage.

First, though, let us consider an atypical sale of publicly traded securities—that is, one attempted during extraordinary circumstances, in which the financial markets are roiled by volatility. In those moments when stock prices might be plummeting, the would-be seller of ordinary stocks and bonds might have a difficult time finding any willing buyer. Or certainly a buyer willing to pay an attractive price. Mutual funds, by contrast, must buy back their shares no matter what the circumstances of the market.[32] A fund shareholder, importantly, redeems her shares *directly to the fund*, not to other voluntary participants in the market. And so there will always be a willing—or, if not exactly willing, then a legally obligated—buyer for fund shares. Indeed, this returning of mutual fund shares to the fund is why we refer to the practice as a redemption rather than as a sale.

Second, consider other common kinds of investments. The shares of privately held companies—such as Facebook or Twitter before those businesses went public—are not traded on any stock market. If an investor holding those shares needs to turn them into cash, the process of selling them could take days or weeks, if it ever becomes possible.

Similarly, the most common investments for Americans are not financial assets but concrete assets like automobiles and houses.[33] Converting those kinds of chattels and realty into cash can take a distressingly long time, certainly far longer than the few days of a mutual fund sale. Selling cars and houses can also involve Craig's List or realtors, open houses, tidying up old stains, and all sorts of other unpleasantness.

Finally, think again of one's own, homemade attempt at building a portfolio. If you had assembled a diverse selection of thirty, five hundred, or five thousand individual stocks, then liquidating those investments would involve a great deal of time and aggravation—far more than one single and simple mutual fund redemption order.

Now that we know what mutual funds are and why they are so popular, we can more comprehensively attempt to dissect one.

2

STRUCTURE

No, you have to explain it to me more. I'm not being difficult. I understand this less well than you think I do, and I want to know.
—Supreme Court Justice Stephen Breyer
at oral argument in
Janus Capital Group v. First Derivative Traders, 2010

The anatomy of mutual funds is complicated and counterintuitive. So much so that many investors are unaware there even is a structure about which to be confused—after all, aren't funds just something offered by a financial firm, like a bank account or a certificate of deposit? They are not. And they do have a structure, one sufficiently complicated to confuse even a number of well-briefed Supreme Court justices.[1]

Stephen Gerald Breyer earned degrees from Stanford University; Magdalen College, Oxford; and Harvard Law School. He then served for many years as a member of the faculty of Harvard Law School, where he was a leading expert in the notoriously abstruse field of administrative law. His legal acumen won him a seat on the U.S. Court of Appeals for the First Circuit and then a brisk elevation to the Supreme Court of the United States. Nevertheless, during the oral argument for a mutual fund case before the Supreme Court in 2010, Justice Breyer said to an advocate, "You have to explain it to me more. I'm not being difficult. I understand this less well than you think I do, and I want to know."[2] Toward the end of that same argument, Justices Alito and Ginsburg appeared to lose track of which set of shareholders was actually seeking recovery in this legal farrago of investors and investments.[3]

The Supreme Court case was brought by shareholders in a public company (Janus Capital Group, Inc.), which owned a subsidiary (Janus Capital Management LLC), which in turn advised a mutual fund (Janus Investment Fund). Hmm, that's a lot of similar-sounding businesses. Indeed it is—let confusion reign!

Investors in Janus Capital Group argued that they had been duped because the firm's subsidiary, Janus Capital Management, published a prospectus declaring that, as the investment adviser of Janus Investment Fund, the adviser did not allow market timing in the fund. As it happened and in exchange for illicit remuneration,

Janus Capital Management did allow market timing in Janus Investment Fund, which harmed the shareholders in that fund. When this market-timing scheme was publicly revealed, investors in Janus Investment Fund bolted, draining revenue from Janus Capital Management, and thereby draining profits from its parent, Janus Capital Group. So when, in the dying moments of an hour-long oral argument, Justices Alito and Ginsburg inquired about the shareholders of Janus Investment Fund in a lawsuit filed, in fact, by the shareholders of Janus Capital Group, one was left to wonder how well they had followed these mutual fund involutions. Not well, it appeared. But grasping the structure of a mutual fund can be difficult for anybody.

The organizational blueprint of even a standard mutual fund can resemble an angry baby's adventure with knitting yarn, and the architects of this chaos have little incentive to untangle it for us. Jonathan Swift decried the murky bog of England's investment industry over three hundred years ago—little has changed: "Through the contrivance and cunning of stock jobbers there hath been brought in such a complication of knavery and cozenage, such a mystery of iniquity, and such an unintelligible jargon of terms to involve it in, as were never known in any other age or country in the world."[4]

Yet the structure of these funds is something we must understand—and can, with a few helpful diagrams—if we are fully to appreciate the incentives and vulnerabilities in these vital investments that hold so much of our money.

Like a doctor diagnosing a patient, we must learn some basic elements of our subject's anatomy. Not with hundreds of sleepless nights over four years of medical school, but with just a few illuminating diagrams and descriptive explanations.

The Structure and Operations of Mutual Funds

For all the popularity and ubiquity of these funds in our economy, they remain a curious species of financial instrument whose inner workings are alien to many Americans.[5] Mutual funds are, structurally and operationally, like neither the quotidian American businesses nor the omnipresent bank accounts with which we are all more familiar. To appreciate the variety of ways in which funds—and our enormous investments in them—can go awry, we should first spend a moment exploring their unique design and operation.

On the one hand, Americans constantly interact with myriad companies in our economy that provide us with all the goods and services we need to go about our daily lives. Ford sells us cars, Exxon sells us petrol, and Uber drives us if we don't happen to like driving Fords or buying petrol. Within the world of investment funds, these companies are known as *operating companies*, and they are categorically distinct from mutual funds. If we invest our money to buy shares of equity in Ford, Exxon, or Uber, we expect those companies to use our money to build more cars, drill for more oil, or inflict another software update on us whenever we just want a ride somewhere. The financial arrangement is straightforward: as stockholders in an operating company, we will benefit if the company's performance—or, perhaps more accurately, its perceived performance—improves. Mutual funds do not provide goods or services to customers in this way but, rather, as *investment companies*, they provide their users with a means for investing in other securities.

On the other hand, many of us regularly engage in arrangements with financial institutions such as banks to deposit our money or to purchase certificates of deposit. Contrary to what banks might like us to believe, account holders provide banks with a service by depositing their money in the banks. Banks can, and do, use those sums to generate profits for the banks' benefit, typically by lending depositors' money to borrowers at a specified rate of interest. In exchange, banks often promise a certain rate of return to their depositors, a rate lower than the one the bank is charging its borrowers. Thus, in our retail dealings with banks as account holders, we are guaranteed a certain return, albeit one that might be quite low or one that varies in accordance with agreed-upon interest-rate benchmarks. If a bank refuses to pay that specified return, we as depositors will have a legal cause of action that we can force the bank to pay us. When a mutual fund produces a disappointing return, by contrast, investors enjoy no such legal recourse.

Mutual funds thus differ in critical functions and categories from both operating companies and other financial instruments. To understand these differences, we will dissever a mutual fund to identify each of its essential moving parts and players. We will return to this anatomy lesson repeatedly in the chapters ahead, as we explore the variety of ways in which mutual funds can be exploited to divert money away from their investors.

As we address ourselves to the financial specimen before us, perhaps the most striking overall characteristic of a mutual fund is its remarkably passive helplessness. If we celebrate American businesses for their entrepreneurial dynamism and the drive of their energetic corporate officers, we must acknowledge mutual funds to be the docile marionettes they are. Funds are the financial equivalent of patients in a vegetative state, kept alive only by a complex array of external machines and doctors. To understand funds, then, we must understand this cast of economic actors who surround and animate them.

Let us begin with the central actor in the birth and life of a mutual fund. That actor is not, alas, the investor. As much as we, the American investing public, might wish to think of ourselves as the central objects around whom the industry revolves, the truth is that the sun in this financial solar system is actually our counter-party: the investment adviser.

The Investment Adviser

The term *investment adviser* is an unfortunate one. The phrase inevitably conjures the misleading image of a human, probably middle-aged and sporting a combover, strapped to a desk, and gushing with "exciting investment opportunities!" Those individuals do exist aplenty—and they do indeed advise clients with investments—but for our purposes, we'll give them the title of *financial planner* or *financial adviser*, not investment adviser.[6] In the mutual fund industry, the term *investment adviser* refers not to an individual human being but instead to a business entity. These businesses typically comprise many individual humans who think of themselves as investment experts and who do, indeed, manage investment portfolios.

In this country, many investment advisers are household names. They advertise widely in the pages of *The New Yorker*, the *Atlantic*, and other sensible magazines consumed by middle-class and middle-age savers. They also insert their commercials into the coverage of golf and tennis tournaments. Exemplars include Fidelity Management and Research, which manages the Fidelity funds; the Vanguard Group, which manages the Vanguard funds; Capital Research and Management Company, which runs the American funds; Pacific Investment Management Company LLC, which manages the PIMCO funds; and Franklin Advisers, which manages the Franklin Templeton funds; as well as T. Rowe Price Associates, BlackRock Advisors, J.P. Morgan Asset Management; and many others. Of course, we cannot omit the adviser we met earlier in this chapter, Janus Capital Management LLC.

A few of these investment advisers, such as Fidelity, are independent, private companies, in which case their owners might be a relatively small group of individual shareholders. Many other investment advisers, such as J.P. Morgan, are divisions of massive, multinational financial houses, in which case they are likely to be wholly owned subsidiaries of corporate shareholders—that corporate parent, if publicly owned, might in turn have hundreds of thousands of its own public shareholders. And the shareholders of an adviser are a different population from the shareholders of funds managed by that adviser. In all of these cases, however the advisers are organized, they owe fiduciary duties to their own shareholders and to the funds they manage.

Example #1: Figure 2.1, Fidelity Investments, is a privately held company owned by a limited number of individual shareholders (SH).

Example #2: Figure 2.2, Janus Capital Management, is a wholly owned subsidiary of Janus Capital Group, which is a publicly traded company owned by a large number of shareholders.

We begin with the investment adviser for two reasons. First, the adviser is the brains of the operation. Second, the adviser initiates the entire process of launching a mutual fund. In many entrepreneurial stories, customers have a need and

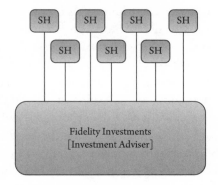

Figure 2.1 Private Investment Adviser and Shareholders.

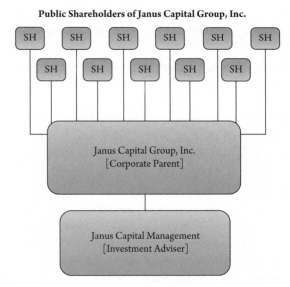

Figure 2.2 Public Investment Adviser and Shareholders.

seek out businesses to fill it (e.g., "Who can build me a house?") or businesses create a need for their customers (e.g., "You must have the ability to fling wingless birds at swine!") and then fill it (e.g., Angry Birds by Rovio Entertainment). In the land of mutual funds, however, investment advisers create their own customers.

Investment advisers form a mutual fund in the same mundane way that functionaries at many large businesses create new operating companies in this country every day. That is, the investment adviser typically hires a law firm, which often assigns a paralegal to the matter, and that underling in turn hires a vendor such as

CT Corporation or Corporation Service Company in Delaware to complete the necessary legal paperwork to create a brand-new business entity.

Already we are in unexpected territory. To many typical investors, mutual fund investments do not conjure images of separate and distinct companies. Instead, funds at first blush appear to be more like the bank accounts or certificates of deposit (CD) we discussed earlier. That is, a financial instrument by which the investor enters some sort of explicit understanding with the investment adviser. In a bank account or CD, depositors give their money to the bank as part of a contractual arrangement in which the bank promises to pay the account holder an obligatory return on her savings. The amount of that return might be a fixed percentage or might instead vary in accordance with prevailing interest rates, but the arrangement is very much between the bank and the account holder. Legally, we would characterize these arrangements as contractual debt transactions. The bank cannot simply decline to pay the promised amount without risking a lawsuit for breach of contract. The account holder, in turn, enjoys legal recourse to hunt down any amounts promised to the account but unpaid by the bank.

A mutual fund investment, by contrast, is an equity arrangement. That is, fund investors are shareholders, not creditors nor account holders; they hold stock, not debt. The consequences of this legal status are important, primarily because they permit substantial—even total—loss in the investment. Equity, with its potential for outrageous fortune and total loss, is an inherently riskier proposition than debt, with its limited interest payments in good times and higher bankruptcy priorities in bad times.

But in whom do fund investors invest?

Not the investment adviser, contrary to what one might expect. One might reasonably believe that handing over $1,000 to Fidelity constitutes, if not a banklike promise, then some sort of investment in Fidelity itself; after all, Fidelity is the name on the investment. Sad to say, a Fidelity mutual fund investment is not an investment in Fidelity itself, which is a shame because investing in Fidelity and other advisers over the past few decades would have been a brilliant decision. The stock of many investment advisers has performed tremendously well over the past few decades.[7] Shares in mutual funds, however, are not investments in the adviser itself.

The confusion is understandable—perhaps even intentional. The funds managed by investment advisers almost always come with the advisers' names plastered all over them. Funds managed by Fidelity include the Fidelity Value Discovery Fund, the Fidelity Select Air Transport Fund, the Fidelity Spartan 500 Index Fund, and hundreds of other funds with the name *Fidelity*.[8] Funds managed by Janus include the Janus Fund, the Janus Enterprise Fund, the Janus Venture Fund, and approximately thirty other funds with the name *Janus* in their title.[9]

But, again, a fund investment is most decidedly not an investment in the adviser. Instead, mutual fund investors are shareholders in the new, separate company that the investment adviser has just created. But if the fund is a separate company, why does it bear the same name as the investment adviser? Isn't that perhaps some sort of trademark violation? No, not for any practical purposes. A trademark violation is a violation only if the victim complains. And, in this case, the putative victim would be the entity that specifically created the new fund and willingly named it after itself.

When a person creates a new Massachusetts business trust or Maryland corporation or Delaware statutory trust—which are among the most popular choices of business entity for new mutual funds—the formation documents require just a few pieces of information. The first of those is a name for the new business. At the investment adviser's direction, the person filling out the paperwork enters a name for the fund that both describes the fund and includes the adviser's name. Why? Because the adviser explicitly wants to be connected with the fund for marketing and advertising purposes. The adviser wants the investing public to associate the new fund with the adviser's reputation and existing complex of perhaps dozens or hundreds of other funds. That goal of instant recognition is why all the Fidelity funds feature the name *Fidelity*. We'll see later that advisers may disavow this warm embrace of their funds when disgruntled plaintiffs come searching for someone to pay legal liabilities incurred by funds.

But if the fund and the adviser are not the same entity, what precisely is the connection between the two of them? The answer to that question depends on the moment at which you ask it. At the earliest stage in the life of a fund, after the adviser has just created it and is attempting to establish it—long before the investing public knows about or is permitted to invest in the fund—the adviser is the only shareholder in the fund. Legally, then, the fund is a wholly owned subsidiary of the adviser, as we see in figure 2.3. This early stage in the life of a fund is known as the *incubation period,* and it contains two critical events in the development of a fund.

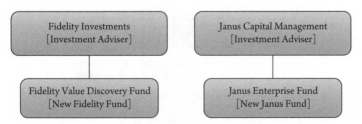

Figure 2.3 Investment Advisers and New Fund Subsidiaries.

The Board of Trustees

Being the founder of a new business is a little like being a new parent, with perhaps a little less crying, more sleep, and fewer soiled diapers. But fund founders, like parents, must bring those new lives into being and give them names. And founders who form a fund must also fill out an incorporation document that is something like a birth certificate, providing pertinent details about the new creation. Those formation documents include, in addition to the new fund's name, the membership of the fund's board of trustees.

In this respect, the formation process for an investment company is similar to the formation of an operating company. Founders of an operating company must also list a name and identify which humans are going to serve as members of the board of directors of the new corporation. In this country, Boston has been something of a spiritual home and center of the mutual fund industry ever since the first trio of American funds was created there in the 1920s.[10] Many of those earliest mutual funds were created as a legal entity known as a *Massachusetts business trust* rather than as a corporation or partnership or sole proprietorship.[11] This form of business organization granted its users with comparative flexibility and has, perhaps through inertia or path dependence, remained a common choice for mutual funds.

The supervising body of a Massachusetts business trust is still today known as the board of trustees. And like a corporation's board of directors, a fund's board of trustees possesses the authority to make decisions on behalf of the business for the benefit of the fund's shareholders, as shown in figure 2.4.

The members of this board are thus important human repositories of the fund's perspective on the world. Federal laws require 40 percent of a fund's board to be "independent" from the investment adviser.[12] Of course, that leaves 60 percent of the board members who can be very dependent upon—indeed, employees of— the investment adviser. The legal definition of independence requires the trustee to eschew certain financial connections with the adviser, but it does not eliminate the broad array of common, indefinable ways in which humans can be good

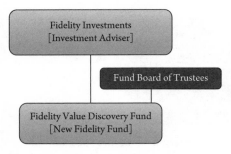

Figure 2.4 New Mutual Fund and Board of Trustees.

and loyal friends.[13] Remember that the investment adviser during the incubation period is the fund's sole initial shareholder and, as such, has the power to appoint by fiat all the trustees, independent or otherwise. Under such an arrangement, it is hard to conceive of an investment adviser going out of its way to appoint antagonists or troublemakers to the board.

In *The Way We Live Now*, Anthony Trollope describes the board meetings of the South Central Pacific and Mexican Railway with a liberal dollop of caricature, but the spirit of ingratiating camaraderie may survive in some measure:

> At the regular meetings of the Board, which never sat for above half an hour, two or three papers were read by Miles Grandall [the company secretary]. Melmotte himself [the chairman of the board] would speak a few slow words, intended to be cheery, and always indicative of triumph, and then everybody would agree to everything, somebody would sign something, and the "Board" for that day would be over.[14]

More recently in nonfiction, the *Wall Street Journal* has referred to the position of fund trustee as "the most lucrative job you've never heard of," noting that trustees for Fidelity funds are paid more than $400,000 each year for their pains of meeting every month or so.[15]

Of course, in exchange for this remuneration the fund trustees are expected to police the interests of the fund's shareholders. As our tour of malfeasance in subsequent chapters will demonstrate, some trustees have performed that role better than others. One of Trollope's board members, Lord Alfred Grendall, offers us an admonition that investors might do well to remember: "Does not every one know that a director of a company need not direct unless he pleases?"

The Advisory Agreement

For the board of an operating company, one of the first orders of business is to hire corporate officers such as the chief executive officer, president, treasurer, and secretary. Those individuals are the people who will actually undertake the business of the company. But a fund is different. And, with respect to management operations, the difference between operating companies and investment companies is profound.[16]

A fund's board of trustees does not hire officers or employees to run the business. Instead, the board essentially outsources the entire management of the fund's business. The board does so by entering into an investment advisory agreement on behalf of the fund, pursuant to which the fund retains the services of an external vendor—an investment adviser—to provide investment advice to the fund.[17] If this structure is beginning to sound circular, that's the point; it *is* circular.

The phrase "investment advice" may sound a little precatory, like some well-intended encouragement from a concerned aunt, but in practice it is far more mandatory. Investment advisers run mutual funds.[18] They manage and direct almost every facet of the executive authority of the business. The Securities and Exchange Commission has noted that "the term 'investment adviser' is to some extent a misnomer" because an adviser is "no mere consultant" but "almost always controls the fund."[19]

Here, then, is the first and most critical piece of life support for our fund: with no ordinary officers or employees of its own, the fund relies entirely on management provided externally through an investment adviser. This contractual connection, like an umbilical cord, is created during the early incubation period,[20] when the fund's board consists entirely of appointees of an investment adviser. And which investment adviser do we think a mutual fund's board of trustees will hire to oversee the operations of this new fund?

Why, the investment adviser that just created the fund and appointed the members of the board, of course.

The investment advisory agreement is a contract pursuant to which the adviser operates the fund in exchange for *a percentage of the assets of the fund*. Does this arrangement seem conflicted or underhanded somehow? Certainly, a subsidiary entering into a contract with its parent is far from an arm's-length business transaction. But because the relationship at this time is only that of a parent and a wholly owned subsidiary, there are no other parties to the arrangement who might be harmed by an ill-advised contractual agreement. Remember, at this early stage, no outsiders are investors in the fund yet.

The only investor in the fund at this stage is the investment adviser, and the adviser's investment comes in the form of an infusion of perhaps a few million dollars of its own money to seed the fund.[21] In a curious albeit temporary arrangement, depicted in figure 2.5, the investment adviser manages its own money through this newly created fund.

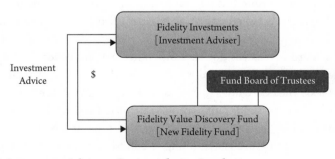

Figure 2.5 Investment Advisory Contract during Incubation.

The Incubation Period

Wouldn't an investment adviser prefer to manage other people's savings and thereby to make money off those other people? Of course, it would. But a few reasons explain why an adviser may choose to begin with this incubation arrangement before welcoming the outside investing public into the fund.

One of those rationales is understandable and perhaps even commendable. Recall that investment advisers will be selling their investment expertise to the public via this mutual fund. Bear in mind also that investment advisers often manage large numbers of funds, with a broad range of distinct investment objectives. If the investment adviser creates a new fund and purports to manage it with the purpose of making returns from, say, Japanese equities traded on the Tokyo Stock Exchange, the investing public might reasonably wonder just how good the investment adviser is at that strategy.

As with a restaurateur opening a new kitchen, the public's first question is likely to be, "How good is the cooking?" The incubation period, then, is a trial phase during which the investment adviser can develop and experiment with its new investing recipe using its own assets. An investment adviser like Fidelity, for instance, may already possess enough market recognition and reputation to attract money into a new fund immediately, even without this trial period. But if its investment strategy turned out to be a poor one, the adviser could harm those early investors and besmirch its reputation with a precipitate launch. By running the fund privately and internally for a few months, the investment adviser can attempt to perfect its investment strategy while developing a track record that it can eventually show to the investing public as a way to demonstrate its skill.

Of course, the investing public will be impressed with that track record only if it is a good one. And that brings us to another, perhaps less benevolent reason for these incubation periods. Investment advisers regularly launch several new funds concurrently, aware that not all of them will necessarily perform well during the incubation period. If a few of those new funds do poorly, as is often the case, the adviser can eliminate them privately before ever revealing their poor results to the public. Thus, incubation could also allow advisers to cherry-pick their best new funds to present what might appear to be an infallible track record to the investing public.[22]

At some point, of course, the investment adviser will make money only if it does invite the outside investing public into the fund. So, following the incubation period, the investment adviser will choose to take certain funds public. As the investing public flows into the fund, the adviser can draw out its own seed investment. Thus, the process of taking a fund public both establishes the business model in which investment adviser receives money for managing other people's money and terminates the parent-subsidiary relationship between the adviser and the fund.

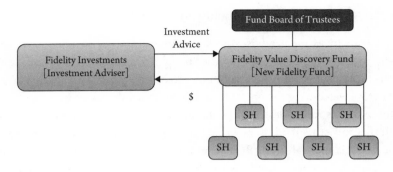

Shareholders in the Fund

Figure 2.6 Investment Advisory Contract after Fund Goes Public.

With the investment adviser now out of the role of fund shareholder, the fund thus ends its status as a subsidiary of the adviser. But the newly orphaned and public fund still possesses important and lasting legacies from the gestational period of adviser dominance, which is shown in figure 2.6. First, the composition of the board of trustees remains the same. Second, the investment advisory contract between the adviser and the fund remains in place.

Incoming shareholders who object to those arrangements could, of course, decline to invest if they found them troublesome. To do so, those investors would need to possess some knowledge about the board and the contract. A leading legal expert in this field, John Morley of Yale Law School, has stated: "I know of no director election or other important matter that has ever been contested by the impetus of shareholders in the ninety-year history of the open-end mutual fund industry."[23]

The Structural Conflict Between Investment Advisers and Fund Investors

Before we go further, let us clearly identify the structural conflict between investment advisers and fund investors. The U.S. Congress, when legislating new rules for mutual funds, offered a startling verdict on the relationship between many advisers and their funds: "potentially incestuous."[24]

Recall that, legally if not practically, advisers are business entities separate from the funds they manage. Whether an adviser is a subsidiary of a large financial house or a public company or a privately held business, it will have its own shareholders, a population distinct from the investors in funds managed by the adviser. These relationships are important because, as a matter of corporate law, the human directors and officers of investment advisers owe their adviser and its shareholders fiduciary duties. Courts have interpreted those duties to encompass somewhat gauzy concepts of loyalty, care, and good faith, as well as entirely con-crete concepts like an obligation to maximize profits for shareholders.

And note the critical element in this arrangement. Investors in a mutual fund are not generally shareholders of the investment adviser; instead, they are related only through a contractual arrangement. If the management of an investment adviser attempts to maximize the profits of its shareholders, it will find itself in a raw and stark conflict of interest. All profits for an adviser's shareholders must necessarily come from the assets of fund shareholders. Thus, an adviser who maximizes the adviser's shareholders—as opposed to the fund shareholders—transfers wealth from the fund shareholders to the adviser's shareholders.

An old joke—and dark truth—in the mutual fund industry is that the average investor in an investment advisory firm has done enormously better than the aver-age investor in a mutual fund over the past several decades. That is, the profits of investment advisers have wildly surpassed the performance of the average mutual fund.[25]

The conflict between managers and owners is a very old one and can be stub-bornly intractable. In Melville's *Moby Dick*, Captain Ahab illustrates the schism nicely. When the *Pequod* is damaged, the chief mate, Starbuck, urges Ahab to heave-to and repair the leaking hold: "Either do that, sir, or waste in one day more oil than we may make good in a year." Ahab, desperate to pursue his own cetacean interests, dismisses Starbuck with a "Begone!" Starbuck asks, "What will the own-ers say, sir?" Ahab replies with a meditation upon the conflict between principals and agents:

> Let the owners stand on Nantucket beach and outyell the Typhoons. What cares Ahab? Owners, owners? Thou art always prating to me, Starbuck, about those miserly owners, as if the owners were my con-science. But look ye, the only real owner of anything is its commander.[26]

Legislators have attempted to redress this imbalance between commanders and owners in mutual funds. In 1970, the U.S. Congress passed a federal law that created a fiduciary relationship between an investment adviser and the investors in that adviser's mutual funds. Section 36(b) of the Investment Company Act of 1940 states that an investment adviser "shall be deemed to have a fiduciary duty with respect to the receipt of compensation" paid by fund shareholders.[27] In the chapters ahead, we will see how helpful, if at all, this legislation has been to fund shareholders.

The market, too, has created alternative structures: most notably, in the Vanguard fund complex, the funds are managed by an investment adviser that is owned by the Vanguard Funds themselves. Perhaps not coincidentally, Vanguard's average fees are among the lowest in the industry and its assets under management are among the highest.

The Distributor

The process of taking a fund public brings us to our second important player in the structure and operation of mutual funds: the distributor. What a fund distributor distributes are shares in the fund. The parties to whom the distributor distributes those shares are investors who wish to become shareholders in the mutual fund. If the investment adviser's job is to invest the money in a fund wisely, then the distributor's job is to persuade new investors to pour their money into the fund.

The distributor's role of facilitating an exchange between businesses that want to raise money and investors who want to acquire stock is a common one in the financial world. And, just as in the romantic world, this role of matchmaker can be an essential one.

At some point in the successful growth of operating companies such as Facebook and Uber, the company's management decides to raise a war chest of millions or billions of dollars to expand its operations. At the same time, many investors desperately want to be part of a hot new venture. The financial matchmaker who brings those two groups together is known as the *underwriter*, a term also used for mutual fund distributors. Every operating company that goes public hires an underwriter to oversee the complicated task of pricing the company's stock and distributing its shares. But with operating companies, the process of going public is a singular, discrete event.

When Facebook wanted to go public, it hired an underwriter to manage a consortium of investment banks to buy its offering of shares to the public. Typically, an underwriter is an investment bank that coordinates a syndicate of other banks that purchase all the shares a company wants to sell. Some junior bankers at the underwriter put in a few intense months of diligence and negotiation, then everyone hopes for a geyser of an initial public offering (IPO). A vertiginous IPO is celebrated with dry-aged porterhouses and flights of single malt at Morton's, and Lucite deal toys for all. And, as far as Facebook and other operating companies are concerned, the project of underwriting ends there.

When an ordinary individual wishes to own shares in Facebook, she is highly unlikely to have any dealings with Facebook itself—instead, investors from the proletariat have to buy shares from other people who already own the shares, like second-hand buyers in an enormous used-book market. This process of buying and selling shares on the public stock markets is similar to how the United States itself issues paper currency into our economy: a U.S. mint prints sheets of crisp new bills, which are circulated to Federal Reserve banks, which then pass the bills to major commercial banks, which in turn distribute the bills through their tellers and ATMs to the American public. Ordinary U.S. citizens do not collect their starched new greenbacks directly from our sovereign.[28] With mutual funds, on the other hand, ordinary investors do collect their shares from the funds that offer them.[29]

Mutual fund shares do not trade on any secondary market. Investors who wish to invest in a mutual fund receive new shares issued just for them. And when mutual fund shareholders want to end their investment in a fund, they do not "sell" their shares to another interested investor, as a shareholder in an operating company might do. Instead, they "redeem" their shares by returning them directly to the fund itself.

So, with a mutual fund, the process of continually issuing and redeeming shares requires a perpetual underwriter, and the mutual fund distributor fills this role, as shown in figure 2.7. Indeed, for a fund, the process of going public is a chronic condition and, once begun, continues indefinitely. Mutual funds thus often have an underwriter of their own, who works exclusively to distribute the shares of only one family of funds.

Distributors pursue two projects in their goal of boosting the distribution of a fund's shares: the popularization of the fund to potential investors and the provision of easy ways for investors to buy the fund's shares. To succeed at these joint tasks of encouraging and facilitating distribution, distributors typically explore several routes.

The first is simply to advertise their funds, in print magazines, on television, radio, online, and through the ordinary avenues of commercial marketing. Anyone who has ever watched a televised yachting regatta, a polo tournament, perchance, or other programming redolent of disposable income may have seen mutual fund commercials. The pages of magazines enjoyed by America's investing demographic are also well populated by the marketing efforts of fund distributors.[30]

Of course, plenty of other businesses advertise in those pages also, sometimes with serendipitous and contrary messages: for example, pages 2 and 3 of the May 2015 issue of *Real Simple* features a confident woman striding toward Fidelity's slogan "More Power To You"; then pages 4 and 5 show three young friends having

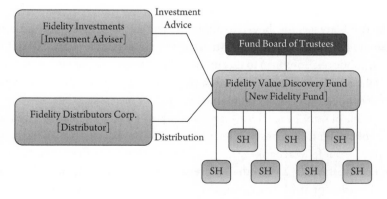

Shareholders in the Fund

Figure 2.7 Investment Adviser and Fund Distributor.

a good time with their Chevy Malibu under the tagline, "Mutual Funds or Mutual Friends?" The self-evident answer, one presumes, is "OMG, friends, right!? Funds are lame!" Distributors, nevertheless, attempt to do the best they can with the advertisement of their funds' shares.

In addition to marketing their funds, the distributor must ensure that willing investors have avenues to buy shares in the fund. Underwriters can help provide retail investors with a common array of channels through which to acquire fund shares, such as: (1) directly from the fund complex itself via an account with the investment adviser; (2) through the menu of options included in employers' 401(k) plans or individual retirement accounts (IRAs); and (3) through the array of market investments offered by online brokers such as E*Trade or Ameritrade and brick-and-mortar firms of certified financial planners and broker-dealers such as Edward Jones, Charles Schwab, and Merrill Lynch. A fund's distributor is responsible for establishing all of these investment avenues. And for making them work.

We'll see later in the book that distributors can get into trouble in their exertions to make these channels work too well—usually when they use investors' money to make undisclosed payments to the gatekeepers of each channel. Nevertheless, the boards of trustees of mutual funds regularly enter into distribution agreements, as they enter into investment advisory agreements, on behalf of their funds. And, once again, the compensation is a percentage of the assets in the fund.

The investment adviser and the distributor are the two most important service providers for any mutual fund, but boards of trustees commonly retain another trio of more minor vendors to complete the array of operations that a fund needs performed on its behalf.

The Custodian

Mutual funds are legally obliged to retain the services of a custodian. Not a janitor to clean up their messes—though, in extremis, fund complexes have been known to hire a public relations firm to tidy up after them; this custodian is, instead, a large financial institution charged with taking legal custody of a fund's assets. Typically, this role is filled by a major commercial bank. Not necessarily because banks are impregnable or unimpeachable—several regularly go bust and, in this day and age, many more suffer from a besmirched reputation—but because banks are intensely regulated by our federal banking laws. As the legal holder of all of a fund's cash and portfolio investments, a custodian segregates the fund's assets from the adviser's assets. In order for any transactions to occur in the fund's portfolio, the custodian must receive lawful instructions from the fund's investment adviser.[31]

This rather clumsy choreography, in which an adviser must transmit orders to the custodian instructing the custodian to release certain fund assets for the acquisition of particular stocks for the fund's portfolio, is intended to thwart fraud and theft in a mutual fund. No process is capable of perfectly eliminating all fraud, of course, but the use of custodians does create a paper trail of investment decisions. A custodian also stands as a heavily regulated third party between the adviser and the fund.

These steps are intended to help reduce cases in which an investment adviser simply pockets investors' money and flees with it to an undisclosed island in the Caribbean. Bernie Madoff's Ponzi schemes were operated in lightly regulated or, indeed, unregulated private investment funds that did not require custodians. We cannot know whether Madoff's perverse ambitions would have foiled even a diligent custodian, but the presence of any custodian might have made his machinations more difficult to perpetrate or more easily traceable. Indeed, of the problems from which mutual funds suffer, rarely do they have anything to do with corrupt custodians.

The Transfer Agent

A fund must retain the services of a company that can manage the humdrum requirements of administering thousands upon thousands of client accounts for all of the shareholders in a fund.

In a mutual fund, it's always important to bear in mind which pool of investments we are talking about at any given moment. Remember that investors who participate in a mutual fund buy *fund shares* and are *fund shareholders*—that is, their shares represent a small slice of the overall performance of the fund. By contrast, the money they contribute goes into a massive combined pool of money that the adviser then uses to buy and sell other investments, such as stocks, bonds, real estate—these investments are called *portfolio securities*.

So, fund shareholders own shares of the mutual fund (such as the Vanguard Total Stock Market Index Fund), while the mutual fund owns the portfolio securities (such as Ford or IBM). And each fund shareholder invests in the hope that a fund's portfolio securities will increase in value in order to raise the corresponding value of her fund shares. (And note that the custodian, above, holds the portfolio securities.)

Fund shareholders need regular statements of their holdings and sporadic shareholder notices, access to websites filled with disclosures about the funds, and toll-free telephone numbers staffed by operators who can interact with the investing public. These unglamorous but necessary operations are typically the province of a transfer agent.[32]

The Administrator

An investment adviser might choose to outsource some of the back-office tasks associated with running a mutual fund. An administrator will then be responsible for preparing and filing materials with regulators such as the Securities and Exchange Commission, with taxing authorities such as the Internal Revenue Service, and with any other demanding governmental agencies.[33]

These five primary services providers are the fingers that animate a mutual fund. Like the strings on a puppet, these players provide life to the fund externally; without them, the fund would essentially be an inert bucket of cash.

Often, several of these companies are sibling affiliates within a single, larger financial institution. Consider, for example, the J.P. Morgan family of funds: the adviser is J.P. Morgan Investment Management Inc.; the distributor is JP Morgan Distribution Services Inc.; the administrator is J.P. Morgan Funds Services; and the custodian is JPMorgan Chase Bank.[34] (And, yes, all those versions of J.P. Morgan are spelled differently.)

In essence, one large company can—through separate subsidiaries—provide the entire constellation of functions required by a single family of funds, as figure 2.8 demonstrates.

Other Service Providers

Of course, like any other public financial entity, mutual funds need the services of other usual supporting cast members. A fund needs an accountant to conduct

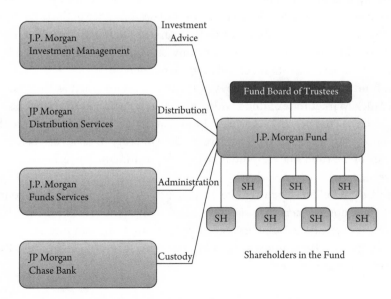

Figure 2.8 Mutual Fund and Family of Related Service Providers.

periodic audits of all the money flowing in and out of the fund and the public statements of the fund's financial condition. A fund also needs legal counsel to ensure that it is complying with the extraordinarily complex web of state and federal regulations that govern mutual funds. And, at certain rocky times in their history, funds will engage not only public relations firms but also the services of their law firms' litigation departments.

Building the Fund's Portfolio

Finally, we must consider the primary business of a mutual fund: investing. And here we are focusing on the investing that involves a fund's portfolio securities. Ninety million fund shareholders have poured $16 trillion into 8,000 mutual funds—we must give thought to where all that money goes.

For the most part, investment advisers use all that treasure to buy the stocks and bonds of our country's publicly traded corporations and the debt of America's federal, state, and municipal governments. In an indirect and sort of unsatisfying way, all of us Americans who own small pieces of mutual funds own even smaller pieces of America's largest corporations and our governments' debt.[35]

As anyone who has dabbled with buying and selling a few stocks knows, the process is fraught not only with the risk of picking losers but also with the certainty of paying fees simply to play the game. Even enormous mutual funds pay commissions to brokers for buying or selling securities for their portfolios. And since those portfolios can amount to billions of dollars, the commissions that funds pay can themselves amount to millions upon millions of dollars each year. So, the brokers who execute those trades at the direction of investment advisers provide another critical external service to mutual funds. And, like each of the external service providers we have already discussed, they don't do it for free.[36]

Structural Costs and Complexity

The costs associated with all these services are of critical importance to fund investors because these expenses ultimately come out of the investors' assets. Every dollar invested in a mutual fund, then, loses value immediately from the costs associated with our mutual fund structure. In order to break even, a mutual fund must generate positive investment returns that at least surmount their operating costs. As important as the amounts these service providers charge, we shall see, is the manner in which they charge for their work. The method as much as the magnitude can create particular incentives—at times, perverse—which investors in mutual funds must appreciate in order to protect their investments.

As a parting thought on the structure of mutual funds, let's consider our Supreme Court case once again: Whatever happened to those disgruntled Janus shareholders? Recall that they wanted Janus held responsible for making public misstatements about the way in which its subsidiary, an investment adviser, man-aged a mutual fund. Our discussion of fund structures above and figure 2.9 should help us understand what troubled those Supreme Court justices:

Knowing what we do now about the management of a mutual fund, we understand that, although the Janus Investment Fund and its investment adviser are legally separate entities, the adviser—and nobody else—controls all business operations on behalf of the fund. Janus Capital Management estab-lished the policy to prevent market timing, Janus Capital Management wrote the prospectus banning market timing, and Janus Capital Management—for illicit gain—subsequently allowed someone to market time the Janus Investment Fund.

What did the Supreme Court justices—once they realized that fund share-holders were not involved in this lawsuit—decide? A bare majority of five justices ruled that Janus Capital Management was not responsible. They reasoned that the fund is, after all, a distinct legal entity and it has its own board of trustees. Alas, only someone willing to disregard how much an adviser dominates both its funds and their boards could be comfortable with such a formalistic conclusion.

But who, then, was responsible for the falsehoods in the Janus Fund prospec-tus?[37] Janus won its Supreme Court case arguing that the *adviser* should not be responsible.[38] Earlier in the same litigation, at trial, Janus also argued cheekily and successfully that the *fund* shouldn't be responsible for those misstatements, either[39]—a fund, as everyone knows, doesn't really conduct any business on its

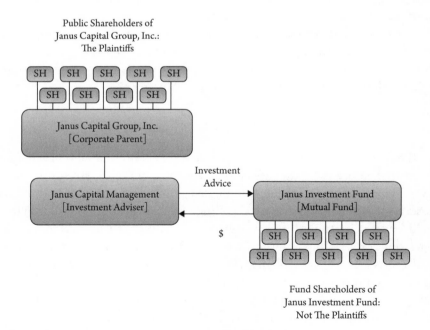

Figure 2.9 Public Shareholders and Fund Investors in the *Janus* Case.

own behalf. What sort of outfit could make these two diametrically opposite arguments in the same litigation? Janus, of course, whose logo shown in figure 2.10 is the two-faced Roman god.

Figure 2.10 Janus Logo.

In the structure of mutual funds, legal distinctions—no matter how formalistic they may be—can be powerful bulkheads for protecting investment advisers from liability and simultaneously barring shareholders from recovery.

3

ECONOMICS

Here is something every non-rich American family should know: The odds are that you will run out of money in retirement. . . . The standard prescription is that Americans should put more money aside in investments. The recommendation, however, glosses over a critical driver of unpreparedness: Wall Street is bleeding savers dry.
—Eduardo Porter, *New York Times*, 2015

The economics of a mutual fund are not terribly different from a leaky bathtub. And, at the moment, America's funds dribble out approximately one hundred billion dollars each year.[1]

As investors, we pour our money into a fund in the hope that the fund's adviser will make prudent—perhaps even prescient—decisions that will lead the fund's portfolio to accumulate investment gains. In effect, we want our investment adviser to raise the level of water in the tub for all our financial benefit. Alas, before a fund even commences its primary mission of investing, money has already begun to seep away.

Our exploration of the structure of mutual funds revealed the intricate nexus of legal contracts that connect investment advisers and all their affiliates to funds. Just as with dubious plumbing, most of the leaks in a mutual fund system will appear where the contractual pipes fit together. As we examine the ways in which advisers and their sibling entities arrange their compensation, we will see that their fees inevitably draw down assets in the fund. No matter how well or poorly a fund is performing, it is always bleeding money in the form of fees. To generate positive returns for fund shareholders, then, an adviser must first do well enough to earn back the fees it charges. But no matter how sagacious an adviser's decisions, in good times its fees diminish any gains; in bad times they exacerbate losses.

Any plumber who attempts to triage a leak must first determine two important aspects of the problem: first, where is the water coming from; second, how much water is escaping. That two-step diagnosis is also how we will examine the economics of mutual funds. In this chapter, we will identify the sources of the money leaking from funds, then, in the next chapter we will examine the magnitude of the spill.

The people and companies that manage mutual funds must, of course, be compensated for their services. Indeed, the management fees that fund advisers charge are conceptually little different from the executive compensation paid to the business people who run operating companies. Though America has lavished a great deal of attention on—and at times, indignation at—the size of corporate America's executive compensation, comparatively little notice has been taken of fund management fees. To some critics of fund fees, however, Galsworthy's inscription on the altar to the God of Property are apt:

Nothing for nothing, and really remarkably little for sixpence.[2]

Perhaps even more important than the actual amounts advisers are paid is the particular manner in which they are paid. The structure of how someone is compensated often creates the incentives governing how that person will behave.

How Advisers Are Paid

Consider a coffee barista. Can his pay tell us anything about his performance? If we learn that he takes home $20,000 a year, we remain ignorant about how tasty any given cappuccino he pours might be. If, instead, we discover that he is paid based on the number of shots he pulls, we might reasonably expect that he will place a premium on speed over quality. If, on the other hand, his salary is raised or reduced based on customer reviews, we might expect the taste of his creations to improve, perhaps at some cost to his speed. Management might prefer one arrangement, aficionados of the bean might prefer the other. As it is, most baristas are paid by the hour, so they may just be killing time and, perhaps, a lot of cups of coffee. To understand the incentives for the investment advisers of mutual funds, let us begin by examining the way in which they are paid.

Is investment advice simply a product, like an iPhone or one of those cappuccini? No, most decidedly not. First, even the most undiscerning customer can eventually figure out whether a phone or coffee was any good; investments, on the other hand, can take decades to declare themselves a success or failure. Second, with a standard product, customers hand over an amount of money that represents the seller's notion of what the product is worth. Or, perhaps, what the seller believes the market's notion is of the product's worth.

By the time a customer hands over hundreds of dollars for the latest iPhone, Apple has already spent millions to design, manufacture, and advertise the new gadget. Where does Apple get all that loot up front? One source, of course, is the trove of billions we gave them so that we could gorge on all the previous models. But another source, particularly for companies not quite so capable of addicting

America to its wildly popular products, is the capital market. That is, companies can borrow the money they need from lenders or raise it from investors in exchange for shares of equity. With that money in hand, companies can then pay for the raw materials and services they need to develop their wares.

In a mutual fund, shareholders are simultaneously the source of raw materials and the customers. An investment adviser that wishes to manage a fund portfolio needs both a pool of money to manage and compensation for its labor. If we wished to earn a few hundred dollars in gains from a mutual fund, we cannot simply pay the adviser a few dollars in fees; we must hand over the tens of thousands of dollars that the adviser needs to use to earn those gains. From that pile of dosh we hand over, the adviser will deduct its fees.

This arrangement may seem obvious and unsurprising, but consider its application in the normal dealings we have with operating companies. Imagine if the only way to buy an iPhone were to hand Apple $10,000, to wait a year, and then to receive the $10,000 back together with one of those magical white boxes.

Purchasing products and investments are fundamentally different undertakings. As we shall see again and again, granting an investment adviser control over all those thousands—indeed, trillions—of dollars in order to generate marginal gains and fees creates enormous temptation for our investment advisers. Some resist better than others.

So, an adviser's fees come directly out of our investment. How exactly? Through a basic multiplication formula. Advisers—and their affiliated service providers—charge a fee expressed as a percentage. To determine the fee in dollars, that percentage is multiplied against all the assets under the adviser's management in a fund. So:

$$\text{Advisory fee} \times \text{assets under management} = \text{adviser's revenues}$$

Before we examine the amount of fees in percentages and, more important, the amounts of earnings in greenbacks, let us take a second to note that this formula immediately tells us something fundamentally important about mutual funds. The formula reveals to us hints about how the coffee brewed by a fund adviser is going to taste. That is, it reveals the adviser's incentives in the way it runs the mutual fund.

Let us assume as our premise that a primal drive of financial institutions is to make more money. Under our simple mutual fund formula, an investment adviser can adjust only two variables if it wishes to increase its revenues: the size of its fee or the amount of assets under its management.

As with any multiplication task, the result will grow if either multiplicand is enlarged. But in the world of funds, the ease with which an adviser may increase the two variables is not equal. Increasing fees—like raising prices in any business—is never going to be popular with paying customers, and advisers generally would rather avoid doing so publicly.

Increasing assets under management may not be quite as simple as hiking a fee, but it can be done in a pair of ways that are less likely to bother shareholders: either by making incisive investment decisions that capture gains in the market or by persuading investors to pour more money into the fund.

The first of these approaches requires outstanding investing expertise or luck—traits that innumerable academic studies show mutual fund advisers are incapable of demonstrating consistently.[3] The second requires marketing, a task to which the advisory industry applies itself diligently.

But note the critical difference between these approaches to investors in a fund. The simple increase of assets in a fund may or may not represent an increase in gains to investors in that fund. Consider a fund that doubles in size over the course of a single year. And, for the sake of simplicity, let's imagine that the increase came entirely from either one mode or the other.

If the fund doubled in size without taking in a single penny of new investment, then the increase must have come only from rising values of the securities in the fund's portfolio—that is, the fund's adviser has, indeed, been wise or fortunate. And the fund's investors all benefit also, as the value of their shares in the fund are likely to enjoy something close to a 100 percent increase.[4]

If, on the other hand, the fund doubled in size without any gain or loss in the portfolio's securities and, instead, solely because the adviser persuaded new investors to send in more money; then, the investors in the fund will enjoy zero increase in the value of their fund shares. Though the fund's assets have increased, its assets per share have remained constant. Yet in this case, the adviser's revenue will still double.

So, to inflict a little math on the problem, here are the two approaches rendered in simple numbers:

	January 1	December 31	Gain to shareholders
Approach 1:	$\dfrac{\$100 \text{ in fund}}{100 \text{ investors}} = \$1$	$\dfrac{\$200 \text{ in fund}}{100 \text{ investors}} = \$2$	From $1 to $2 = 100 percent
Approach 2:	$\dfrac{\$100 \text{ in fund}}{100 \text{ investors}} = \$1$	$\dfrac{\$200 \text{ in fund}}{200 \text{ investors}} = \$1$	Stays at $1 = 0 percent

So, the fund's investment adviser will double its earnings in either case.

Here, then, is a foundational divergence in the interests of fund shareholders and fund advisers. Fund shareholders benefit only when a fund actually generates investment gains; fund advisers benefit by increasing the assets under management any way that they can. As we will see, less than scrupulous advisers have devised a panoply of creative ways to increase assets under their management that do not benefit fund investors—indeed, several that actually harm those investors.

Other Possible Ways to Compensate Fund Advisers

If our current approach to compensating fund advisers creates these perverse incentives, are there no other ways in which they could be compensated? Certainly there are. But, unfortunately, perhaps not any better ways.

First, investment advisers could treat their advice like other services and simply charge an annual flat fee unconnected to the amount of assets. Customers can pay a standard price for tax preparation or pest control or lawn care, and fund investors could pay a set price for investment advice. Investment advisers might be content with that arrangement because, if a fund were to lose huge amounts, the adviser's compensation would not be adversely affected. Of course, if the fund were to perform magnificently, the adviser would not share in any of those gains, either. What, then, would be the adviser's economic incentive under such an arrangement? In essence, the adviser would gain only by bringing in new investors and new investment, not by managing the fund's money successfully. Excellent returns could certainly attract new investors, but good performance is hard for advisers to achieve consistently. Marketing is more straightforward. So, a flat fee might cause advisers to be even less concerned with generating positive investment returns for fund shareholders.[5]

A second alternative would be for investment advisers to charge a fee based on actual investment profits they generate for their funds. Performance fees, as this sort of arrangement is known, are a staple of other collective investment pools, such as private equity funds, venture capital funds, and hedge funds.[6] Advisers of those funds typically earn 20 percent or more of the gains they generate, which explains how Mitt Romney could afford to run for president so often[7] and how a hedge fund manager can buy priceless masterpieces and a Fifth Avenue mansion in which to house them.[8] Successful hedge and private equity fund advisers can earn billions in a single year.[9] Of course, the investors in those funds pocket the other 80 percent of gains and appear to do perfectly well also, so why don't mutual funds adopt this approach?

Quite simply because performance fees reward risky behavior.[10] Performance fees generate money for an adviser only if there are profits in the fund—and the larger those profits, the more spectacular the adviser's earnings. In essence, they are the home runs of the investing world, and as such, they encourage the behavior of Sammy Sosa and Mark McGuire.[11] Not necessarily the corking and juicing so much as the swinging for the fences, strike-outs be damned. An adviser rewarded by a share of profits will take more risks to generate those gains. Sluggers in baseball take bigger cuts at the pitches they face, and when it works, we enjoy the spectacular long ball; when it fails, we witness the flaccid strike-out. Investors with a lot of money can afford strike-outs; investors who are scrimping for retirement generally cannot.

In the United States, our representatives and senators in Congress have determined that mutual funds ought to be an investment option primarily for ordinary retail investors, and consequently, they have enacted laws severely limiting performance fees.[12] So, we are left with our imperfect mechanism for compensating the investment advisers of mutual funds.

The decision to try to keep mutual funds a safe if uninspiring investment for the general public has many consequences. When Americans invest, just as when we travel by air, we face two sets of rules. For the great masses flying commercially on sardined Airbuses, the federal government imposes tight security and heavy restrictions on our freedom; if something goes awry aboard one of those planes, the lives of many people are at risk. For the opulent few flying privately on Gulfstreams, word is that the limousines pull right up to the jets' staircases without a single representative of the federal government on hand to pat a body down; if something goes awry aboard one of those planes, only the lives of a few people who can well afford good pilots and mechanics are at risk.[13]

In investment funds, this regulatory dichotomy also exists. As a broad matter, mutual funds are more heavily regulated than private funds offered only to wealthier investors.[14] More specifically, federal laws limit the ability of mutual funds to use performance fees, to build portfolios comprising riskier investments (such as derivatives), and to engage in more hazardous investment techniques (such as leverage).[15]

If mutual funds are the comparative jalopies on our financial highways buzzing with hedge-fund Ferraris, then they have been designed to be so. Mutual funds are intended to deliver their passengers in safety, not necessarily in haste and certainly not via an adrenaline-drenched ride.

Finding out What Advisers Are Paid

So, how do we find out where the leaks are? Now that we know *how* investment advisers and other service providers are paid, where can we find out *what* they are paid? This question should be an easy one to answer. After all, federal regulations require all advisers of mutual funds to send their investors prospectuses and to file public reports containing detailed lists of their fees.[16] But the task of figuring out the exact amount of a mutual fund's fees remains a surprisingly difficult one. First, despite federal disclosure requirements, many investors do not know where to look to find the fees.[17] Second, the fees, when located, are not simple to decipher.

Where can we find those fees? If you are an investor in the fund already, the adviser should have mailed you a hard copy of the prospectus soon after you purchased your first shares in the fund.[18] Like other financial and sordid materials, these mailings typically arrive in generic or anonymized envelopes to protect your privacy. And like so many other mass mailings, most prospectuses promptly find their way into the garbage. But prospectuses sent after a purchase are, in any event, of no use in discovering the fees of funds that we are considering prospectively, before we actually hand over our money.

Like everything else today, we can find fees on the Google—and like so many things Google, its Finance page can be very helpful—but we need to know what to search for. The name of the document in which a fund's fees are disclosed is the fund's *prospectus*. A typical fund prospectus can easily run to forty, fifty, or more pages in length, bloated with legalistic scrapple. All legal prospectuses must contain a section entitled "Fees and Expenses," which includes a table listing the expenses that investment advisers and the other service providers charge the fund. In recent years, to lessen the unavoidable morass that such a long disclosure form inflicts on lay readers, regulators have also required a new document called a *summary prospectus*.[19] So, a quick Google search of a fund's name and the word *prospectus* should bring you to the correct document.

Alternatively, investment advisers such as Vanguard and Fidelity maintain websites that list information about all the many offerings in their sprawling fund families. On those websites—as well as on the sites of independent, third-party aggregators of fund information, such as Morningstar and BrightScope—the prospectus and summary prospectus can often be found under the heading of "Filings" or "Reports." As we get closer to our goal, though, the challenges mount.

In nutrition, one of the most notable revolutions has been the Food and Drug Administration's requirement that dietary tables appear on the packaging of all food items sold in the United States.[20] Fee and expense tables are often compared to those FDA labels, but we'll see some important differences. The first, of course, is that we always know when we're looking at the appropriate FDA label: the one on the box matches the stuff in the box. It's not necessarily so simple with tables for mutual funds.

When we have a prospectus in hand, we must first realize that a single document can serve as a prospectus for many separate mutual funds. The prospectus shown in figure 3.1, for example, covers seventeen different J.P. Morgan funds.[21]

Prospectuses require information about the performance and fees of each fund, and also about the adviser and the risks of investing each fund. If the risks of several funds are similar, then an adviser may produce information common to many funds only once in the prospectus. Accordingly, some portions of a prospectus break out specifics for each fund, while other portions apply only to all the funds covered by that prospectus. That means, within a single document, we must keep alert to make sure we are examining the fees of the particular fund we have in mind.

But even when we have the correct fund, we are confronted by the fact that many mutual funds offer a variety of classes of shares in the same fund. So, the

Prospectus

J.P. Morgan U.S. Equity Funds

Class A, Class B*, Class C & Select Class Shares
November 1, 2014, as supplemented November 5, 2014

JPMorgan Disciplined Equity Fund
  Class/Ticker: A/JDEAX: Select/JDESX
JPMorgan Diversified Fund
  Class/Ticker: A/JDVAX; B/JDVBX; C/JDVCX; Select/JDVSX
JPMorgan Dynamic Growth Fund
  Class/Ticker: A/DGAAX; C/DGXCX; Select/JDGSX
JPMorgan Equity Focus Fund
  Class/Ticker: A/JPFAX; C/JPFD; Select/JPFSX
JPMorgan Equity Income Fund
  Class/Ticker: A/OEIX: B/OGIBX; C/OINCX; Select/HLIEX
JPMorgan Equity Index Fund
  Class/Ticker: A/OGEAX; B/0GEIX; C/OEICX; Select/HLEIX
JPMorgan Growth and Income Fund
  Class/Ticker: A/VGRIX; B/VINBX; C/VGIC.X; Select/VGIIX
JPMorgan Hedged Equity Fund
  Class/Ticker: A/JHQAX; C/JHQCX; Select/JHEQX
JPMorgan Intrepid America Fund
  Class/Ticker: A/JIAAX C/JIACX; Select/JPIAX

JPMorgan Intrepid Growth Fund
  Class/Ticker: A/JIGAX ;C/JCICX; Select/JPGSX
JPMorgan Intrepid Value Fund
  Class/Ticker: A/JIVAX; C/JIVCX; Select/JPIVX
JPMorgan Large Cap Growth Fund
  Class/Ticker: A/OLGAX; B/OGLGX; C/OLGCX; Select/SEEGX
JPMorgan Large Cap Value Fund
  Class/Ticker: A/OLVAX; B/OLVBX; C/OLVCX; Select/HLQVK
JPMorgan U.S. Dynamic Plus Fund
  Class/Ticker: A/JPSAX; C/JPSCX; Select/JILSX
JPMorgan U.S. Equity Fund
  Class/Ticker: A/JUEAX; B/JUEBX; C/JUECX; Select/JUESX
JPMorgan U.S. Large Cap Core Plus Fund**
  Class/Ticker: A/JLCAX; C/JLPCX; Select/JLPSX
JPMorgan U.S. Research Equity Plus Fund
  Class/Ticker: A/JEPAX; C/JEPCX; Select/JEPSX

*   Class B Shares are no longer available far new purchases.
**   Closed to new investors.

Figure 3.1 Prospectus for J.P. Morgan U.S. Equity Funds.

adviser may offer one set of shares to retail investors, another set to investors who are investing through a retirement account, yet another set to institutional investors, and so forth. Some advisers, such as Fidelity, assign inscrutable names to their different classes: Investor shares, Admiral shares, and so on. The J.P. Morgan prospectus shown in figure 3.1 covers up to four different classes of shares for its seventeen different U.S. equity funds: Class A, Class B, Class C, and something called Select Class. (A different prospectus covers three more classes for those very same funds: Class R2, Class R5, and Class R6.) The array is almost as baroque as the caste system used by our airline industry: First Class, Executive Platinum, Preferred, Emerald, Gold, Priority.

Here, then, is another barrier to the lay investor. Do you know what precise class of shares you own in each of your mutual funds? Do you know in which classes you might be eligible to invest? Do you even know why an adviser would offer multiple classes of shares in the same fund? The answer to those questions is highly salient to determining fees because, as we shall see when we examine a sample table, the chief difference among share classes is the amount they charge. Our single J.P. Morgan document contains information for fifty-seven different investments.

Fee and expense tables are divided into two major sections: Shareholder Fees and Annual Fund Operating Expenses. All fees gnaw away at an investor's money, but conceptually these fees differ in that Shareholder Fees are like cover charges that a patron might pay to get into a club, while the Annual Fund Operating Expenses are more like the bill for drinks the patron actually orders. These different fees can also be categorized by the people whom they are intended to compensate: Shareholder Fees go to the bouncers, the people who provided an investor with access to the fund; Operating Expenses go to the people who run the establishment.

Shareholder Fees

The first category, colloquially known as "sales loads" or just "loads," are an increasingly rare phenomenon.[22] But when they do exist, they are a significant burden on investors and, like all cover charges, are easy to resent. Typically, loads can take effect at two points in time: when an investor purchases shares (front-end loads) or when an investor redeems them (back-end loads). The proceeds from these commissions go to the brokers who execute these trades. In Las Vegas, taxi drivers who deliver patrons to bars, restaurants, gun ranges, and other desert delights are often rewarded with similar commissions. In Vegas, the establishments seeking the customers pay those commissions; in mutual funds, investors pay the commissions. Loads are sufficiently galling that many investors have rebelled against them, and most fund families now offer no-load share classes. And for the average investor, avoiding loads is often a sound first step when investing in mutual funds.

Annual Fund Operating Expenses

The section of the fee and expense table for Annual Fund Operating Expenses is where to find information about the most salient—and unavoidable—mutual fund fees. All the prospectuses tell us in the subtitle that these are "expenses that you pay each year as a percentage of the value of your investment." Mathematically, it makes no difference whether your investment is reduced directly from your money or proportionally from your money when mixed with everyone else's money; the result either way is less money for you. But this particular category of expenses relates not to your gaining admittance to the fund but to the ongoing operations of the fund.

Complicating the Simple, for Fun and Profit

Before we marvel at the difficulties of reading a simple chart, let us take a moment to consider the challenges of figuring out how much something costs. And the human ingenuity that can go into making that task remarkably difficult.

In a robust and diverse market, such as the one for computers, for example, customers typically make purchases based on a range of sometimes complicated considerations: *How much does the computer cost?*, of course, but also, *Am I a Mac or a PC person? Is a more expensive Mac still a better deal than a cheaper PC?* The decision, possibly, depends on how much of one's psyche is invested in those brands—or in just having a computer that works. In markets such as these, the companies that sell the products usually make it pretty easy to figure out how much they cost.

Now, consider the markets for fungible goods, like pork bellies or crude oil. In these markets, prices from different sellers should be truly simple to compare because, by definition, what they are selling is identical. From whom should Smithfield Farms buy pork bellies for the bacon it makes? Why, the cheapest seller, if those bellies are in fact the same. From whom should Southwest Airlines buy its jet fuel? Again, the cheapest barrels would make most sense.

And what is the most fungible of all commodities in our economy? Not necessarily pork bellies or crude oil. Depending on the discrimination of one's palate, perhaps the pork bellies of Iowa savor just that little bit more of a fine *terroir* than whatever is oinking out in North Carolina. Likewise, some crude oil is sweeter—that is, less sulfurous—than others. But there is one commodity that is, indisputably, exactly the same throughout our entire economy: money.

The almighty and perfectly consistent dollar. Accordingly, if someone wants to borrow or lend some money, zero consideration need be paid to the taste or quality of the greenbacks; only price should matter. And the price of money should be really easy to communicate: most often, we just express that price as a particular percentage. When the U.S. Treasury wants to borrow money for thirty years, it states unequivocally what it is willing to pay: 2.98 percent, for instance, as of January 4, 2016.[23]

This notion of transparent pricing for fungible commodities is all very compelling in theory. But anyone who has ever borrowed money for a household mortgage has endured a different experience. Figuring out the best price for a mortgage from a variety of lenders can be an incredibly difficult challenge. But can't one simply compare the percentages from three or four different competitors and choose the lowest?

If only we could. Whichever company offered that lowest rate would soon attract all household borrowers and dominate the market. Yet our market teems with different lenders. Either all the lenders are charging the same amount or some borrowers are paying more for their loans than they need do. If one lender did charge the lowest rate and borrowers knew that, then the scores or hundreds of other lenders charging more would quickly have to match that

Annual Fund Operating Expenses[1] (expenses that you pay each year as a percentage of the value of your investment)

	Class A	Class B	Class C	Class N	Class Y	Class I
Management Fees[2]	1.18%	1.18%	1.18%	1.18%	1.18%	1.18%
Distribution and/or Service (12b-1) Fees	0.24%	1.00%	1.00%	0.50%	None	None
Other Expenses						
Other Expenses of the Fund	0.25%	0.25%	0.25%	0.25%	0.25%	0.06%
Other Expenses or the Subsidiary	0.01%	0.01%	0.01%	0.01%	0.01%	0.01%
Total Other Expenses	0.26%	0.26%	0.26%	0.26%	0.26%	0.07%
Acquired Fund Fees and Expenses	0.05%	0.05%	0.05%	0.05%	0.05%	0.05%
Total Annual Fund Operating Expenses	1.73%	2.49%	2.49%	1.99%	1.49%	1.30%
Fee Waiver and/or Expense Reimbursement[3]	(0.29%)	(0.29%)	(0.29%)	(0.29%)	(0.29%)	(0.29%)
Total Annual Fund Operating Expenses After Fee Waiver and/or Expense Reimbursement	1.44%	2.20%	2.20%	1.70%	1.20%	1.01%

1. Expenses hare been restated to reflect current fem..
2. "Management Fees" reflects the gross management fees paid to the Manager by the Fund and the gross management fee for the Subsidiary during the Fund's most recent fiscal year.
3. After discussions with the Fund's Board, the Manager has contractually agreed to waive fees and/or reimburse Fund expenses in an amount equal to the indirect management fees incurred through the Fund's investments in funds managed by the Manager or its affiliates. This fee waiver and/or expense reimbursement may not be amended or withdrawn for one year from the date of this prospectus. unless approved by the Board. The Manager has also contractually agreed to waive the management fee it receives from the Fund in an amount equal to the management fee it receives from the subsidiary. This undertaking will continue to be in effect for so long as the Fund invests in the Subsidiary and may not be terminated unless approved by the Fund's Board.

Figure 3.2 Sample Chart of Oppenheimer Annual Operating Expenses.

price or go out of business. But they don't appear to have done either. So, what is going on?

Mortgage lenders know that a price war could drive down profits for them all. And they have figured out how to make it difficult for borrowers to determine how much lenders are charging to rent their money: opacity.

Anyone who has taken out a mortgage has waded through innumerable variables involved in lending. First, there's the variety of different terms: fixed or variable; five, seven, fifteen, or thirty years; points down or nothing due at closing; and on and on. But even when one keeps those variables constant, comparing lenders remains difficult. They all seem to charge a different blend of administrative fees, application fees, origination fees, appraisal fees, processing fees, underwriting fees, fees to copy and courier you materials, and on and on.

As Princeton economist Alan Blinder has noted in his analysis of the 2008 financial crisis, complexity is a weapon that financial firms can deploy against less sophisticated investors.

> Why create such a complex system? Didn't anyone remember the KISS principle? (*Keep it simple, stupid.*) The answer is, in fact, simple, and not at all stupid: Complexity and opacity are potential sources of huge profit. The more complex and customized the security, the harder it is to comparison shop for the best price. And without comparison shopping, there is little effective competition.[24]

So, when the actual price of a mortgage is inscrutable, how is a borrower to decide among different lenders? Perhaps decisions are based on which lender the borrower has heard of before (i.e., marketing, not price); or based on which loan officer is friendlier or more helpful (i.e., customer service, not price); or based on whose website is easier to navigate (i.e., convenience, not price).

If our economy can obfuscate the price of something so universally constant as a U.S. dollar, then muddying the cost of mutual funds with their myriad investment strategies, performances, investment advisers, share classes, and so on should be a simple project. Indeed, for those so inclined, it can be.

Let us consider the annual fund operating expenses for a fund called the Oppenheimer Commodity Strategy Total Return Fund, shown here as figure 3.2. With the table for the appropriate fund, we must be sure to run our finger down the column that corresponds to the correct class of shares. This table lists six different share classes.

When we examine the contents of the table, the first thing we may notice is that the expenses appear to be minuscule numbers. They are expressed as percentages—and small ones at that. A number like 1.70 percent or 2.49 percent would be on the high end, and it's not uncommon to find numbers less than a 1 percent. One percent of 1 percent is known in the financial industry as a *basis point,* or "bp" (pronounced *bip*). So, 1 percent is 100 basis points. On our chart, some of the expenses are expressed as single-digit basis points—surely, these must be minuscule numbers.

What joy, this whole cautionary tale has been hugely overblown! If these are the pittances that are at stake, what could all the fuss be about? Yes, these numbers are indeed tiny. But investment advisers don't take home percentages, they take home those percentages multiplied by the assets under their management. And, remember, only one of those two multiplicands needs to be a large number to generate a large result. In the fund industry, some expense ratios may appear to be small, but that does not mean the adviser's remuneration is. If a person is entitled to 1 percent of the water in a river, we will not know her take until we know the size of the river; if the river happens to be a big one, she will be gorged silly.

The money flowing through mutual funds is a $16 trillion Amazon River. So, even with the ostensibly small percentages listed in the expense tables, the fund industry pockets nearly $100 billion each year. (In the next chapter, we will focus on the magnitude of fund fees; here, we are primarily concerned with identifying their source.)

Investors might better appreciate the amount they are paying for investment advice if it were expressed in real dollars. Another chart in a fund's prospectus does attempt to convert these relatively abstract percentages into more concrete dollar amounts. But they do so only in connection with a hypothetical $10,000 investment.[25] If an investor has a larger amount in the fund, she must factor that difference into computing the actual fees that she pays. Nowhere in a prospectus or statement are investors told of the actual dollar amount they pay each year.

In figure 3.2, the first entry is entitled Management Fees. These are the amounts charged by the investment adviser for managing the fund. As we saw in chapter 2, the investment adviser serves as the cerebrum that controls the operations of a mutual fund. Accordingly, the adviser's management fees are often the largest amounts charged to the fund and, consequently, to its shareholders.

The second item in figure 3.2 is something called a 12b-1 Distribution Fee. (Chapter 4 will discuss the propriety of fees such as these.) For now, we need note only that the distributor also receives a stream of money out of the fund in a manner similar to the investment adviser.

So far, the expense table shown in figure 3.2 has been relatively precise about the destination of the expenses: first, to the investment adviser; second, to the distributor. But the next entry is for something labeled, rather generically, Other Expenses. What might that mean? In practice, this heading relates to charges for the administrative and recordkeeping services of a fund's transfer agent or custodian. Those costs might include paying for an interactive website that investors can use to track or manage their investments, for telephone operators who can answer investors' questions, and for sending statements to apprise clients of their investment performance.[26]

Consider, though, whether those charges should ever be linked to the assets under management. For a simple illustration, imagine if a mutual fund had only one shareholder: if the assets of the fund doubled or tripled, would the fund incur greater administrative expenses? No new website would be needed, no additional telephone operators or customer statements would be necessary. Yet, if the fees are based on assets, then the administrator would nevertheless incur a windfall of double or triple its fees. These kinds of fees are not always tied to assets, but when they are, investors should beware.

The table for this Oppenheimer fund is complicated by additional breakdowns for the other expenses and for something called the Subsidiary (whose definition an investor must hunt for elsewhere in the document), as well as for Acquired Fund Fees and Expenses, which materialize when one fund invests in another fund.

But the next row in this table is, at last, a sum total of the foregoing amounts and is known as the *expense ratio*. Here, then, is the single number that tells us what we are actually paying. Expense ratios are the "prices" that investors, industry analysts, and information services such as Morningstar most regularly quote when discussing funds.

But we can also see that the expense ratio is not the final number in this table. And here is where we move firmly into a mortgage-like morass of obfuscation. The next line is entitled Waiver and Expense Reimbursement, which may sound promising to investors: words like *waiver* and *reimbursement* suggest that money might be coming back their way, and indeed the bracketed numbers in that row are negative amounts that do act to lower the expense ratio. Lower expenses— just like lower prices—certainly sound better for investors. But note also that this portion of the table is where footnotes begin to sprout like unwelcome fungi. In financial reports, as with so many publications, footnotes rarely herald the coming of a transparent discussion.[27]

In figure 3.2, the footnote explains that the fund's investment adviser has contractually agreed to reimburse the fund the stated amounts, "for one year from the date of this prospectus, unless approved by the Board." Apparently, this fund is enjoying a boon! The investment adviser, for some undisclosed reason, is effectively lowering the fees that it charges. What could be possibly wrong with that? Let's find out.

If an investment adviser wanted to lower its fees, there is another, more obvious way to do that: it could simply charge a lower management fee. Why impose higher fees in the first part of the table, only to lower them later on? Something in the roundabout nature of this discount seems curious. Here are three potential explanations—one benign, two insidious:

1. The adviser may have some compelling reason for reducing its fees temporarily, for one year. In this prospectus, however, the adviser offers no reasons for that temporary discount. And why not just lower its fee today, then raise it again a year from now? The adviser will be legally obligated to generate a new, updated prospectus in a year's time anyway.[28] If the adviser decided to raise its expenses at that time, it would not incur any additional printing costs to disclose the new fees to its investors. As it is, this ostentatious fee reduction has a whiff of the used-car salesman: "Hey, our price is usually 249 basis points, but I can knock off 29 . . . just for you, baby!" Or, we must ask ourselves, is the price really just 220 bps?

2. Investment advisers who raise their fees are obliged to notify investors of that fact and to obtain their approval, but advisers who eliminate waivers and reimbursements need only update their prospectus. Query, how many current fund shareholders read updated prospectuses? So, an adviser can effectively raise its fees in two ways, either by expressly increasing its management fees or by quietly eliminating a waiver or reimbursement. The first of those approaches will be highly visible to the adviser's customers; the other may not be. In effect, advisers

can use waivers and reimbursements to advertise low introductory rates for their funds, then raise those rates without scaring away investors. Recall that the footnote's language says the waiver and reimbursement may be eliminated at any time within a year, with the approval of the Board. Here, then, is a device for allowing advisers to raise their fees *sotto voce*.

3. Consider what this waiver has done to the expense ratio of this fund. What now is the fund's actual expense ratio? Is it the first total set of fees or that total minus the waivers and reimbursements as listed at the bottom of the table? If it's the latter, then for how long will that remain the accurate total—for a year or for some unknown, perhaps far shorter portion of a year? The insertion of a price reduction for an unknown and unknowable duration might possibly represent a better deal for investors—or might not, depending on how long it stays in effect.

If an adviser truly wanted to lower its fees, it could do so more directly and clearly. The waiver approach, on the other hand, simply obfuscates an already complicated chart that should have provided a simple answer to every investor's fundamental question: How much will it cost to invest in this fund?

Dollars

The most striking visual consequence of quoting mutual fund fees and expenses in terms of percentages is that their costs inevitably appear small. If even the most expensive mutual funds rarely cost more than 2.5 percent, that's just a measly 2.5 percent. Just two-and-a-half things out of every one hundred! A trifle, surely.

But let's consider an alternative. What if these fees and expenses were quoted in the way in which investment advisers actually experience them: as hard currency? We can replicate this process with a very simple piece of multiplication, so the conversion isn't intellectually challenging. But there are two problems: first, the presentation of data can make a great deal of difference in its emotional— or perhaps even rational—impact; second, one of the two pieces of data necessary to perform our simple piece of multiplication is missing from the summary prospectus.

We can determine a reasonable estimate of the amount of money an investment adviser or distributor pockets annually by multiplying the percentage of its operating expenses by the assets under management in the fund. But the assets under management in the fund are not quantified in the summary prospectus. With a little bit of looking elsewhere, we can determine for the fund presented in figure 3.2 that the net assets were approximately $330 million in 2015. With a total expense ratio—while our old friend, the waiver, remains in effect—of 220 basis points, the service provider pockets more than $7 million each year.

One may consider $7 million a lot or a little for the practice of managing this fund's portfolio. But consider the following scenario. If this fund is on the menu of a corporate 401(k) plan, retirement contributions are almost certain to flow into the fund automatically every year. If those contributions eventually double the size of the fund to $660 million, the service provider will then pocket almost $15 million each year. Does it make sense for it to double its revenues simply because the fund has gotten larger? Remember, our hypothetical increase considers growth due only to the addition of new investments, not to a growth in the value of the portfolio's investments.

Perhaps—one might think—a larger fund will impose a greater administrative burden on its service providers. More money in the fund might, for instance, correlate with more fund shareholders, which might mean more people will require monthly statements, more people will use the website, or more people will call the toll-free telephone number. Perhaps that could happen, but there are two issues here.

First, one component of the expense ratio relates explicitly to administrative costs. The other components cover only investment advice and distribution efforts. And there is little reason to expect that a version of the fund that has doubled its size will involve twice as expensive investment decisions or marketing efforts. Certainly, a fund that grows to enormous proportions might become a challenge to manage, but those costs are unlikely to grow proportionally, particularly for funds linked to indices, which computer algorithms manage automatically.

Second, it is unlikely that even the administrative costs of a fund would grow in direct proportion to the size of a mutual fund. Producing one hundred thousand statements will almost certainly be cheaper, per statement, than producing one thousand statements. As funds grow larger, we should expect them to enjoy economies of scale and for pro rata expenses to decline. Some investment advisers do recognize this phenomenon and claim to share those savings with their investors. But any such savings are not reported in this kind of prospectus.

Fees and Expenses Not Specified in the Table

Though there are a slew of numbers included in a fund's table of fees and expenses, many of the most important ones are not identified. Yet the quality of the operation of a mutual fund may turn on these costs—and they will, of course, ultimately be borne by the fund's shareholders, even if they go unspecified.

Consider a relatively obvious example. We already know that mutual funds are highly regulated investment entities—and indeed, we can see some of the fruits of that regulation in such legally obligatory filings as the prospectus, summary prospectus, annual report, and statement of additional information—so, we know that lurking somewhere behind all these documents and legal compliance must be a lawyer. Usually far more than one. A fund must, therefore, pay legal fees as a regular component of its operating expenses, and they do. But those fees are merely lumped in with the Other Expenses in the prospectus.

Similarly, funds are required to report financial data in their prospectuses, as well as in their annual reports and proxy statements. Like all publicly traded companies in this country, some of those financial numbers must be verified by professional auditors to ensure their accuracy and impartiality.[29] Like lawyers, then, accountants regularly perform work on the financial statements of mutual funds and, of course, submit bills for their efforts. Again, fund shareholders bear the costs of those accounting expenses, but those fees, too, are not broken down in the prospectus.

Perhaps legal and accounting fees, when amortized across the size of a large mutual fund, simply do not add up to an amount worth troubling the average investor. Or perhaps motived shareholders can discover what they need to know with enough digging into other obscure disclosure documents, like Statements of Additional Information, semi-annual reports, and proxy statements. Perhaps, but there are other expenses that no investor can choose to ignore—yet, these numbers are also elided from the prospectus.

A particularly large operational number is the brokerage burden. Recall for a moment the primary business of a mutual fund: to invest in stocks, bonds, and other securities. Doing so necessarily involves transactions costs, even if those investments are in ordinary, unexotic securities. Just as retail investors must pay E*Trade, Charles Schwab, or some other broker a fee for buying or selling securities on their behalf, so too must a massive mutual fund that buys and sells millions, if not billions, of dollars in securities. Brokerage fees for mutual funds regularly add up to millions of dollars each year.[30] Again, however, investment advisers are not required to disclose these fees in a fund's prospectus.

Instead, they appear in the pages of a very thick and highly obscure document called a Statement of Additional Information (SAI). Advisers are not legally required to send SAIs to fund investors (unless requested), and they do not do so. Instead, SAIs can be found—by a determined investor—in the crannies of the Internet. And for the very determined investor, brokerage fees can be retrieved from somewhere deep within the entrails of an SAI.

Perhaps, a contrarian might argue, numbers as important as these are not included in the prospectus because, unlike an adviser's expenses, they are not inevitable; conceivably, they could be zero. A fund might not make a single trade in a year. Perhaps that might be the case in a passive index fund, but in an actively managed fund, the number never is zero. And like all the other fees that trickle out of the money we keep in mutual funds, these amounts add up to significant dollars.

Indeed, when compounded over time, fees and expenses on mutual fund investments aggregate to far more than irksome leaks—they can amount to hundreds or thousands of dollars flowing out of the average investor's account and into the coffers of investment advisers. Fees, of course, will always be with us, but investors might understand them far better if the complexity of our current tables were simplified to a single number. Advisers could decide what to include in that fee, within reason, but they should present investors with precise, uncomplicated information. Like the calories in a chocolate bar, the cost of a fund should be clear. Currently, the true cost is hidden in a forest of figures.

PART II

DISEASES AND DISORDERS

Central to the fund scandal: Some fund executives placed hauling in
assets—and profits—above the interests of fund shareholders.
—Tom Lauricella, *Wall Street Journal, 2014*

Our exploration of the structure and economics of mutual funds in the first
part of this book reveals a number of surprises for ordinary investors: professional investment firms manage our money under a burden of incentives
that are structural and perverse. In part II, we will go beyond considering
merely potential conflicts to examine more direct threats to the wealth and
welfare of fund investors. This series of chapters illustrates and explains
the startling array of ploys—at times breathtaking in their creativity—by
which investment advisers and their affiliates can peculate the savings of
investors.

These pages are not intended to be an indictment of the mutual fund
industry but, rather, to provide a map for ordinary investors of where be the
dragons. An inventory of misbehavior may unavoidably convey some sense
that mutual funds are the fruits of a witch's kitchen. And, indeed, much that
has been written on our financial markets in recent years evokes the aftermath of Melmotte's downfall in *The Way We Live Now*: "Very many men
started up with huge claims, asserting that they had been robbed, and in the
confusion it was hard to ascertain who had been robbed, or who had simply been unsuccessful in their attempts to rob others." Outright burgling is
rare, but mutual funds are the way we save now, so we must confront their
foibles if we are to enjoy their fortes.

4

FEES

If you want to steal a lot of money and get away with it, steal a little
from a lot of people. They will probably never notice. If they do, they
may not think it worth the effort to complain.
　　　　　　　　　　　　　—Floyd Norris, *New York Times*, 2003

Funds and fees go together like balloons and needles. Fees cause money to leak
out of funds, and their aggressive application can dramatically deflate investment
returns and ruin the party. Indeed, the combination is sufficiently inharmonious
to wreak discord upon one of more famous duets in the study of law and economics in America.

Frank Easterbrook and Richard Posner are two of the most respected and influential stars in America's legal firmament, and they share a remarkable amount
of their professional *curricula vitae*.[1] They have both won tenure twice over: first,
as members of the faculty of the University of Chicago Law School, and then as
federal judges appointed for life by President Ronald Reagan.[2] They have also
achieved something like tenure of the wallet in business together as consultants
for the highly successful consulting firm, Lexecon.[3]

Philosophically, they have been intellectual comrades for many decades,
scouting together much of the path of law and economics. It's fair to say that
Easterbrook and Posner are intellectual blood brothers. So, when they found
themselves in a pointed argument with one another, on the public record, concerning a question of law and economics—well, America's legal academia har-
kened to the spectacle. The topic of the contretemps, as it happens, was the size of
fees charged by a mutual fund.

Countless articles, books, and parental lectures warn us to be ever-vigilant
about the expenses we pay for our mutual funds.[4] And like most parental lectures,
this advice often goes unheeded, in spite of its soundness. All financial transactions involve the confrontation of self-interested counterparties, as Trollope
reminds us: "Each lady was disposed to get as much and to give as little as possible, in which desire the ladies carried out the ordinary practice of all parties to

a bargain."[5] But the costs and consequences of fees are particularly acute with investment funds.

Our exploration in chapter 3 of how and where fees leach out of funds has provided us with basic training as investment sentinels. But now we switch our focus from reading the simple blueprints that show the operation of fees to investigating the alarming ways that some investment advisers impose those fees. Advisers of mutual funds possess the power to select the level of fees, the source of fees, and the use of fees. In all three spheres, adviser decisions can prove detrimental to investors in their funds.

First and perhaps most intuitively, the level or magnitude of fees is the most direct source of peril for a fund investor. Because fees paid to advisers come directly out of the money we invest, the more an adviser charges, the more those expenses hurt us financially. Any savings lost to fees today also lose the compounded returns they might have generated over subsequent decades. So powerful is the magical power of returns upon returns that Charles Dickens deified it in *Bleak House*: "The name of this old pagan's god was Compound Interest."[6] So, to echo the sages' sound advice, investors should certainly shop around to avoid being mulcted by their mutual funds. Figuring out what is too much, however, is a somewhat more complicated project than it appears.

Second, investors must be alive to the source of the fees. But what could be the issue here—surely there is only one possible candidate, no? If we, the investing public, don't pay a fee, then nobody does. Well, not quite. The more accurate financial answer is that if some investors do not pay for a service, then other investors must or the business providing the service must functionally pay by absorbing that cost.

When it comes it to the distribution of fund shares, the question of who should pay is a gnawing one. Many fund advisers and distributors believe that fund shareholders should pay for the cost of marketing, advertising, and distributing the shares in a fund. Such advisers and distributors, accordingly, impose the so-called 12b-1 fees we saw in the fee and expense tables discussed in chapter 3.[7] But plenty of fund investors—who have, by definition, already made their way into a mutual fund—have a hard time appreciating why they should subsidize the enlightenment of others who have not.

Finally, the destination or use of fees can be controversial. The element of fund distribution that involves advertising may bring to mind marketing campaigns in the booze-soaked and smoke-filled company of charismatic Don Drapers and brilliant Peggy Olsons. But the glamour dissipates quickly when one learns that fees for distributing funds have at times been used for what looks alarmingly like the payment of kickbacks. Fund distributors routinely give money to financial intermediaries for recommending specific funds to customers. So, it may be more *Boardwalk Empire* than *Mad Men*.

Let's take a closer look at all three of these topics on fees, beginning with the amount of money that we pay.

Problems with the Magnitude of Fund Fees

In 2007, a group of investors, Mary Jones, Jerry Jones, and Arline Winerman, sued the adviser of their mutual fund investments, Harris Associates, for violating Section 36(b) of the Investment Company Act.[8] The trio claimed that Harris was charging excessive fees. But as important as the reason for their complaint was the location they chose for their lawsuit: Chicago, Illinois.

Because the Investment Company Act is a federal law and because Harris Associates is based in Chicago, our plaintiffs sued the adviser in a federal court, the U.S. District Court for the Northern District of Illinois. And when our trio of plaintiffs subsequently lost their trial, they appealed to the U.S. Court of Appeals for the Seventh Circuit, the federal appeals court covering Illinois, Wisconsin, and Indiana, and subordinate only to the Supreme Court of the United States in that jurisdiction.

Though Section 36(b) cases have been quite numerous across the United States since the provision was enacted in 1970,[9] not many had made their way up to the Seventh Circuit, and none involving an open-end mutual fund. Certainly none before this one had found its way to the docket of Chief Judge Frank H. Easterbrook, when he sat in judgment of *Jones v. Harris Associates L.P.* as the highest-ranking member of a three-judge appeals panel. When asked, in this lawsuit, whether he thought Harris Associates had charged too high a fee, Easterbrook had a ready and sharp answer.

"There's no such thing as too high a fee in a mutual fund," he concluded in his ruling.[10] Easterbrook gave the back of his hand to a quarter-century of prior rulings from a sister court of appeals because he thought that precedent "relies too little on markets." His economic analysis cut through existing case law with a simple rubric: in a competitive market, a fiduciary such as an investment adviser can charge whatever the market will pay. "A fiduciary must make full disclosure and play no tricks but is not subject to a cap on compensation." In the absence of fraud, then, any fee that an investor pays is—as a matter of Easterbrook's interpretation of the law—reasonable.

But how could Easterbrook be so sanguine about prices, particularly in an industry that pits investing greenhorns against extremely sharp financial professionals? Because markets.

"Today, thousands of mutual funds compete," noted Easterbrook. "The pages of the Wall Street Journal teem with listings" and all those funds "come much closer to the model of atomistic competition than do most other markets." Easterbrook noted the power of shareholder exit in such a self-evidently competitive market: "An adviser can't make money from its captive fund if high fees drive investors away." Investors "vote with their feet and dollars." Investors "can and do 'fire' advisers cheaply and easily by moving their money elsewhere."[11]

Easterbrook's Neoclassical Law and Economics

Well, to anyone familiar with Easterbrook's oeuvre, this swashbuckling analysis was a classic exemplar of his style of neoclassical law and economics.[12] That school of economic analysis of the law presumes that most investors and participants in the market are rational human beings with stable, well-ordered preferences.[13] And, further, that their behavior in the market reflects those preferences. In this case, when Arline, Mary, and Jerry chose to invest in those funds, neoclassicists would presume they did so rationally.

The legal consequence of a court using the lens of neoclassical law and economics is often for the arbiter to recuse itself, functionally, and to allow the market to determine the correct result in any particular circumstance. So, when Chief Judge Easterbrook stated that the market was functioning well and that nobody here was deceived, he was inexorably syllogizing toward a predictable conclusion: that the court should not intervene to alter the bargain between the investors and the fund adviser. And that ruling, of course, meant that he would countenance no redress for our plaintiffs' pleas of wrongdoing.

This legal methodology is one that has long been shared and advocated—even more vociferously on occasion[14]—by Easterbrook's colleague on the bench and in the halls of academia, the Honorable Richard A. Posner. Indeed, it was Judge and Professor Posner who in 1973 wrote the field's seminal text, *Economic Analysis of Law*, now in its ninth edition.[15] As a consequence of that intellectual pedigree, many observers were astonished when Posner disagreed so publicly with Easterbrook's analysis. But he did—here's how.

The Seventh Circuit comprises eleven judges, though as is customary only a three-judge panel—of Easterbrook and two others—sat in judgment of the *Jones v. Harris* appeal.[16] Posner was one of the eight others who did not, so he had no opportunity to vote against or to dissent from the ruling when the appellate panel decided the case. But once Easterbrook and his fellow panelists announced their ruling and circulated it to the other Seventh Circuit judges, any judge on the court became entitled to call for the entire court to rehear the case *en banc*.[17] That is, to call for the parties to reargue the case before all eleven judges of the Seventh Circuit. One judge—whose identity is always unknown to the public—did call for a rehearing *en banc*. All eleven judges then voted on the procedural matter; rehearing *en banc* would be granted only if a majority voted in favor.[18]

But for some reason, also unknown to the public, one judge—Kenneth Ripple—recused himself from the decision.[19] Then five judges voted in favor of the petition for rehearing *en banc*, but five did not. Five out of ten is awfully close, but it is not a majority. So, the petition failed by the narrowest possible margin. The vote thus left Judge Easterbrook's ruling as the law of this part of the land.

But Posner was not quite done. He took one final opportunity to make his point heard. He wrote a highly unusual judicial opinion—a dissent from the denial of rehearing *en banc*—which four other judges joined. With the case at this point so resoundingly lost, further protestations by parties or even judges are almost always unavailing. So, a dissent at this stage in the proceedings is extremely rare in the world of the federal judiciary.[20] And that rarity helped make Posner's opinion so interesting, so pointed, and—by the rather senescent standards of appellate jurisprudence—so enthralling.

Posner's Behavioral Law and Economics

Posner's dissent was a measured but emphatic disagreement with his friend's ruling. He began by scratching his head over Easterbrook's quixotic approach to the whole issue. Twenty-five years earlier, the U.S. Court of Appeals for the Second Circuit (covering New York, Connecticut, and Vermont) handed down a ruling in a similar case, *Gartenberg v. Merrill Lynch*,[21] that had become the dominant legal precedent in this field. Posner was puzzled by Easterbrook's dismissal of the *Gartenberg* precedent, noting that it had set forth such a difficult standard for plaintiff investors that the preceding twenty-five years of litigation "in excessive fee cases has resulted almost uniformly in judgments for the defendants." So, why was Easterbrook going out of his way to push the bar for plaintiffs even higher? Or, to lower it further for defendants? "It's not as if *Gartenberg* has proved to be too hard on fund advisers," noted Posner.

Then, challenging Easterbrook's assertion that advisers cannot make money "if high fees drive investors away," Posner questioned the premise: "That's true; but will high fees drive investors away?"[22]

Posner was striking directly at Easterbrook's contention that the market for mutual funds worked efficiently. And he was doing so with a newer strain of legal analysis, known as *behavioral economics*. This lens, unlike its neoclassical cousin, emphasizes not the rationality of market participants but their irrationalities. And it isn't so quick to assume markets are competitive.

Indeed, Posner counterclaimed by suggesting that competition did not have salutary effects in this setting: "Competition in product and capital markets can't be counted on to solve the problem because the same structure of incentives operates on all large corporations and similar entities, including mutual funds." Moreover, those "funds are a component of the financial services industry, where abuses have been rampant." Posner published those words in August 2008, just weeks before the bankruptcy of Lehman Brothers triggered an explosion in coverage of the abuses in the financial services industry.[23]

Do Mutual Fund Investors Fire their Advisers over Fees?

Let us pause to consider this question that both judges asked, implicitly and explicitly, about whether high fees drive investors away. Do investors sell fund shares—and thus "fire" their adviser—on the basis of fees? Perhaps some do, though hopping in and out of a fund is plausible behavior only for investors who know what they are doing, who have the time and inclination to scrutinize the fee and expense tables of various funds, who comprehend the good and bad alternatives to the fund, and who know how to execute the transfer.

These operations are not quite as simple as Easterbrook makes them out to be. Most investors in mutual funds have day jobs and other lives—they may not have the time to research and effectuate their market-disciplining exits and entrances to funds. Financially, many of the investors in mutual funds are not subjects whom economists would deem to be sophisticated investors.[24]

But Easterbrook pointed out that the fees Harris Associates charged were in line with the fees charged by the advisers of other funds: "It is undisputed that these fees are roughly the same (in both level and breakpoints) as those that other funds of similar size and investment goals pay their advisers." Posner dismissed the usefulness of this comparison to other players in the industry: "The governance structure that enables mutual fund advisers to charge exorbitant fees is industry-wide, so the panel's comparability approach would if widely followed allow those fees to become the industry's floor."[25]

Posner's argument was, in essence, that if fund advisers charged all ordinary investors artificially high rates, a comparison of those rates would be an unhelpful check on inflated fees. The discovery that the amount you spend is the same as everyone else spends on taxes, protection rackets, or movie popcorn does not answer whether those amounts are efficient or, instead, universally too high. But Easterbrook rejected the notion that ordinary investors might need help: "It won't do to reply that most investors are unsophisticated and don't compare prices. The sophisticated investors who do shop create a competitive pressure that protects the rest."[26]

This argument has two flaws. I'll identify one; Posner supplied the other.

First, let's acknowledge that relying on sophisticated investors to protect the herd is an elegant solution—and one that neoclassical economists often make[27]—to address the challenges facing unsophisticated investors. In many contexts, the effectiveness of this simple dynamic seems manifest. Not everyone who buys an iPhone, for instance, need be an electrical engineer. Not everybody who dines at a Michelin-starred restaurant has to be a food critic. Apple Incorporated and chefs of haute-cuisine will still put out the best phone and food that they can, the theory goes, because they fear that someone in their audience might be an engineer or a critic. And, if served electronic or comestible garbage, those sophisticated parties would object, perhaps loudly, which would cause embarrassment and loss to the smartphone makers and chefs in our economy.

That story makes intuitive sense. But the solution works only if the predators on the herd have no way of distinguishing between sophisticated and unsophisticated. Yet they often do. When, for instance, a chef recognizes the food critic of the *New York Times* at one table and a herd of grubby tourists at another, the chef can serve the critic a delicious concoction of micro-gastronomical foam while tossing gruel and stones at the Clampetts. This distinction isn't simply a matter of culinary snobbery; it's also an economic one: the restaurant can make more money by saving the finest ingredients for only its sophisticated clientele.

In the world of mutual funds, Easterbrook overlooked the fact that it is easy for fund advisers to determine who is and who is not sophisticated. Indeed, our entire financial industry—including important portions of the federal securities regulations[28]—relies on a common proxy for sophistication—namely, the amount of money an investor has. If she has a lot, we generally deem her a sophisticated investor. Often this proxy may be far from accurate (see, e.g., Justin Bieber or the sisters Kardashian), but we also decline to worry about wealthy investors who have enough money to afford to lose a little or to hire expert advisers to protect their interests. How would the investment adviser of a mutual fund know how wealthy one of the fund's investors is? Because we investors announce the fact every time we buy fund shares. If we invest $500,000, we are, by crude categorization, sophisticated. If we invest $500, we are not.

And this phenomenon leads us next to Posner's objection. If fund advisers know how to discriminate between sophisticated and unsophisticated investors, they can all charge a higher price to the unsophisticated. Posner did allow that a comparison of fees would be useful, but not between the rates that ordinary investors pay in different mutual funds; rather, it was between the rates that advisers charge their sophisticated investors and the rates they charge their unsophisticated investors: "A particular concern in this case is the adviser's charging its captive funds [unsophisticated] more than twice what it charges independent funds [sophisticated]."[29]

Let us also consider for a moment Easterbrook's claim that mutual fund investors, if sufficiently sophisticated, can simply hop out of funds whenever they want to. Is that true? Not quite. Several barriers stymie this breezy notion of investment mobility. First, think about the millions of investors who invest in mutual funds through 401(k) plans. Their options may be narrowed to just the limited array of funds within their retirement plan. Second, bear in mind the tax consequences of redeeming fund shares. Leaving precipitately or at an inopportune time might trigger tax penalties for an investor. Trading in and out of funds could impose significant tax liabilities. So, even genius investors, perfectly able to interpret the fund disclosure charts, may not be able to protect themselves as readily as Easterbrook suggested.[30]

Easterbrook made one other spurious claim about the industry in his opinion. To rebut the relevance of these glaring discrepancies between what retail and institutional investors pay for mutual funds, he said "[a]s it happens, the most substantial and sophisticated investors choose to pay substantially more for investment advice than advisers subject to § 36(b) receive."[31] He was referring to hedge funds, in which high net-worth investors often pay "their advisers more than

1 percent" in fees, "plus a substantial portion of any gains from successful strategies." But this argument is profoundly misleading and unhelpful for explaining
how mutual funds work.

Easterbrook was saying, essentially, that the great unwashed shouldn't complain that they pay $15 for movie tickets, compared to famous members of the
academy who get to watch movies for free, because those famous people pay thousands of dollars for home theaters. Hmm. Objection, your Honor, relevance? The
fact that rich investors pay high rates for hedge funds—a far riskier and completely
different kind of investment—has zero application here. The claim of unfairness in
this case is that advisers charge sophisticated players far lower rates than they
charge ordinary investors for the *same* investments. And, as it happens, recent
reports suggest that several of the most sophisticated institutional investors actually have little idea of the fees they pay for their exotic private fund investments.[32]

Do sophisticated investors pay less to invest in the exact same funds as ordinary investors? Yes. Researchers and commentators report that "expense ratios for
institutional funds are roughly half of the expense ratios borne by retail funds."[33]

That statistic is jarring. And it can't be explained away by distinguishing the
costs of serving retail and institutional clients. Yes, retail clients might be more
expensive were they to require more toll-free phone representatives, more website
coding, more individual monthly statements. But it's also possible that institutional clients might actually drain more resources: a huge university endowment
with tens of millions to invest is likely to command more time and attention from
an investment adviser's CEO and portfolio managers than hordes of mom-and-
pop investors. As it happens, we don't actually know which kind of investor is
more expensive . . . because fund advisers aren't willing to disclose the data.[34]

But quibbling over these expenses is actually beside the point because these costs
of servicing clients would all be covered by the *administrative fees* that advisers charge.
And our startling statistic is that the *management fees* are twice as high for retail
investors. That is, the fee for choosing investments for the fund is twice as high, even
though the adviser's investment choices for both groups of investors are the same.

Competition in the Market for Mutual Funds

Let us take a moment to consider the larger question that Judges Easterbrook and
Posner are debating—namely, Is the mutual fund industry competitive? Some
studies—such as one cited by Judge Easterbrook in his opinion[35]—suggest so.
Yet certain phenomena in the market for mutual funds confound the idea that this
industry is humming along like a paragon of Adam Smith's invisible perfection.[36]

Consider, for instance, the scores of different funds that track the S&P 500
Index. Here we have more than one hundred different funds attempting to replicate
the performance of a common index, yet they charge a wide array of prices.[37] Sure,
some of the funds use sampling techniques or weight their holdings differently,

but they all purport to offer the same thing: an investment that simply emulates the best-known measure of American stock market performance, the Standard & Poor's 500. A market in which largely fungible investments cost wildly different amounts—from a few basis points to over 125 bps[38]—would appear to suffer from pricing or informational problems. In an efficient market, we should not expect to see such price discrepancies. Like pork bellies, soybeans, and barrels of oil, we expect largely similar commodities to trade at comparable prices.

Ordinary investors should be more distressed to learn that the mutual fund industry also suffers from an inverse relationship between price and performance.[39] That is, the more one pays to invest in a mutual fund, on average, the lower that fund's investment returns will be. Over many decades, several studies have found this perverse relationship.[40] Consider this finding for a moment and imagine its bizarre application to the other things we buy. What would we think of a world in which the most expensive computers still required DOS commands or the most expensive Bordeaux grands crus were the most undrinkable plonk. Okay, none of us can really be sure about the wine . . . but investments are not just for social poseurs; we quite reasonably expect more expensive investments to generate greater risk-adjusted returns.

The inverse relationship is the opposite of what you would anticipate from an efficient market. We expect expensive cars to be faster, expensive computers to be more powerful, and expensive investments to produce better returns. A market in which the most expensive funds perform the worst confounds Easterbrook's notion of an investing Eden. But it does contain one dose of cheer.

While high fees correlate to low performance, low fees also correlate to high performance. So, ordinary investors without the time or tools to scrutinize the performance of thousands of funds—and knowing, as we all do by now, that past performance is no guarantee of future results—can nevertheless seek a certain refuge by hewing to a simple heuristic: funds with lower fees generally perform better.[41] As Jack Bogle says, "you get what you don't pay for."[42] That is, what an adviser doesn't take out of your investment remains yours and can compound for decades into the future.

So, while Easterbrook cited one study to support his proposition that the fund market is competitive, plenty of other studies and phenomenon suggest otherwise. One can delve into the considerable mounds of empirical analysis and retrieve support for both positions. And one can argue either side of the debate until one is blue in the wallet. As an alternative conception, perhaps the market can be both competitive and uncompetitive at the same time.

If we acknowledge that the mutual fund market is a large, complicated, and sprawling investment system, we might concede that it contains multitudes. Consider America's crime statistics. A critical visitor to the United States might accuse the country of being a dangerous place, citing the high number of murders nationally. A loyal citizen could argue the contrary by pointing to the innumerable bucolic burgs free of crime. To demand "Which is it—is America safe or not?" would oversimplify the inquiry. Crude, blanket generalizations are unhelpful with both crime rates and mutual funds.

Some portions of America are safe, some are less so. Similarly, some neighborhoods in the fund industry are competitive safe havens for investors while others are not. Advisers like Vanguard and Fidelity appear to engage in a great deal of healthy competition, while some other advisers appear to ply their funds at high prices to unsophisticated investors in less friendly segments of the industry. Both can exist at the same time. Like many complicated ecosystems, broad and sweeping characterizations do little to shed light on nuanced circumstances.

What, Emphatically, the Law of Fund Fees Is

One final question from *Jones v. Harris*. If the case was done, dusted, and lost, why did Posner take such pains to make his disagreement known in his dissent from denial of rehearing *en banc*? Why argue, as he did, that flaws in Easterbrook's opinion "warrant our hearing the case *en banc*"[43] when he had already lost that vote? Couldn't he have simply buttonholed Easterbrook over the watercooler? With three to choose from—at the University of Chicago Law School, in the chambers of the Seventh Circuit, and in the hallways of Lexecon—he certainly didn't lack for watercoolers. To many observers, the prominence of Posner's disagreement was not really intended for Easterbrook's edification. It was intended to grab someone else's attention. But whose?

Why, that of the Supreme Court of the United States. Public disagreements between Posner and Easterbrook are rare. Public disagreements in their shared area of legal scholarship—economics—are even rarer. Many interpreted Posner's dissent to be an effort to persuade his bosses—the nine justices of Supreme Court—to hear the case. And, of course, to overturn Easterbrook's ruling. Given that the Supreme Court takes only eighty or so cases out of ten thousand petitions each year, the justices' attention needs grabbing.[44] Posner pointedly invoked several of the Court's favorite code words, emphasizing in his dissent "the creation of a *circuit split*, the *importance of the issue* to the mutual fund industry, and the *one-sided character* of the panel's analysis."[45]

And Posner succeeded. The Supreme Court did take the case.[46] They then curtly reversed Judge Easterbrook's ruling in a unanimous eleven-page decision that largely reaffirmed *Gartenberg* as the law of the land.[47]

In a deflating postscript, when the case returned to Judge Easterbrook's panel on remand for judgment consistent with the Supreme Court's ruling, the Seventh Circuit reaffirmed its original decision against the plaintiffs. But only after more than five years! The court apologized for the delay, explaining that "the papers were placed in the wrong stack and forgotten," but expressed hope that "at least some good will come from the delay."[48]

Problems with the Source of Distribution Fees: Rule 12b-1

Imagine yourself at a terrific little nightclub, tapping away in a completely unembarrassing way to the stirring tunes of your favorite musical artist. After a few enjoyable hours, a server sidles through the atmospheric murk of the club and presents one of those black vinyl booklets to you. The curly slip of paper inside lists a charge for something called "distribution."

"What's this?" you ask, over the background music.

"Your bill," comes the answer.

"But I paid a cover at the door," you say.

"Yes, that was to get into our lovely spot."

"And I bought a ticket for the show," you say.

"Yes, that was for the talent up on stage."

"Then what is this charge for?" you ask.

"Distribution."

"Yes, I see that," you call a little more loudly. "But what is this 'distribution' of which you speak?"

"It's all perfectly legal," your server reassures you. "Rule 12b-1 of something or other permits it."

"Okay, but what's it for."

"It's for marketing and advertising," comes the explanation. "So, we can persuade other patrons to come in to the show."

"But I don't want other people in here," you protest. "I'm already enjoying the show."

"The club will make more money."

"How would that benefit me?"

"More customers will mean the club can buy more things in bulk for cheaper wholesale prices," says the server. "It's called economies of scale."

"So, when more people come, you'll charge me less for my drink?"

A pause.

"Maybe."

In the world of mutual funds, perhaps the most perplexing and troubling fee that investors pay is the distribution fee. We have mentioned this fee before,[49] listed in the expense table of a fund's prospectus (figure 3.2), and seen that it can amount to a significant portion of a fund's overall expense ratio.

When we first met the fund distributor, we noted that two of its chief functions are to make sure new investors know about and are able to buy shares in the distributor's mutual funds. Boards of trustees regularly enter into agreements on behalf of their funds with fund distributors. Just as with investment advisers and so many other service providers, the fund pays the distributor a percentage of its total assets to compensate the distributor for its efforts. The Securities and Exchange Commission authorized these payments in 1980 through the promulgation of Rule 12b-1 of the Investment Company Act of 1940. Today, they are known in the trade as 12b-1 fees.[50]

Investors who learn that they are paying 12b-1 fees are often chagrined to realize they are underwriting someone else's financial edification. Anyone who is already an investor in a mutual fund does not, quite obviously, need a tutorial on the benefits of investing in that particular fund. Yet 12b-1 fees are—indeed, they can only be—assessed on those investors who are already in the fund. The proceeds, though, are used explicitly to attract new investors.[51]

Why Would an Existing Investor Want to Pay to Enlarge the Fund?

Consider that fact for a moment. A fee is being charged to promote a mutual fund. The only people eligible to pay that fee are people who currently invest in the fund. Each of those investors is being charged a fee to attract other investors to the fund. And, as we've seen in chapter 3, managers receive greater remuneration when their funds expand, no matter how those funds expand. But why would any investor in the fund want to give away their money to attract other people?

That question has no self-evidently compelling answer. The only reply, proffered by the fund industry, is that if a fund grows sufficiently large,[52] it may accrue greater bargaining power and enjoy economies of scale in its fund operations. If a million-dollar fund grows into a billion-dollar fund, for example, it might be able to enjoy discounts from its vendors, which might theoretically lead to savings for investors. Of course, this proposition is readily testable: one need only check to see whether funds do increase in size and, if so, whether any savings are in fact passed through to investors as funds expand in size.

As it happens, economists and other academics have undertaken such studies.[53] Indeed, Dr. Lori Walsh, a financial economist in the SEC's own Office of Economic Analysis, conducted the most prominent one in 2004, entitled "The Costs and Benefits to Fund Shareholders of 12b-1 Plans."[54] In it, she concluded that 12b-1 fees certainly are effective at increasing the size of funds: "funds with 12b-1 funds do, in fact, grow faster than funds without them." But that may be the only thing that 12b-1 fees accomplish as planned. Walsh went on to conclude that "shareholders are not obtaining benefits in the form of lower average expenses or lower flow volatility. Fund shareholders are paying the costs to grow the fund, while the fund adviser is the primary beneficiary of the fund's growth." Government reports are notorious for burying clear verdicts beneath bureaucratic equivocation and vagueness. Not Dr. Walsh's report: "shareholders do not obtain any of the benefits from the asset growth. This result validates the concerns raised by opponents of 12b-1 plans about the conflicts of interest created by these plans."

On the issue of passing along bulk discounts to investors more generally, fund advisers have not covered themselves in glory. To the contrary, a decade ago federal authorities charged fifteen fund firms for failing to honor other, more explicit bulk discounts they had promised to fund investors.[55]

Inasmuch as possible savings from 12b-1 distributions are not explicitly promised, investors will have an even more difficult time determining whether they are ever honored. Without access to all the records of the fund, investors will always have trouble detecting whether any economies of scale are materializing and, if so, whether the adviser is passing all, some, or any savings through to investors. For now, the Walsh study finds that savings do not make their way to investors and are simply pocketed by the fund firms.

In 2014, fund investors pay $12.4 billion dollars in 12b-1 fees,[56] so the scope of this issue across the industry is enormous.[57] And 12b-1 fees have proved immovable in the face of several waves of proposed reform. Yet, as deep as the 12b-1 pool is, some advisers appear to find it insufficient: a recent SEC enforcement action alleged that First Eagle Investment Management, with access to a 12b-1 plan authorizing $200 million of shareholder monies to be spent on distribution and marketing, found "that amount to be insufficient" and illegally "dipped into the funds further."[58]

But perhaps the elimination of 12b-1 fees would be fruitless. Were this category of expense to be eliminated, might not the industry simply raise their other fees a commensurate amount? And if they did, the then-larger management fees would be opaque buckets hiding a compendium of costs for which we at least enjoy a modicum of transparency now. Perhaps, but at least the fund firms would then have to own that their management fees are higher.

They would also lose the imprimatur of the SEC for inflicting these divisive fees on the investing public. The presence of Rule 12b-1, in effect, sanctions the use of these payments, despite their dubious value to investors. And advisers can argue that, if such payments really were detrimental to investors, surely they would not be permissible.

So, now we have a sense of how the rest of our conversation at the nightclub would go. After paying the bill for distribution we have been handed, a regular at the next table might lean over and say.

"This place used to be really cool, but now it's too crowded."

"At least the drinks are cheaper," you reply. "Right?"

"No. Why?"

Problems with the Use of Fees: Revenue Sharing and Shelf Space

Now that we know the problems with the size and source of fund fees, let us examine one of their most controversial destinations. Judge Easterbrook, in his *Jones v. Harris* ruling, made a claim that will help us shift our focus to the uses to which an adviser may put mutual fund fees. Easterbrook maintained—perhaps to mollify the plaintiffs against whom he was ruling—that "the Oakmark funds' net return has attracted new investment rather than driving investors away."[59]

But no matter how honorable, no judge in the *Jones v. Harris* case had any way of knowing what caused new investment in the Oakmark funds. Inflows may have been attributable to the funds' net return or to some other cause entirely. Our foregoing discussions about the prominence and payment of fund distribution should indicate to us that money can flow into a mutual fund for reasons other than a portfolio manager's efforts and talent. A dedicated distributor, for instance, might possess a more effective touch through marketing, advertising, and inspiring salespeople.

That is, the promotional efforts of Oakmark funds' distributor, even more than investment decisions of the funds' adviser, might have been what attracted any new money. But how satisfied should investors be with the way in which distributors attract new investment?

Where Do 12b-1 Fees Go?

The answer to this question might turn on what it is precisely that distributors do with 12b-1 fees. First, they use those fees to pay for television commercials and print advertisements geared to the investing public.[60] Second, they arrange channels through which investors can buy shares in the fund through other financial intermediaries, such as brokers, financial planners, and investment sales professionals.[61] But, more specifically, they offer what can charitably be called "promotional incentives" to those salespeople to recommend the fund to new investors.

Again, the usual justification for spending Peter's money to attract Paul is that, if a fund grows sufficiently large, the fund will be able to enjoy economies of scale. Then, through the trickling down of economies of scale, the fund will be able to pass savings back to Peter, Paul, and everyone else in the fund. As we have seen, alas, this aspirational chain runs afoul of documented reality.[62]

But even if investors were assuaged by such savings, they might nevertheless be discomfited by the more unsavory uses of 12b-1 fees. Some distributors, it seems, have developed creative—indeed, at times illegally imaginative—ways to promote sales of their funds. The euphemism for this practice is "revenue sharing."[63]

How Are Mutual Funds Like Breakfast Cereals?

Consider the magnitude of the challenge for a fund distributor: it must distinguish its funds from among the many thousands for sale in the United States. Simply making a fund available for purchase through an investment mega-market like Charles Schwab or E*Trade or Edward Jones is not, by itself, likely to guarantee sales for that particular fund. In this sense, funds are a lot like competitive breakfast cereals.[64]

Dozens, if not hundreds, of cereals are available for purchase by the finickiest of breakfast connoisseurs in this country. And, like fund distributors, companies in the business of selling cereal must find effective means for distributing their tasty morsels to the shopping public. What might be a great way to do that? In addition to bombarding children with commercials during Saturday morning cartoons, getting boxes of their Chocolate-Frosted Sugar Bombs[65] onto supermarket shelves would surely be helpful.

But supermarkets have only a limited amount of shelf space on which to stock their wares. For some tasty, irreplaceable comestibles—like Heinz ketchup and Kraft macaroni & cheese—supermarkets may voluntarily set aside shelf space to ensure that shoppers come in the door to buy those indispensable staples . . . and linger to shop for all the other needs of their pantries. But for more fungible foods—like, say, breakfast cereal—a supermarket may conclude that its customers are less militant about insisting that the store stock any particular brand.

In those cases, the store need not accommodate any particular cereals; instead, it is the cereal sellers who must persuade the store to make space for their boxes. After all, for the cereal peddler, the difference between getting its boxes onto a supermarket shelf versus stockpiling them in a warehouse could mean huge dollars in sales. So, shelf space has a concrete value, and cereal producers willingly pay for the privilege of getting their boxes onto the shelves of major grocery stores. Indeed, for Chocolate-Frosted Sugar Bombs, the cereal maker might pay quite a premium to get its boxes not just on any old shelf but on one precisely at the forty-inch eye line of our nation's iron-willed, sugar-addicted five-year-olds.

Similarly, in our sprawling market of mutual funds, fund distributors know that investors are more likely to buy more of the most prominently displayed funds. And so those distributors, too, might be eager to get their funds stocked on well-trafficked shelves. But where, exactly, are the popular shelves in the world of mutual funds?

Shelf Space for Mutual Funds

Some of the busiest shelves are in the storefronts where most investors come to shop for advice about investing their money, such as investment brokers like E*Trade online and Edward Jones in real life. In fact, every day, clients walk into the 8,000 branch offices of Edward Jones to ask how they should invest their money.

As it happens, Edward Jones had a helpful way to answer that question. In the early 1990s, the firm developed a program called Preferred Mutual Fund Families, which it described on its public website in this way: "With nearly 11,000 mutual funds available, it can be difficult to know which fund(s) to pick. That's why at Edward Jones, we focus on seven preferred mutual fund families that share our commitment to service, long-term investment objectives, and long-term performance."[66]

So, the most coveted shelves at Edward Jones and other brokers are these exclusive lists of "preferred funds." A glossy handout with just a few investing options vetted by a broker like Edward Jones is sure to attract far more attention than the eye-numbing inventory of 8,000 funds.

Another particularly busy set of shelves for mutual funds is the menu of offerings provided through America's $6.8 trillion of defined-contribution plans. Employers that offer 401(k)s and similar plans also typically provide their employees with a limited menu of a score or so of mutual funds from which to choose. Again, and not surprisingly, employees in defined-contribution plans overwhelmingly direct their attention and money to shares in those funds.[67]

Recall again the chief functions of a fund distributor: to make sure new investors know about their mutual funds and are able to buy shares in those funds. Getting funds onto a broker's preferred-fund list or a 401(k) menu are highly effective ways for a distributor to accomplish both of these goals. But what could persuade the gatekeepers of a preferred list or a 401(k) menu to include a specific fund on their hallowed shelves? Well, what would persuade a radio disc jockey to play a particular song on the station's coveted airways (thus ensuring higher sales for the artist)?[68] And what persuades a supermarket to grant shelf space to a box of cereal? The answer is always the same.

Money.

Specifically, the brokers receive payments from the 12b-1 fees that ordinary investors pay.

The idea that a mutual fund distributor would pay money—the fund investors' money, no less—to a financial intermediary to be included on its preferred fund list may sound a tad unsavory. To some, the quid pro quo looks very like a bribe. Indeed, to explore this side of the investment abattoir, one must develop a firm constitution.

The Legality of Revenue Sharing

Yet this pay-to-play practice of paying for shelf space is legal.[69] Fund firms have nevertheless fallen afoul of the law by failing to disclose these arrangements to their investors. Perhaps those failures to disclose were mere oversights. Or perhaps the advisers feared that disclosure of the shelf-space payments, so redolent of kickbacks and bribery, might make their investors queasy.

Edward Jones, as it happens, paid $75 million for its sins. The broker failed to disclose to its clients that its seven preferred fund families were preferred only because they paid Edward Jones a considerable douceur.[70] But Edward Jones is certainly not the only set of shelves to have solicited—but not disclosed—such payments. Morgan Stanley paid $50 million to settle the allegation that, "Unbeknownst to Morgan Stanley's customers, Morgan Stanley received monetary incentives—in the form of 'shelf space' payments—to sell particular mutual funds to its customers";[71] Ameriprise paid $30 million to settle charges that it received "tens of millions of dollars each year" from mutual fund families "for selling their mutual funds";[72] Citigroup paid $20 million to settle charges that its Smith Barney brokerages accepted, but again did not disclose, payments from seventy-five mutual fund complexes for shelf space.[73]

Fund distributors, of course, stand on the other side of these transactions, and they, too, are obliged to disclose any payments they make, whether from 12b-1 fees or out of their own assets. But, alas, sometimes it slips their mind. PIMCO paid more than $11 million to settle charges that it failed to disclose its payments to brokers for promoting PIMCO fund shares.[74] MFS also paid $50 million to settle similar allegations.[75] (Please note, this MFS settlement in March 2004 was a different one from the $225 million it paid the preceding month to settle market-timing charges.[76])

Lest we think these arrangements are skeletons from the distant past, consider the SEC's recent accusation of two investment advisers in Oregon for reprising the practice more recently. In 2012, the chief of the SEC Division of Enforcement, Bruce Karpati, noted that these payments to intermediaries "for recommending certain types of investments may corrupt their ability to provide impartial advice to their clients."[77] Then, in late 2015, J.P. Morgan paid $307 million to settle charges that its banking units impermissibly directed clients into J.P. Morgan's own funds. "The undisclosed conflicts were pervasive," said Andrew Ceresney, the director of the SEC Division of Enforcement.[78] The SEC learned of these practices from a whistle-blower inside J.P. Morgan, Johnny Burris, whom the firm subsequently fired. J.P. Morgan cited three complaints against Mr. Burris as the basis for his termination; the *New York Times* reported that all three complaints were drafted by an employee of J.P. Morgan.[79]

Remarkably, the SEC stops worrying about any possible corruption if the fund firm includes a generic disclosure deep within its least-read materials. MFS today inoculates itself against further prosecution by placing the following statement in its Statement of Additional Information:

MFD [the distributor] and/or its affiliates may pay commissions, Rule 12b-1 distribution and service fees, and 529 administrative services fees (if applicable), shareholder servicing fees, and other payments to financial intermediaries that sell Fund shares as described in APPENDIX J.[80]

Appendix J, on the seventy-third page of the SAI, does not reveal any amounts MFD actually paid. But it does list the names of fifty-seven financial intermediaries to whom MFD might have given money, including—not at all surprisingly—Edward Jones, Morgan Stanley, and Ameriprise.[81]

Before we depart the sordid demimonde of fund fees and influence peddling, let us consider one final unhealthy consequence of the practice. Just as payola in the music industry can lead to airtime for appalling earworms while true artists languish in silence, the use of 12b-1 and revenue-sharing payments in mutual funds can lead to the promotion of funds that are poor choices for ordinary investors while far better investments are ignored.

Happily, some fund families—such as Vanguard and Dodge & Cox[82]—decline categorically to participate in these revenue-sharing arrangements. So, the diligent investor who is willing to inquire does have a way to escape the vapors of unwholesome payments.[83] Were the SEC to ban the practice, all investors might be so lucky.

|| 5 ||

SOFT DOLLARS

This witch's brew of hidden fees, conflicts of interest, and complexity in application is at odds with investors' best interests. We all know we can do better. That's why I've asked Congress to consider legislation to repeal or at least substantially revise the 1975 law that provides a 'safe harbor' for soft dollars.

—Christopher Cox, *Chairman, Securities and Exchange Commission, 2007*

Loyalty programs can inspire some curious behavior. In December each year, frequent fliers start booking circuitous itineraries to distant but inexpensive destinations. A flight from Newark to London and back again after a two-hour stroll around Heathrow? Sure, if it preserves a flier's cherished Elite status. The joy of striding across that yard of red carpeting is evidently worth a layover in Ouagadougou. Airlines, of course, are delighted by this bizarre conduct because it proves that their mileage programs are doing precisely what they were intended to do: distorting people's decisions in the airlines' favor. We'll give you all sorts of swag, goes the pitch, so long as you use our airline devotedly. Business travelers are more than pleased to gobble up the perks of a favorite airline and, so much the better, to spend their employers' money to do so.[1]

In the world of mutual funds, we can also find loyalty programs with a remarkable array of perquisites. Trusty customers can amass points known as "soft dollars" for their steadfast patronage; then they can redeem them for all sorts of awards. In his testimony before Congress in March 2004, Harold Bradley, chief investment officer at American Century Investments, explained the marvelous buying power of this new currency, which can be used to purchase goods and services from companies like Compaq and Dell, Ernst & Young and PricewaterhouseCoopers, the Kellogg School of Management and the Wharton School, and even the Standard Club of Chicago, "a private retreat of luxury and tranquility . . . home to Chicago's fashionable society and the business elite for over 125 years."

Wonderful, how do we enroll? We don't. These programs are not for the investing public. Rather, they are for investment advisers. Like business travelers, the decision makers at fund advisers are spending other people's money to win themselves rewards. In this case, the money that advisers spend belongs to the fund and is contributed by ordinary investors, but the rewards go to the advisers.

For fund investors, soft dollars are not at all the gentle, soothing tender their euphemistic name would suggest.[2] Jack Bogle, founder of Vanguard, offered this characterization of soft dollars: "Like 'negative amortization' and 'carried interest,' 'soft dollars' is a seemingly benign term designed to put a happy face on practice that is harmful—even indefensible—to clients of institutional managers."[3] Eric Roiter, formerly general counsel of Fidelity and now lecturer in law at Boston University, has called soft dollars the "least transparent" use of investor's money.[4] They may also be the least understood.

So, how does an adviser amass these loyalty points?

Assembling a Mutual Fund Portfolio

Consider the central activity of a mutual fund adviser: investing the fund's money—specifically, by buying and selling securities for the fund's portfolio. Recall that in the world of mutual funds, we have two important and distinct species of stock: *fund shares*, bought and redeemed by shareholders who want to invest in a fund; and *portfolio securities*, bought and sold by the fund's investment adviser using money raised from fund shares with the goal of generating returns for the fund. The fund's distributor focuses on matters pertaining to fund shares, but the investment adviser—our subject here—focuses on the management of portfolio securities.

Portfolio investing for a mutual fund actually comprises a variety of tasks, some performed by people within the investment adviser and some done with the help of vendors outside the firm. The investment process often begins with junior analysts who work for the adviser, researching and analyzing the financial prospects of particular companies whose securities the adviser might choose to acquire for the fund's portfolio. With the recommendations of analysts in hand, a portfolio manager might then consider a fund's cash reserves and tax position before approving a decision to buy new shares on behalf of the fund. Then, the purchase of those shares must take place. And here is an interesting point of convergence between the way ordinary investors buy stock and the way massive multi-billion-dollar mutual funds do so.

All of us need to get in touch with someone to broke stocks for us.[5] Ordinary investors might use a retail stockbroker like E*Trade or Merrill Lynch to buy the shares for our account. Mutual funds do something similar, with a few important variations. In whichever way we acquire the shares, we all must pay our broker a fee for executing the transaction.

With $16 trillion to invest,[6] mutual funds undertake an enormous volume of trading, so their brokerage commissions amount to a commensurately substantial pile of money. For most mutual funds, commissions are a significant—if little appreciated—expense. And like frequent flyers, credit card shoppers, and coffee addicts, fund firms are regular customers at the brokerage institutions they patronize.

So, which brokerage firms do fund advisers use for their trades? Some of the same ones individuals use: Bank of America Merrill Lynch, Wells Fargo, and J.P. Morgan, for instance. And some brokers that don't befoul themselves with retail custom—Goldman Sachs, most famously. The number of these institutional broker-dealers is relatively small, with just about a score of major firms executing a huge proportion of all trades for America's retail and institutional investors.

Information about the brokerage transactions for each mutual fund appears in its supplemental—and almost universally ignored—disclosure document called the Statement of Additional Information (SAI). Investment advisers don't circulate SAIs to fund shareholders, but with some Googling, we can pull up an SAI online and find the information as shown in figure 5.1.[7]

In the SAI for one of America's largest mutual funds, Vanguard's Total Stock Market Index Fund, for example, we see that the fund paid over $5 million in brokerage commissions in 2013. In the same chart, we see that the Vanguard Small-Cap Index Fund spent approximately $4.5 million that year. So, between just those two funds, Vanguard spent almost $10 million on brokerage commissions in a single year. The Vanguard fund complex contains more than 120 other funds. Even if those others spend notably less on commissions, this single investment adviser is clearly an enormous consumer of brokerage services.

So, if investment advisers are dropping tens or even hundreds of millions of dollars at a dozen or so broker-dealers each year, what might they reasonably expect in return? Some well-executed trades, naturally. But at these levels of patronage, a variety of perks and rewards also seem inevitable. In many parts of our economy, a customer bringing even a fraction of that sum into a business would receive generous rewards for loyalty—certainly, oodles of credit card points, frequent flyer miles, or two-for-one lattes. As long as our investment advisers swill their ocean of financial coffee at just a handful of cafes, those cafes will be eager for their business. And, of course, generous with their rewards.

The question for us, of course, is to whom do those rewards for loyalty flow?

Brokerage Transactions

Before we explore the rather disappointing answer to that question, let's first consider this business transaction from the broker-dealer's perspective. How eager might those firms be for a slice of the mutual fund business?[8]

Very. Many of a mutual fund's trades are simple to execute through computerized algorithms, yet they still generate hundreds of millions of dollars in annual

During the fiscal years ended December 31, 2012, 2013, and 2014, the Funds paid the following approximate amounts in brokerage commissions:

Vanguard Fund	2012	2013	2014
Total Stock Market Index Fund	$3,955.000	$5,089,000	$5,671,000
500 Index Fund[1]	617,000	1,008,000	742,000
Extended Market Index Fund	1,096,000	1,303,000	1,152,000
Large-Cap Index Fund[2]	92,000	58,000	39,000
Mid-Cap Index Fund[3]	749,000	2,370,000	840,000
Small-Cap Index Fund[3]	1,391,000	4,451,000	1,538,000
Value Index Fund[3]	286,000	391,000	169,000
Mid-Cap Value Index Fund[3]	125,000	233,000	138,000
Small-Cap Value Index Fund[3]	383,000	1,349,000	410,000
Growth Index Fund[3]	373,000	830,000	265,000
Mid-Cap Growth Index Fund[3]	84,000	207,000	68,000
Small-Cap Growth Index Fund[3]	780,000	1,816,000	805,000

Figure 5.1 Brokerage Expenses from Vanguard Statement of Additional Information.

revenue for the brokers.[9] How might we expect them to compete with one another for clients? Price, of course, should be an important factor. If a mutual fund's portfolio manager wants to buy 100,000 shares of General Motors, for instance, she is likely to solicit a quote from a few different brokers. If GM is trading at $40 per share, the stock itself is going to cost $4 million, but the fund must also pay the brokerage fee. When the SEC conducted an investigation into brokerage commissions in 1998, it found that mutual funds paid an average of six cents per share, with most commissions falling between three and nine cents per share. Today, commissions are more likely to be between one and four cents per share.[10]

Let's imagine, then, that Goldman Sachs tells the portfolio manager that they will charge 6 cents per share, or $6,000 for the trade; Morgan Stanley offers 3 cents per share, or $3,000; and J.P. Morgan quotes 1 cent per share, or $1,000. So, the adviser has an easy choice. J.P. Morgan made the low bid and will win the order, no?

Hmm, not quite.

But surely no one would pay $6,000 for a trade that could be had for $1,000. Well, that depends—let's listen to the rest of the brokers' pitches. Goldman hastens to mention that their $6,000 price includes more than just the mere execution of the trade. They will happily throw in something else to sweeten the deal. What, pray, does Goldman Sachs have that our mutual fund does not?

For one thing, an army of eager young equity analysts who earn their lavish salaries by doing something unpleasant for 120 hours a week: analyzing, relentlessly.[11]

Indeed, Wall Street's largest investment banks—who are to a significant degree also the country's largest broker-dealers—boast highly vaunted research departments. A quick surf through the shouting heads on television's business shows often reveals "Goldman's buy recommendation" on a particular stock, or "Morgan Stanley's hold recommendation" on another, and so on. Those recommendations to buy, sell, or hold represent the collective wisdom of an investment bank's analysis of a particular stock. Many critics have challenged the accuracy and impartiality of that wisdom—indeed, some have prosecuted it[12]—but few serious participants in our markets care nothing whatsoever for the thoughts of Wall Street analysts.

Why might the investment adviser of a mutual fund, with its own staff of analysts, care for the research of an investment bank? Isn't research and analysis what the investment adviser is purporting to sell to its own mutual fund investors? Indeed it is, but many fund advisers are comparative generalists in the investment world, willing to defer to the superior expertise and greater economies of scale of specialists at investment banks.[13] A bank might have a greater number of analysts in particular segments of the economy—analysts with greater expertise in those areas. Certainly, the leading analysts at Wall Street banks have extraordinary—some might even allege extralegal[14]—access to management at the country's most important corporations. At all events, mutual fund advisers might reasonably want to know what the leading analysts are thinking about particular economic sectors and specific stocks, if only to anticipate the reactions of other investors to those recommendations.

But let's also assume that some of the proffered research turns out to be entirely useless. Would that change the fund adviser's cost-benefit analysis? J.P. Morgan is offering to execute the trade for $1,000; Goldman is offering to do so for $6,000 and throwing in a folder of investment research of unknown quality. You and I might hesitate, might ask Goldman for some reassurances about the value of that folder's contents. But, then again, you or I would actually be paying the bill. A fund adviser isn't paying the bill—the investors in the fund are. So, what is the marginal cost of accepting Goldman's bid—to the adviser? Very little. As we know from the world of medical insurance, when patients do not pay their bills, they want the best possible procedures and medications, and lots of them, without regard for the cost. Investment advisers, too, are happy to use other people's money to "pay up" for extra services.

The Regulatory Safe Harbor

As it happens, brokerage bargains like our example occur every day in the trading of a mutual fund's portfolio securities. And they are perfectly legal.[15]

Now this assertion of legality may seem both erroneous and dubiously emphatic. Possibly erroneous because fund advisers are fiduciaries, and a basic principle of fiduciary law is that a fiduciary may not use its client's assets for the fiduciary's own benefit.[16] Spending a mutual fund's assets to pay inflated brokerage prices for extras would seem to violate that prohibition.

The assertion may be dubiously emphatic because fiduciary principles are notoriously nebulous and lawyers infamously cautious about offering such concrete legal conclusions. Nevertheless, Section 28(e) of the Securities Exchange Act of 1934 provides a safe harbor, in which a mutual fund investment adviser can use fund assets to pay for brokerage commissions that include "research." And the SEC has explicitly ratified that permission through a series of subsequent interpretive releases underlining the point.[17] Of course, the SEC has also described soft dollars as "hidden from investors."[18]

But why should fund shareholders pay for things that the adviser wants, needs, or uses? Because, goes the rationale behind Section 28(e), investment research ultimately redounds to the benefit of investors in a mutual fund. If a fund adviser can better educate and inform itself about the state of the market, that adviser should perform its task of providing investment advice more effectively, which will in turn benefit investors in a fund managed by our newly enlightened adviser.[19] Call it trickle-down enlightenment.

The Best Execution Requirement

But hang on a moment; fiduciary duties aren't always so gauzy, and acting in the best interest of clients isn't the only impediment to fund advisers' spending more than necessary on brokerage commissions. What about that other fiduciary principle requiring a money manager to seek the "best execution" when trading securities for a client?[20]

Indeed, the best execution rule is a cornerstone of money management. And, ostensibly, it would seem to limit our adviser's ability to pad the bill—even if doing so might be defensible through the circuitous route of indirect benefits. Doesn't the best execution rule require the fund adviser to choose the $1,000 bid from J.P. Morgan?

Well, that depends on what "best" means.

Consider a scenario in which you are selling your home. Someone offers $500,000; another bidder offers $475,000. You'll take the higher bid, right? Obviously. Or perhaps you'll ask a few more questions.

Those questions might reveal that the $475,000 bid is all cash, for a closing a week from today, from a buyer who is a member of the city's professional football team; while the $500,000 bid is from a student, employed part time at his first job, who is "really looking forward to learning about how to get one of those mortgage things." And so, we see that price is by no means everything—and at times not even the "best" thing.

Of course, we already knew that buying the cheapest version of something isn't always the best policy. John Ruskin warned long ago that "[i]t's unwise to pay too much, but it's worse to pay too little." Haircuts? Brain surgery? Tacos? When you lunge for rock-bottom prices, you often pay for those savings one way or another, sooner or later.

But in the world of securities trading, isn't mammon God? Isn't a trade a trade? The stock either gets bought or it doesn't, so there shouldn't be much else to consider about execution. Indeed, using electronic trading platforms, a fund can execute trades for less than a cent a share.[21] So, in this particular context, perhaps the "best execution" rule should force them to use the cheaper methods.

Ah, but not quite. A mutual fund might very well care about more than simply commission price when placing a buy order. If one of the larger funds in America is the buyer, for example, it will have hundreds of billions of dollars under management. So, its order might be to buy many millions of dollars of a stock. An order that huge cannot simply be executed with the click of a mouse. The buyer—or rather, the buyer's broker—will almost certainly need to acquire the stock in chunks as it become available from willing sellers. But a clumsy broker could place large buy orders on the market in a ham-fisted way that telegraphs to other market participants that this particular stock is in demand. Stock in demand has a very nasty habit of quickly becoming more expensive. Other market participants who understand what is happening and who are able to trade quickly can place orders before the fund—that is, they can front-run the fund's buy orders—which will drive up the stock's price.[22]

So, in the hands of a stock-broking oaf who charges rock-bottom commissions, a large order could end up being far more expensive for the fund—through "market impact" costs—if the stock's price rises during a maladroit buying process. Any cost savings from cut-rate brokerage commissions would thus be squandered through poor execution and infelicitous market impact.

Trollope alluded to this challenge of buying large blocks of stock without moving the price adversely. His savvy but unscrupulous American, Hamilton K. Fisker, tried to buy as much stock of the South Central Pacific and Mexican Railway as he could without driving the price up: "I'll buy every share in the market. I wired for as many as I dar'd, so as not to spoil our own game."[23]

So, it is the concept of "best"—and most emphatically not "cheapest"—execution that allows money managers such as fund advisers to factor in variables other than commission price when determining which brokerage to use for a trade. Speed, adroitness, and market impact are some of those other variables. So, too, might be the aforementioned loyalty programs and their soft dollars in this business.[24]

Soft-Dollar Programs

Soft-dollar programs work in a variety of ways. But one useful comparison is to the points program on a credit card. As an investment adviser uses fund assets to pay for brokerage commissions, all the dollars it spends are recorded, in just the same way that a credit card company keeps track of how much money a cardholder spends.

In both scenarios, the dollars spent represent a form of currency. And, as with a credit card, broker-dealers offer their reward points according to a ratio. So, just as gas and groceries might be worth triple points on a credit card, the SEC's investigation found that brokerage commissions generate soft dollars at an average of 1.7 to 1.[25] That is, for every 1.7 dollars a mutual fund spends on commissions, the fund's adviser earns one soft dollar. Incurring brokerage commissions, then, is how soft dollars are accumulated. How are they redeemed?

Again, like a credit card company, the broker-dealers offer their clients an array of possible rewards on which they can spend their soft dollars. Recall the testimony the chief investment officer at American Century, who provided Congress with a remarkably concrete guide. He submitted a list maintained by broker-dealers that included vendors whose products and services could be paid for using soft dollars.[26] The list included 1,200 names, many of firms specializing in financial research. But accounting, computer, and telephone companies were on the list, too. And let's not forget that "private retreat of luxury and tranquility," the Standard Club of Chicago.[27] Hmm, we seem to drifting away from conventional understandings of "research" and well outside the safe harbor of Section 28(e).

The Defense of Soft Dollars

In 1998, the SEC concluded that this shadow economy of soft dollars amounted to more than $1 billion each year.[28] In 2004, money manager Whitney Tilson estimated that investors pay more than $6 billion in extra fees each year.[29] If this system of racking up credits with investors' money and cashing in benefits for advisers sounds a little seedy, perhaps we should eliminate the Section 28(e) safe harbor that permits it. Why do Congress and the SEC permit these sorts of convoluted and conflicted arrangements?

One response is that conflicts of interest—such as the temptations here for an adviser to misuse investors' money for the adviser's benefit—are merely potential sources of problems. A conflict does not, by itself, demonstrate actual harm to fund investors.[30] To show that harm, we would need either to find proof that an adviser chose a poor brokerage firm because of soft dollars or to see examples of soft-dollar redemptions that provided no benefits to the fund shareholders. We will.

But first let's acknowledge that conflicted transactions do, in theory, have an ability to benefit shareholders. Consider a corporation in which the chief executive officer authorizes payments to her relatives in the form of rent for office space. The conflict is obvious: an officer using corporate assets to enrich the officer's relatives is engaging in a conflicted insider transaction. But now let us hypothesize that the corporation in question is just a fledgling start-up with two employees selling cupcakes from a food truck, and the office space in question is the garage of the CEO's parents. In that scenario, we would be far less suspicious. And we might change our mind entirely about this conflicted insider transaction if we learned that the parents were offering the space for a price well below, not high above, the fair market value.[31]

So, in principle, conflicted transactions might not necessarily harm—indeed, they might even benefit—shareholders. In mutual funds, all that excellent research might pay for itself by inspiring a fund adviser to excellent performance and greater returns for fund investors.

Maybe.

Violations of the Safe Harbor

In practice, we have seen advisers and brokers paddling well outside the Section 28(e) safe harbor. When the SEC conducted an investigation into soft dollars in the mutual fund industry, it found investment advisers using them to pay for travel, airfare, hotels, meals, employee salaries, and cellphone bills. Other lowlights included bottled water, limousines, interior design, and round-trip airfare to Hong Kong for an executive's child. Though soft-dollar abuses may be rare, they are not just artifacts from a sordid past.[32]

In 2005, SEC Commissioner Paul S. Atkins reported that investment advisers had used soft dollars to pay for conferences in Bermuda, for rent, and even for college tuition.[33] In 2013, Instinet, a New York brokerage, redeemed soft dollars from its customer, J.S. Oliver Capital Management, by paying $329,365 to the ex-wife of the adviser's president; $65,000 in rent payments for J.S. Oliver "offices" in the president's home; and $40,094 for upkeep on the president's New York City timeshare.[34] It's awfully hard to see how payments like these provide the slightest benefit to investors in a fund managed by J.S. Oliver Capital Management.

The Problem with Soft Dollars

Critics of Section 28(e) and the entire soft-dollar subculture argue that our current system of opaque payments—which so resemble kickbacks—inevitably leads to these sorts of abuses.[35] And fund investors will have a difficult time policing them to discern potentially beneficial transactions from actually harmful ones. Nowhere in the compendious disclosure documents required of fund firms are soft dollars reported or their number and uses disclosed. In the 296-page *Fact Book* prepared in 2015 by the fund industry's trade association, the Investment Company Institute, which contains sixty-seven tables of data on every aspect of the business, soft dollars are mentioned precisely never.[36]

So, how might we muck out these abuses from our investment stables? The most direct step would simply be to prohibit soft dollars and require advisers to pay only "hard dollars" for anything they receive from a broker-dealer. Or, if we think all that patronage is a valuable asset, the SEC could limit its use to additional brokerage commissions. Like "cash-back" credit cards, broker-dealers could reward mutual funds with free trades. Those savings would inure directly to the benefit of fund investors. But for any research, business tools, or trips to Hong Kong, our regulators could require investment advisers to spend their own money. We typically expect American enterprises to pay for their own infrastructural needs and business expenses, and the fund industry certainly has the cash.

We should expect the industry to claim, as it regularly does, that a change such as the elimination of soft dollars would lead to a rise in other fees.[37] After a while, the regulation of mutual funds can begin to feel like a hostage negotiation. But if fees must go up, then at least fund investors will know what investment advice costs—and will not have to hope they receive third-hand benefits from perquisites surreptitiously paid to their advisers. Nor will fund investors have to worry that soft dollars are perverting their adviser's judgment about how best to invest.

6

FAIR VALUATION

Somewhere along the line, the name of the game became gathering a
lot of assets. If it can bring in a lot of assets, a fund company can make
money no matter how the funds themselves perform for investors.
—William H. Donaldson, *SEC Chairman, 2005*

St. Michael's College is a small Catholic school close to the shore of Lake
Champlain in Colchester, Vermont. The college was founded in 1904 by priests
of the Society of Saint Edmund, who had fled France fifteen years before, during
another of the country's paroxysms of anti-clericalism. A century later, in 2009,
members of St. Michael's faculty attempted another flight when they decided
to transfer their savings from one retirement plan to another. Such a pedestrian
transaction shouldn't really have been very dramatic, but, it produced years of
class-action litigation and amounted to another exodus for St. Michael's.

To effect the transfer of their savings, the faculty members attempted to close
out their accounts in the plan they were leaving, which was administered by the
Teachers Insurance and Annuity Association of American—College Retirement
and Equities Fund (TIAA-CREF). TIAA-CREF is a nonprofit organization
widely known as an enormous provider of retirement services to academics and
medical professionals across the United States. Subsequent allegations in a class-
action complaint filed against TIAA-CREF, however, accused the investment
adviser of far from charitable behavior.[1]

Professors at St. Michael's noticed that TIAA-CREF was taking a long time to
process their transfers. Recall that mutual fund sales should, by law, be settled by
the third business day following a client's request. Yet the professors' transactions
at TIAA-CREF were taking far longer. And the stock market in 2009 was moving
dramatically.

During some of the delays, the stock market rose notably. In some instances,
the professors were still able to access their accounts online and to watch as their
holdings grew—"in some cases by thousands of dollars"[2]—during the delay
between when they had submitted their transfer request and when TIAA-CREF
actually closed the accounts. Yet the subsequent transfers by TIAA-CREF did
not reflect those corresponding gains.

The complaint filed in federal court alleged that TIAA-CREF wrongfully "kep[t] customer accounts open for days or weeks after receiving instructions to close them, and retain[ed] all investment income earned in the interim for itself."[3]

When the plaintiffs' attorneys suspected that TIAA-CREF was treating other people's accounts in a similar, dilatory way, the lawsuit swelled into a class action involving "as many as 40,000 employees at private colleges with TIAA-CREF accounts."[4] In the summer of 2013, a federal judge granted class-action status to the lawsuit, which accused TIAA-CREF of violating its fiduciary duty of loyalty to these clients. One year later, TIAA-CREF settled the lawsuit, which then covered a settlement class of more than 100,000 investors who had requested but not received their funds within seven days. To atone for its sins to St. Michael's and others, TIAA-CREF paid approximately $20 million.[5]

The accusations leveled at TIAA-CREF were dramatic, involving astonishing delays of several weeks. In a world of instantaneous electronic transfers, those time-frames were positively glacial. But why might they have wanted to hold onto their customers' money? The answer to that turns on how TIAA-CREF is compensated. An investment adviser that inflates the assets it manages—such as by failing to return them to investors promptly—effectively inflates its revenues. Let's see how.

Assets Under Management

The investing experts at mutual funds spend their careers absorbed by figures, but one number stands above all others in their hierarchy of accompts: the precise amount of assets in each of their funds. As we have seen, the formula for remunerating advisers is a simple but powerful one. The revenues an adviser earns each year are equal to the adviser's fees multiplied by the assets under management. So an adviser that charges, say, 0.75 percent (or 75 basis points) to advise a fund holding, say, $1.5 billion in assets would earn $11.25 million each year.

If this example seems a little modest, we need simply add a few zeroes to the assets and add several other funds to the adviser's complex to generate a more impressive return. The figures across the entire industry certainly are more extraordinary, amounting to almost $100 billion in revenues to advisers each year.[6]

In 2014, the average expense ratio in U.S. equity funds was 70 basis points; in bond funds, it was 57 basis points; and in hybrid funds, it was 78 basis points.[7] The corresponding assets that year in equity funds were $8.31 trillion; in bond funds, they were $3.46 trillion; and in hybrid funds, they were $1.35 trillion.[8] So from just these three species of funds, mutual fund advisers generated revenues of $58.2 billion in equity funds, $19.7 billion in bond funds, and $10.5 billion in hybrid funds, for a total of almost $90 billion. They earned billions more from money market and other more specialized funds.

If the professionals who work for investment advisers are like their fellow creatures stalking our financial jungle, then we can assume they are ever eager to maximize their revenues. Under this compensation formula, as we have discussed, they have just two options for doing so: they can either increase their fees or increase their funds' assets. Honestly increasing these two variables can be something of an ordeal.

First, raising fees is a noisy process that can be unpopular with investors: the fund's trustees must be consulted and new disclosure documents are sent out to existing shareholders. Investors are going to notice the change and will likely be unenthusiastic. Second, raising assets under management is a challenging process that requires either marketing efforts or investment success, which in turn requires substantial degrees of effort, skill, and luck.

As we shall see, however, some advisers have been known to pursue a third, ingenious, labor-saving method. How might an adviser—granted, only one liberated from its scruples—attempt to manipulate the compensation formula to its illicit advantage? An unscrupulous adviser can, of course, simply overstate the amount of assets under its management. If the value of the securities in a fund's portfolio were reported to be greater than it actually is, then the assets under management would be higher, and the adviser would thereby earn greater revenues. Let's try our hand at lying about a fund's portfolio securities.

Overstating the Value of Portfolio Securities

To do so, we must begin with the formula for calculating the value of portfolio securities. This equation, too, involves simply the multiplication of two variables: the number of shares that the fund owns and the price of those shares. Alas, these variables are difficult to fabricate, so we may have a difficult time fooling anybody about their value.

Public Investments

If our fund, for simplicity's sake, owned only shares of Google in its portfolio, let's think about how we might overstate their value. We could claim to own a greater number of those Google shares than we actually do. But the fund's custodian, who actually holds the shares, and the fund's auditor, who examines the financial records, would readily discover the true number.[9]

What if we instead claimed that our Google shares were worth more than they really were? Unfortunately, that number too is easily verifiable. Anyone with a computer—and certainly every fund's auditor—can easily determine the exact price of any security that is publicly traded on U.S. stock markets. Those prices are reported quickly and widely all day long.[10] So, our naked effort simply to lie about the value of our portfolio securities will be foiled by the newspapers, television shows, and websites that cast altogether too much illumination on our stock markets.

But let's not give up yet. Fund assets can be overinflated and, on occasion, they have been. So, let's do what all determined criminals do when exposed to too much light—let's move into the shadows and operate in the darker corners of the investment world. To find them, we must move away from public stock exchanges and other investments with transparent and widely reported prices. We need to find some investments whose prices are difficult to determine and rarely reported. Luckily for us, plenty of those investments exist, and owning many of them is completely free from public opprobrium.

Illiquid Investments

Consider the value of shares in a privately held company or investments in real estate or bespoke derivatives. The *New York Times* reported in March 2015 that "big money managers including Fidelity, T. Rowe Price, and BlackRock have all struck deals worth billions of dollars to acquire shares of these private companies [Uber, Airbnb, and Pinterest] that are then pooled into mutual funds that go into the 401(k)s and individual retirement accounts of many Americans."[11] Those investments are popular and widespread, but their prices can be hard to determine and are rarely published. Let's took a look at why.

Think of a company whose stock is held only by private investors. The company need not be some clandestine venture squirreled away in the Cayman Islands; it could be something as open and notorious as Facebook (or Uber, Airbnb, or Pinterest) in the months before its initial public offering.[12] Even in the days before Facebook went public, the company enjoyed millions of users, hundreds of investors, and oodles of press coverage.[13] But its shares were not traded on any public stock exchange, and consequently, their value was difficult to determine at any particular moment in time. The financial community nevertheless regarded equity in Facebook as an excellent investment proposition, and investors clamored to acquire shares. (Goldman Sachs even ran afoul of the SEC in its exertions to squeeze more investors than the 499 permitted as stockholders in a privately held Facebook.[14])

When any company is privately held, the precise value of its shares can be determined with confidence only during a valuation event. The classic valuation event is a sale of shares, either by the company itself during a round of fundraising or by a current shareholder attempting to sell his stock to someone else. But these events are sporadic and may be separated in time by many months. While insiders and observers may have had their own views of what Facebook shares were worth prior to its IPO—and everyone may correctly have assumed that the value was rising continually—the actual price of the stock on any given day was something of a mystery.[15]

This phenomenon of investments experiencing only intermittent pricing events is common also to real estate and over-the-counter derivatives, and it explains why they, too, are difficult to value with regularity. How much is your house worth right now? You could tell me how much you paid for it, but that number can be years out of date. You might be able to tell me how much your neighbor's house recently sold for, but you don't have the exact same house nor the exact same buyer. You could hire an appraiser to offer an opinion, but that appraisal value is simply a professional estimate, and another appraiser might disagree significantly. The most reliable way to price such an investment is to find a buyer willing to make a firm offer. The price that someone is actually willing to pay is, in our system of capitalism, widely accepted as the truest value of an investment.

So an investment adviser—one intent on manipulating the value of its assets under management in any event—can exploit these gaps between pricing events to abet a scheme of pricing puffery.

The Value of Delay

So what if an investment adviser acquired privately held shares or rarely traded securities for the portfolio of its fund, simply waited a while, and then started quietly pumping up the value of those holdings?[16] As the reported value of the holdings increased, so too would the adviser's revenues. If challenged on its valuations, the adviser could protest that no prices were publicly available so its figures could not be disproved.

Hmm, no, that's probably not going to work. That approach should fail, for two reasons. First, the adviser surely would have to support any deviations—upward or downward—in the stated value of its holdings. So, if no public pricing events had actually occurred, then it would have a hard time justifying any revision above the value it paid for the investments. Second, the human eye is attracted to movement. So, when an investment's value changes, investors and auditors are more likely to inquire as to why. An investment rising enough to affect the overall value of a fund would likely prompt the curiosity of fund investors about this success story. And certainly a falling investment would, too.

In sum, surely an adviser could not simply write in a higher price for portfolio securities, could it? Let's consult the professionals.

The UBS Investments

In June 2008, UBS Global Asset Management purchased 54 complex fixed-income securities for the portfolios of various mutual funds that it advised. UBS—or, rather, the UBS funds—paid a total of $22 million for those investments. Alas, for the shareholders of those UBS funds, the summer of 2008 was a particularly poor time to be buying investments on planet Earth.[17] Especially investments that "were part of subordinated tranches of non-agency mortgage-backed securities."[18]

In its cease-and-desist order, the SEC described these investments, politely, as securities whose "underlying collateral generally consists of mortgages which do not conform to the requirements (size, documentation, loan-to-value ratios, etc.) for inclusion in mortgage-backed securities guaranteed or issued by Ginnie Mae, Fannie Mae or Freddie Mac."[19] In the industry, those kinds of investments were known, less politely, as "toxic," "garbage," and other unprintable expletives.[20]

For our purposes, the most important characteristic of those investments was that they "were not listed or sold on any exchange, and there was not an active market for them."[21] So what were the securities worth? With hindsight, we now know the answer was diddly-squat.[22] But in the absence of readily available market quotations, what should UBS have listed as the securities' price in calculating the value of the funds' assets?

A Brief History of Fair Value

The answer to that question has something of a venerable history that reaches back seventy years. The SEC established some of its earliest guidance on how to value investments in response to the machinations of a corporate group "sponsored by George F. Getty, and continued by his son, J. Paul Getty."[23]

The Getty System, as the SEC dubbed the family's elaborate pipeline of subsidiaries in 1943, held stock in a company called Skelly Oil Company. The issue in this case was whether one of the Getty companies was, technically, an investment company under the securities regulations. All investment companies must comply with the onerous regulations that govern mutual funds, which can be an unpleasant burden and one that most operating companies try hard to avoid. Whether this particular Getty company was an investment company turned on the valuation of its holdings in Skelly Oil Company.

Though the stock of Skelly traded on the New York Stock Exchange with readily available prices, the Getty argument was that such prices should be ignored. Their claim was an echo of the universal cry of failed entrepreneurs and angst-ridden teenagers throughout time: the world just doesn't understand!

The value of Skelly shares, it contended, was "considerably in excess of the present market price" of $19.25.[24] Indeed, the Getty corporate parent was proud indeed, arguing that the true value was "not less than the sum of $41 per share."[25] The SEC quickly dismissed this argument, concluding instead that where "the stock of an industrial company is registered and actively traded on the New York Stock Exchange, it seems to us that the only fair value which can be placed on the shares is market value."[26]

Fair Value in Mutual Funds

For UBS in 2008, similar rules applied. The Investment Company Act of 1940 states that the value of securities held in mutual funds is "the market value when market quotations are readily available."[27] But for the illiquid securities UBS had purchased, market quotations were not readily available. The Investment Company Act also covers that eventuality by declaring that, in the absence of market quotations for a particular investment, a fund adviser must use a value that is the "fair value as determined in good faith by the board of directors."[28]

And what was the position of those trustees of the UBS funds? Recall that a fund's trustees are, notionally, distinct from the fund's investment adviser. In this case the UBS trustees' approved procedure was for the adviser to record illiquid investments at their purchase price until the board's valuation committee could make a specific determination of their fair value within five business days. But UBS, the investment adviser, followed something of a different approach.

For two weeks, according to the SEC, UBS valued forty-eight of the securities at "stale"[29] prices provided by friendly third parties, which were higher than the prices UBS paid. Indeed, UBS recorded a majority of the securities at values "at least 100 percent higher than the transaction prices" and recorded some at values "more than 1,000 percent higher."[30]

The SEC was unimpressed. UBS had disregarded the procedures set forth by its trustees, used prices that were artificially inflated, and enriched itself at the expense of its fund shareholders. And these valuation errors triggered a cascade of other problems. When a fund is valued incorrectly, not only is the adviser's compensation incorrect, but so, too, is the price paid and received by every fund shareholder who bought or redeemed shares of the fund during the persistence of the error.[31] Moreover, when a fund's price is artificially inflated, shareholders who redeem will receive too much money at the expense of the shareholders who remain in the fund.

But, as we will see, this puffery by UBS was just a tyro's incompetent effort at deception. The scheme survived only a fortnight before it was discovered. Moving prices up, as we suspected, is awfully difficult to get away with. And when the entire subprime mortgage market imploded a few months later in 2008, UBS surely received a brutally clear lesson about the true value of those securities.[32] For their sins, UBS paid a mere $300,000 to settle the SEC's charges.[33]

A More Subtle Inflation of a Fund's Value

For all its worldly banking sophistication, UBS was something of an amateur at this ruse of distorting fund valuations. Although they presumably recognized the problem with manipulating the value of publicly traded stocks and hewed instead to investments for which there were no readily available market prices, they nevertheless made the mistake of inflating their investments. The truly subtle practitioners of this artful dodge succeed not by changing valuations but by keeping them constant. A price not lowered can be as powerful economically as a price raised . . . but much harder to detect.

Prices that do not reflect drops in value are just as inflated as prices that have been wrongfully raised. Consider, for instance, a fund with investments in a startup company that experiences a business failure. The fund manager could leave the price of those shares unchanged rather than marking them down as circumstances demand. In effect, this inaction by the manager acts to overstate the amount of assets under management and, consequently, inflates the manager's revenues. But outsiders will find it much harder to detect problems with a value that stays constant than with one that an adviser has changed.

An early example of this method of inflating assets by doing nothing involved an investment adviser named Parnassus Investments, which managed the Parnassus Fund.[34] For the portfolio of the fund, the adviser had acquired 565,000 shares of common stock and other securities in a company called Margaux, Inc., a manufacturer of "large, energy-efficient refrigeration units for grocery stores."[35] For two years in the early 1990s, Parnassus valued its investment in Margaux at a constant price.

Yet during that time, Margaux filed for bankruptcy, had its stock delisted from NASDAQ, and endured extremely negative publicity linking Margaux's dodgy refrigerators to the sale of spoiled meat by its largest customer, Food Lion.[36] Only when Morgan Stanley downgraded its rating of Margaux did the Parnassus board reduce the valuation of its investment in Margaux. For their paralysis in the face of these obvious negative influences upon their portfolio, an administrative law judge held that the independent trustees of the board had aided and abetted the overstatement of the fund's net asset value.[37]

The Morgan Keegan Investments

For a far more grandiose effort to distort a fund's valuation in this vein, we must turn to the ambitious executives at the adviser Morgan Keegan. Morgan Keegan's botched investments in toxic subprime securities earned them a $200 million fine from the SEC on top of a package of other highly unusual penalties.[38] So what did they do that was 666 times worse than UBS?

Robert Khuzami, the director of the SEC's Division of Enforcement, summarized their deception with this pithy description: "This scheme had two architects—a portfolio manager responsible for lies to investors about the true value of the assets in his funds, and a head of fund accounting who turned a blind eye to the fund's bogus valuation process."[39]

That portfolio manager, who played the role of villainous mastermind in this scheme, was James C. Kelsoe.[40] Kelsoe managed five Morgan Keegan funds, with aggregate assets of $4 billion, and much of his investment strategy involved stuffing the funds' portfolios with collateralized debt obligations and other poorly rated debt that was "backed by subprime mortgages."[41]

As with the holdings in the UBS funds, these portfolio securities "lacked readily available market quotations and, as a result, were to be internally priced by the Funds' Board of Directors, using 'fair value' methods."[42] Although our nation's mortgage industry was still a year or so away from its complete debacle, the market for these "securities deteriorated in the first half of 2007."[43] Kelsoe was facing a serious problem with the value of his funds and, beginning in January 2007, he began to do something about it.[44]

The funds' stated procedure for valuing illiquid securities such as these was for the board's Valuation Committee to determine a price using fair-valuation techniques. In practice, the trustees abdicated this responsibility in favor of the adviser, Morgan Keegan, who allowed lower-level employees in its fund accounting department—"who did not have the training or qualifications"—to make pricing decisions.[45] This sloppy oversight provided Kelsoe with the opening he needed.

Between January and July 2007, Kelsoe instructed his assistant to send approximately forty emails to the fund accounting department containing 262 "price adjustments" relating to the value of specific securities held in his five funds.[46] Those adjustments did not revise the price of those securities above the price the funds initially paid for them, but neither did they reflect the securities' true, far lower value. Instead, they held at constant or a slight decline the price of securities that were in fact plummeting.

But in the absence of market prices, where did Kelsoe find support for these adjustments? Some were simply arbitrary, the creatures of Kelsoe's own febrile imagination, while others he procured from the broker-dealers from whom he had acquired the securities in the first place. Kelsoe would confer with his contact at a broker-dealer and ask that firm to provide artificially high quotes to support Kelsoe's price adjustments. Keenly intent on keeping their customer satisfied, the broker-dealers regularly helped Kelsoe out. After all, sending along imaginary values to Morgan Keegan wouldn't adversely affect operations at their business. When they declined to abet the fiction, Kelsoe would simply ignore their less than helpful prices.

Bad Bonds

Two particular bond purchases illustrate Kelsoe's modus operandi. In July 2006, Kelsoe purchased something called a "Knollwood collateralized debt obligation" from one of his preferred broker-dealers. Nine months later, in April 2007, Kelsoe reported to his fund accounting department a $92 price for the Knollwood bond using an inflated quote from the broker-dealer who sold it to him. The following month, in anticipation of another routine audit of the price of the bond by his employer, Kelsoe again discussed the price with his salesperson at the broker-dealer. Kelsoe told him "not to provide a quote to Morgan Keegan unless it was $87.50 or higher."[47]

The broker's salesperson replied, two days later, to say that at his firm's trading desk, the bond was being quoted as low as $65. Kelsoe "communicated his unhappiness" about that price "and threatened to stop doing business" with the broker-dealer.[48] A few weeks later, Kelsoe submitted to his audit department a price adjustment of $88 for the bond; again, a figure well above its fair value. Though the broker-dealer wasn't willing to provide such swollen figures, it found itself able to help in other ways. Thanks to the pointed conversation between Kelsoe and the salesperson, the next time the brokerage firm submitted prices of its securities to Morgan Keegan, the number for the Knollwood bond was left blank. As a result, Morgan Keegan continued to price the bond at $88, way above the fair value of $65.

Aiding and Abetting on the Inside

But Kelsoe's scheme would work only if he had a friendly collaborator to accept all his bogus price adjustments. And in Joseph Thompson Weller, he found one. Weller, a certified public accountant, was head of Morgan Keegan's fund accounting department and a member of the firm's valuation committee. The SEC alleged that Weller "knew, or was highly reckless in not knowing, of the deficiencies in the implementation of the valuation procedures."[49] Any diligent fund accounting department, the SEC believed, would have demanded supporting documentation for Kelsoe's pricing adjustments and conducted independent efforts to verify Kelsoe's submissions.

Lest we dismiss these financial fabulists as merely having engaged in some short-cuts in the tedious bean counting of accountancy, consider what their behavior was doing to investors in the real world.

In June 2007, the Indiana Children's Wish Fund invested almost $223,000 in one of the Morgan Keegan funds that Kelsoe managed. Yes, this charity is one of those that grants wishes to children with life-threatening illnesses. Before the year was out, their investment had lost $48,000.[50]

For these brazen sins, the SEC imposed not just the $200 million fine on Morgan Keegan, but it also hunted Kelsoe and Weller personally.[51] Kelsoe agreed to a lifetime ban from the securities industry and to pay $500,000; Weller agreed to pay $50,000. But the case became a landmark for another set of penalties that the SEC imposed.[52]

The Circle of Blame

When the portfolio and price of a mutual fund are so dramatically perverted, who else is to blame? The SEC concluded that the eight members of Morgan Keegan's board of trustees were also responsible. Perhaps that conclusion may seem obvious to one unfamiliar with the history of mutual funds. But the SEC's determination astonished the mutual fund industry.

Once upon a time, not so very long ago, our law enforcers regularly brought criminal charges against individuals who perpetrated financial crimes[53]: the savings-and-loan crisis of the 1980s produced successful criminal prosecutions of more than eight hundred individuals,[54] and the accounting origami of Enron, WorldCom, and Tyco in the 1990s led to the incarcerations of their respective chief executive officers, Jeffrey Skilling, Bernie Ebbers, and Dennis Kozlowski.[55] The English playwright Caryl Churchill anticipated this criminal litany in her 1987 satire, *Serious Money*:

> I'm Duckett. I enjoy the *Financial Times*
> It's fun reading about other people's crimes.[56]

But in more recent years, prosecutions of individuals for financial crimes have dramatically—and, to some, curiously—evaporated.[57] The colossal wreckage of 2008's financial enormities has thus far produced exactly one individual prosecution.

Amid the catalog of scandals afflicting mutual funds in 2003 and thereafter, individual recriminations were rare. And when they did come, they were typically against individuals who worked for the investment adviser. Trustees almost never faced accusations of personal wrongdoing. So the SEC's position in the Morgan Keegan case was dramatic, if perhaps somewhat overdue.

The SEC's order against the trustees accused them of improperly delegating their responsibility to value these securities to the investment adviser without providing guidance or oversight of the process.[58] Robert Khuzami, once again leading the enforcement, offered this pithy epitaph for the sordid episode:

> Investors rely on board members to establish an accurate process for valuing their mutual fund investments. . . . Had the [Morgan Keegan] board not abdicated its responsibilities, investors may have stood a better chance of preserving their hard-earned assets.[59]

Further, added Khuzami, "the eight directors' failure to fulfill their value-related obligations was particularly inexcusable given that fair-valued securities made up the majority of the funds' net asset values—in most cases upwards of 60 percent."[60]

The market also inflicted its own punishment upon Morgan Keegan. By December 2007, funds managed by Kelsoe had hemorrhaged value enormously, prompting Kiplinger to report: "After years of flying high, Jim Kelsoe's bond funds have lost half their value this year."[61] Kelsoe's desperation had been driven by two mutually reinforcing and deleterious phenomena: first, the underlying investments simply tanked; second, in response to those losses, investors rushed to redeem.[62]

Bursts of redemptions are another of the many dangers exacerbated in portfolios stuffed with illiquid securities. No portfolio manager enjoys dealing with large-scale redemptions, but those runs by redeeming shareholders are particularly debilitating for funds with illiquid securities. Since these investments do not, by definition, trade in markets with abundant counterparties, a portfolio manager desperate to sell may have to accept any offer she can find.

So Kelsoe would have had to sell big chunks of his portfolio—at a time when the portfolio's value was plunging—to other investors who knew how desperate he was to sell. Kiplinger's conclusion on this death spiral was categorical: "With the benefit of hindsight, it's clear that illiquid assets such as these are ill suited to open-end funds, which are subject to abrupt and mass redemptions."[63] Ultimately, the debacle at Morgan Keegan resulted in the closure of Kelsoe's five funds and the departure of all eight trustees.[64]

Though the Morgan Keegan swindle was particularly grotesque, it was by no means unique. The SEC maintains a web page dedicated to the Valuation of Portfolio Securities, which lists more than fifty enforcement actions spanning the eighty years from 1943 to 2013.[65] No doubt many more fund portfolios, beyond the SEC's notice, have been unfairly valued in that time.

Ending Unfair Valuations

How then should a portfolio of illiquid securities, if a manager insists on managing one, be valued fairly?

Today, a best practice of conscientious boards of trustees is to obtain the expertise of third-party vendors who specialize in providing values for investments that have no readily available market price.[66] Those vendors develop proprietary methods and algorithms for estimating prices by hunting for correlations between the security in question and other, more transparent metrics. For instance, the value of a particular collateralized debt obligation (CDO) might, historically, have moved in relation to public indices that reflect trends in subprime mortgages. When those indices move, while the CDO's price is stale, an effective algorithm applied to big-enough data could posit a fairer value for the CDO.[67]

Trustees and their vendors can regularly back-test these estimated values by comparing them to the next actual trades of the illiquid securities. If a subsequent market price is wildly different from the value estimated by the vendor, their method or algorithm can be adjusted for future uses.

And, needless to say, no board of trustees should permit a portfolio manager to hypothesize the values of securities in her own fund. No person at the investment adviser could have a more direct and pernicious incentive to distort the performance of a fund.

Ordinary fund investors know very little about this process. And it's unlikely that exhaustive disclosures about a fund's regular fair valuation efforts in the bowels of swollen disclosure documents would enlighten us greatly. But one statistic that might be illuminating would be the margin of error between the values a board uses and the next actual market prices. A fund with regular pricing errors could be one for investors to avoid.

Unless, of course, all those errors by the fund systematically *undervalued* its portfolio and therefore *underpaid* its adviser to the benefit of fund shareholders. Ha ha ha.

Everyday Overstatements of Fund Value

Let's conclude with our less dramatic, but far more common variation on this theme of advisers overstating the assets of their funds. The motto of St. Michael's College is *Quis ut Deus?*—Who is like God? When it came to omnipotence over the professors' savings, the answer was TIAA-CREF.

TIAA-CREF did not inflate the price of the securities in its funds. But it may nevertheless have overvalued its assets under management. How? By holding them longer. Like most investment advisers, TIAA-CREF received a percentage of the assets under its control for every day that it managed those assets. By extending that period, it managed more assets for more days. Any time an adviser drags its feet about transferring funds back to its clients, it is effectively inflating its assets under management and therefore its revenues.

But let's consider arguments that can be made in TIAA-CREF's defense. One might contend that the market could have fallen as often as it rose during any delays in disbursing assets, in which case investment losses might have offset any gains—in which case, the adviser might not have enriched itself very much at all. This defense suffers from several problems.

First, customers who would have realized gains had the adviser not kept them for itself will not be comforted to learn that TIAA-CREF absorbed losses from a different set of investors. Who cares what you did with other investors? They will say, Where are my market gains?

Second, for the past hundred years, our stock markets have risen far more than they have fallen, so any protracted scheme like this will almost certainly accumulate net gains for any financial intermediary that holds onto the money longer than it is permitted to.

Third, and most important, investors continue to pay their expense ratios for every day their money is in the hands of an investment adviser. An adviser who holds onto clients' funds longer than permitted is simply overstating its assets under management in another, creative way.

LATE TRADING

How to Beat the Market: Easy. Make Late Trades.
—Floyd Norris, *New York Times*, 2003

On May Day, 1923, two New York financiers united to form one of the America's most venerable capitalist institutions. Joseph Ainslee Bear and Robert B. Stearns imprinted their names on the investment bank that grew for over eighty-five years to control more than $350 billion in assets. Then, in 2008, Bear Stearns & Co. fell as one of the more notable casualties amid the carnage of the financial crisis. Before its failure and absorption by J.P. Morgan that year, Bear Stearns had become a global financial firm that offered prominent investment banking and brokerage services.[1]

Some of those brokerage services, however, were more full service than many might have imagined. Or than the law permitted. As a broker-dealer, Bear Stearns helped its clients to invest in mutual funds. And sometimes the firm was just a little too helpful. In March 2006, the director of the SEC's division of enforcement, Linda Chatman Thomsen, announced that Bear Stearns had agreed to pay $250 million to settle allegations of wrongdoing: "For years, Bear Stearns helped favored hedge fund customers evade the systems and rules designed to protect long-term mutual fund investors from the harm of market timing and late trading."[2] Thomsen's colleague, Mark Schonfeld, director of the SEC's Northeast Regional Office, added, "Bear Stearns was the hub that connected the many spokes of market timing and late trading—hedge funds, brokers and the mutual funds. Bear Stearns made it possible for hedge funds and brokers to submit orders long after the 4:00 p.m. cut-off."[3] Certainly that behavior sounds unsavory—and for $250 million, it must have been quite a faux pas—but what exactly did the firm do wrong?

First, let us imagine an investor lacking both scruples and a tolerance for risk. Perhaps an extreme version of Mr. Jonas in Dickens's *Martin Chuzzlewit*: "The education of Mr. Jonas had been conducted from his cradle on the strictest principles of the main chance. The very first word he learnt to spell was 'gain' and the second (when he got into two syllables), 'money.'"[4] Is there anything such a scoundrel could do with—or to—a mutual fund? Why, yes, there is. Particularly with the help of Bear Stearns.

As it happens, there are at least three big things. And all three involve the intercession of financial intermediaries willing to sell their access to the back channels of our investment system. The first is a practice called *late trading*; the second and third, which we'll discuss in chapters 8 and 9, involve phenomena known as *market timing* and *selective disclosure*. All three involve sophisticated investors, such as hedge funds, trading illegally in ways that take advantage of long-term investors in mutual funds. Prior to being revealed publicly, late trading alone cost ordinary investors $400 million each year, in the estimation of Eric Zitzewitz, the leading economist of mutual fund scandals.[5]

All three schemes involve financial insiders, at mutual funds or broker-dealers, abetting these illegal trades. What might be the motivation of these accomplices to participate in such schemes? The same as for their confederates—and the same as it has ever been: lucre.

The Pricing Vulnerability that Allows Funds to Be Exploited

One of the antiquarian oddities—and perhaps greatest financial vulnerabilities—of mutual funds is the fact that they are priced just once a day.[6] To understand the intricacies and dangers this practice poses to mutual fund investors, we must explore the idiosyncratic pricing mechanism more closely.

Consider the challenge involved in figuring out the precise value of an entire mutual fund and, consequently, the price of a single share of that fund. A fund, as we know, is a collective investing tool by which thousands of individuals combine their moneys to purchase securities in a wide variety of operating companies. Although the math involved is not terribly complicated in theory, it can be extensive and cumbersome in practice.

The value of a mutual fund—known formally as its *net asset value*, or NAV[7]—is the value of its assets minus its liabilities. Once that value is ascertained, the price per share of a fund is simply the net asset value divided by the total number of shares outstanding. The fund's assets, of course, encompass all the many thousands of shares of Exxon, General Electric, Google, and other securities that the fund owns in its portfolio, plus any cash that the fund's manager has not invested. The liabilities, in turn, include any expenses owed to service providers such as the adviser, distributor, administrators, or lawyers, as well as brokerage commissions generated by buying and selling securities for the fund's portfolio. In concept, these computations should be quite straightforward. But if one returns in time to 1924, when the first mutual fund in the United States—Massachusetts Investors Trust—was launched, the technological impediments become more apparent.

At any given point in the trading day, the calculations involved can be daunting. First, one must begin with an accurate ledger of all the securities the fund holds in its portfolio—that is, a record of exactly how many shares of Exxon, General Electric, Google, and so forth the fund owns at that particular moment. Then, for that particular moment, one must ascertain the precise trading price of each of those corresponding stocks. When those amounts are multiplied by one another accurately and then summed up, one can successfully calculate the total value of the fund. Of course, if one belabors the process by even a few seconds, the prices of all those shares will have changed. Today, even a rudimentary computer with a fraction of the power of a smartphone could instantly compile most of these calculations.[8] But not in 1924. Instead, the pricing process was practicable for a human sporting green eyeshades, sleeve garters, and a moistened pencil only when all those numbers stopped moving.

In the United States, the public stock exchanges typically cease their fluctuations when they close at 4:00 P.M. Eastern Time. After that time, when trading has ceased, a manager can more easily determine the fund's holdings and the final trading price for each of those securities. Historically, then, mutual funds have always been priced after the close of business.

So, if a fund investor places an order at 11:15 A.M., for example, to buy $1,000 worth of a fund or, alternatively, 1,000 shares of a fund, the trade will not actually be effectuated until after the price of the fund is calculated following the close of the stock markets that day. If any order is placed at 4:01 P.M., it will not be filled until after the close of business the next day. This curious system is known as *forward pricing* because fund investors trade at a price that is not known until after the trade is placed, sometimes many hours later.[9]

The Processing of Fund Trades

To understand late trading, we must understand additional details about what happens at 4:00 P.M. and in the hours following that precise moment. First, note that we speak of the price calculated "as of" 4:00 P.M. on any given day, not the price calculated "at" 4:00 P.M. Hmm, do we not have computers capable of calculating the value of a fund's shares within sixty seconds? Of course we do. We now have wristwatches, coffee machines, and thermostats powerful enough to perform that calculation. Even the most rudimentary piece of silicon can multiply the number of securities in a portfolio by their share prices at the close of the market, and add any cash in the portfolio, and subtract any outstanding liabilities of the fund.

But that computation will tell us only the net asset value of the fund. And, in order to execute trades, we need to know the net asset value *per share* of the fund.

That is, we must divide the net asset value by the number of fund shares outstanding in order to know what price the selling fund shareholders will receive and what price the buying fund shareholders must pay. And, as it happens, we do not know the exact number of shares in play at 4:00 P.M. on any given day.[10]

Well, why not? Surely buyers and sellers are using the magical tubes of the Internet and sending their orders in electronically. And surely some computer somewhere can keep track of all of a particular day's orders to buy and to redeem a fund's shares. If a hacker can spam millions of email accounts in a few milliseconds, we must have the technology to do all this monitoring of shares more or less instantaneously.

We do have that technology. But, despite the hegemony of the smartphone, many Americans still do not buy and sell mutual fund shares through a computer. Many Americans still choose to speak with a financial planner in person about the trades they would like to place. A retiree might stop in at a local branch of Merrill Lynch to discuss trades. A busy doctor might place a telephone call to order a trade from her broker. In such old-fashioned, brick-and-mortar dealings, these orders to buy or sell fund shares might actually be written down on an order form.

In some benighted corners of the land, humans still actually fax orders to their brokerage firms. Throughout the course of a business day, a vast menagerie of analog, offline orders can migrate in from all corners of the United States. When the clock strikes 4:00 P.M. on the East Coast, trades for that day are no longer permitted. But fund firms must still gather this multitude of orders from across the land. Like the swelling of a river in a watershed, these individual orders are droplets that flow first into streams, then into rivers on their way to a continental catchment basin. [11]

At the close of business, brokers enter any written orders they have received into their computers. From there, an electronic system known as Fund/SERV, introduced by the National Securities Clearing Corporation in 1986,[12] gathers about 850,000 orders for more than 900 fund firms each day. Fund/SERV funnels orders to buy or to sell a particular fund to that fund's administrator, which can then compute the fund's net asset value per share.

These days, those per share prices must be provided to the National Association of Securities Dealers by 5:30 P.M. Eastern Time. That is, our pricing system allows 90 minutes to gather orders and to complete the NAV calculation. Back at the turn of the millennium, brokers could take until 8:00 P.M. to enter their trades into the Fund/SERV system. That left four hours for things to happen, in both the ordinary world of financial markets and in the underworld of illicit financial intermediaries.

Things such as what?

After the Closing Bell

In the ordinary world of financial markets, good or bad things can happen. Well, naturally. But what we care about are the financially invigorating or depressing things that happen every day. As a common practice, for instance, influential people with important financial news to share regularly make their announcements after the close of the markets. The idea behind this timing is that it allows flighty market participants a night's sleep, away from the manic market, to digest the news soberly before trading upon it. Finance ministers and corporate executives are forever waiting to holding press conferences that announce market-moving news until after the closing bell.

For the average investor in a mutual fund, news that occurs after 4:00 P.M. is often largely irrelevant. If the news were particularly good, for instance, it would be too late to capitalize on. Imagine that, at 5:00 P.M., Apple announces astonishingly gaudy profits from the sale of its iPhone 21. If an investor immediately placed an order to buy shares in a mutual fund specializing in technology stocks, the price he would receive would be the price calculated at 4:00 P.M. the next day, long after the shares of Apple and other tech companies had already risen and been priced into the net asset value of the mutual fund's shares.

Similarly, if the news were particularly bad, it would also be too late to avoid it. Imagine now that, at 5:00 P.M., the chief executive officer of a major financial institution announces that the company is filing for bankruptcy. Again, an investor might think to sell her holdings in any mutual fund heavily invested in the financial sector. But the price she would receive, again, would be the price calculated at 4:00 P.M. the next day, long after the shares of our mythical, not-too-big-to-fail financial firm had plummeted and dragged down the price of the mutual fund's shares.

Beating the Bell

But now consider the underworld of compromised brokers, the world of Bear Stearns. In 1999, Bear Stearns established something it called its "timing desk." The ostensible purpose of this desk was "to monitor and block accounts from trading in mutual funds that did not want market timing trades"[13]—that is, this desk was to be the police department charged with stopping impermissible trades in mutual funds. Of course, that grant of authority also happened to make this desk—like Al Pacino's narcotics squad in the movie *Serpico*—the perfect group to facilitate impermissible trades in mutual funds. According to the SEC, this timing desk "knowingly or recklessly processed thousands of late trades."[14]

In one recorded telephone call, a supervisor at Bear Stearns helpfully explained the scheme to a client:

> Because you're sending trades down some days after what's considered a legitimate time, 4 o'clock New York time, we want, we want to make sure that you know that we need to populate a time prior to 4:00 P.M. New York time. What I'd like to do, we're going to populate either 4:00 P.M. or 3:59.[15]

That is, Bear Stearns would helpfully backdate trades placed after the 4:00 P.M. deadline to an earlier time, so that the client could receive that day's price for the mutual fund.

So, if 4:00 P.M. was no longer the real deadline for certain customers at Bear Stearns, what was? In another recorded conversation, a client asked, "What's the cut-off time?" The head of the Bear Stearns operations department answered [and the SEC noted the accompanying jollity]: "You have plenty of time do trades [laughing]. Pretty much a quarter to six, 5:45 to enter a trade."[16] At Bear Stearns, then, truly platinum clients gained almost two hours of additional time beyond the lawful deadline to trade in mutual funds.

Trading Late

So, when these preferred customers learned of news announced after 4:00 P.M. that was likely to move the market, they could place an order with Bear Stearns that would be backdated sufficiently to allow them to capture the old—and highly valuable—price of the mutual fund. On good news, the client would be able to buy at an artificially low price. And to realize those gains as cash, late-trading clients could simply sell their shares the very next day. On bad news, the client would be able to sell at an artificially high price, a price not yet sullied by the impact of the price-depressing news.

For its favored clients, Bear Stearns made this illegality as convenient as possible by providing them with direct access to the firm's own mutual fund order-entry system. A client need not even be troubled with having one of those awkward conversations about trading illegally. And when mutual fund firms themselves took action to stop problematic trades being placed by misbehaving clients, Bear Stearns helped those clients deceive the mutual funds. Bear Stearns thus provided their clients with a money-making time machine that guaranteed sure-fire gains and avoided certain losses. Late trading is grossly illegal. But so, so tempting because it is, in the words of Eliot Spitzer, betting on a horse race after it has been run.[17]

The Price to Trade Late

What would inspire Bear Stearns to lavish such hospitality upon their clients? The clients were, of course, grateful, in small ways and large. Here is another, truly gruesome conversation that illustrates a measure of the reciprocity:

> TIMING DESK:Oh, I got your e-mail. . ... Thank you.
> HEDGE FUND:You're welcome. I hope—they're supposed to be here tomorrow and he's like, "They're pretty good seats. They're like 25 rows up." He's like "[inaudible] seats." I'm like, "That's what I want."
> TIMING DESK:You're so good to me.
> HEDGE FUND:Hey, no—you're so good to me. It works both ways.[18]

In addition to hot tickets, clients also gave Bear Stearns employees spa gift certificates, meals, and other shows of gratitude.

For a brokerage firm, however, such trinkets are not what the late-trading scheme was for: Bear Stearns wanted a much more valuable *quid pro quo*. For the firm, the true reward was the clients' stream of trading business. Broker-dealers like Bear Stearns enjoy a commission from every trade a client makes, so more trades equals more profit. And helping clients to make winning trades certainly guarantees more trades.

Late Trading through Bank of America: Blatant

A mutual fund adviser, unlike a broker-dealer, is not in the business of profiting off brokerage commissions. But an adviser might nevertheless have its own incentive to permit late trading. And our old friend from Eliot Spitzer's indictment, Edward Stern, of the hedge fund Canary Capital Partners, illustrated another, even more brazen late-trading arrangement in his dealings with the fund adviser, Bank of America.[19]

Bank of America's behavior was possibly more egregious than that of Bear Stearns because the funds being late-traded included those actually advised by Bank of America itself. If one can measure gradations of legality and loyalty, Bank of America abased itself on both dimensions by suborning late trading and betraying the investors in its own funds. Bear Stearns at least had the good grace to impoverish only the investors of other financial firms.

What was in it for Bank of America? Not brokerage commissions, as with Bear Stearns, but a more creative form of remuneration known as "sticky assets."[20] In return for permission to move millions rapidly in and out of Bank of America's mutual funds, Edward Stern and his late-trading operation offered to park other millions of "sticky assets" in other funds in the complex. Although the late-traded mutual funds would bear all the costs of late trading—which we will discuss presently—the fund manager would be compensated via the sticky assets. Recall that managers receive their standard compensation as a percentage of assets under management. So, $25 million in additional assets under management left in place for the long term (that is, a sticky $25 million) would be capable of generating millions of dollars for the investment adviser over time.

So, Stern and his ilk promised to park assets with Bank of America in order to gain the privilege of late trading.[21] Investment advisers, as we have repeatedly seen, are perpetually alive to keeping and attracting new assets under management as a way to maximize their revenues.

Indeed, it was Bank of America who contacted Stern, notwithstanding Stern's own dedication to the practices of late trading and market timing. Ted Sihpol, in the bank's private-client department, cold-called Stern in April 2001 to inquire whether Stern might like to invest in mutual funds through the bank. According to a source quoted by Peter Elkind in his rollicking expose of Stern's misadventures, "it was like a fly cold-calling a spider."[22]

The bank's deal was on the slavering end of generous. Stern would be permitted to late-trade and to market-time Bank of America's own Nations Funds. The bank would provide a credit line of up to $300 million for Stern and his hedge fund to use for their illicit trading activity. The bank would also furnish Stern with derivatives that would permit Canary to short—that is, to bet against—the bank's own mutual funds.

And, like Bear Stearns, Bank of America also granted Stern his own electronic trading terminal so that Canary could plug its trades directly into the national clearing system. That all-access pass allowed Stern to trade as late as 6:30 P.M. and to late-trade not just the Nations Funds but also all of the hundreds of other fund families connected to the system.[23] As Elkind reported: "With its own terminal, Canary could bypass the brokers altogether, submitting late trades almost invisibly, as though it was simply an administrative arm of the bank."[24]

Late Trading through Bank of America: Subtle

The foregoing illustrations of late trading in the happy hunting days—before Spitzer's press conference ruined the party in September 2003—reek of gaudy excess. But late trading can be perpetrated in more subtle ways. Indeed, when Stern first began his relationship with Bank of America, before they became all too comfortable with one another, he took greater pains to disguise his after-hours activity. Stern and his confrères at Canary would submit a variety of "proposed" fund trades to Bank of America prior to the 4:00 P.M. deadline so that they could be time-stamped appropriately. But, upon evaluating market movements after the close of business, Canary traders would then telephone their contacts at the bank with "final instructions." Orders that no longer comported profitably with market developments could be tossed out; orders that remained lucrative could be processed as normal.

So, imagine a simple hypothetical. A trader like Stern places two orders at noon: one to buy a large number of shares in an S&P 500 fund, the other to sell a large number of shares in that fund. Because they are placed at noon, both orders will be time-stamped well before the deadline and thus acquire a lawful pedigree. But, if at 5:00 P.M., the chairman of the Federal Reserve announces a surprising interest-rate cut that is sure to spur the overall market, the trader will certainly not want to sell on that news. So, the trader calls a confederate at the bank and instructs the bank to "lose" the noontime order to sell shares. Conversely, if at 5:00 P.M., the Bureau of Labor Statistics announces shockingly poor employment statistics that are likely to dampen the market, the trader would want to sell on that news. The trader would, accordingly, ask the bank insider to discard the order to buy shares.

In each case, the one remaining order that will be a money-maker proceeds through the system with immaculate bona fides, and the alternative order is lost. In the world of recordkeeping, an auditor will have a much harder time discovering a shredded, burned, or discarded trading ticket than a ticket dated after the 4:00 P.M. deadline.[25]

The Costs of Late Trading

As furtive or as brazen as all this tardy trading may be, is it merely a violation of an arbitrary deadline or does it actually hurt anyone? Yes, it does inflict pain.

Late trading directly enriches the illicit traders by taking money from long-term mutual fund investors. All profits gained from late trading are skimmed from returns that would, in the absence of late trading, have accrued to the shares of investors already in the mutual fund. And all losses a late trader avoids are borne instead by the investors who remain in the fund. Needless to say, investment advisers and brokers do not disclose illegal late trades, so investors also have no way of assessing or pricing in these losses, even if they were willing to pardon the law breaking.[26]

So, if the good news announced after the close of business increases the value of a fund by several million dollars at its next pricing, those millions must now be shared among both the late traders and the long-term investors in the fund. But if bad news decreases the value of the fund by millions, the late traders escape the burden of sharing those losses, leaving them all to depress the shares of long-term investors in the fund. Only the late traders win in a late-trading scheme. Oh, and the investment advisers or brokers who abet them for a fee.[27]

Let's conclude with the discomfiting valediction of Charles Bryceland, Ted Sihpol's supervisor at Bank of America, who offered "accolades" to several of his colleagues in January 2002 for "giving access" to Stern and Canary Capital:

> It is always nice to enter a new year with a success like this. Thanks to all team members who have contributed to this profitable relationship and for thinking across divisional lines to make money for the firm.[28]

No word from Bank of America's management on profits for their mutual fund investors.

MARKET TIMING

Usually, big profits can be earned only if one takes on significantly more risk or uncovers new information. But the late traders and market timers risked little and uncovered nothing, since the news they traded on was already public.... Sometimes speculators really are just greedy and amoral.

—James Surowiecki, *The New Yorker,* 2003

Richard Strong built a career to match his name. Though he was orphaned at seventeen, losing his father to a heart attack and four months later his mother to cancer, he proved resilient. He soon earned a bachelor's degree and MBA in three years apiece, and at the University of Wisconsin's business school, he stood out from his classmates for being married and driven. Early in his career, he formed Strong Financial Corporation to manage money, then devoted years of hundred-hour weeks to forging its success.

Three decades later, Strong Financial employed 1,300 people and managed more than $40 billion in its mutual funds from a magnificent corporate headquarters in suburban Milwaukee. Strong had increased his own fortune to $800 million and was, indisputably, regarded as one of Wisconsin's most successful sons.[1]

Then the investigators came. Lots of them. From the Securities and Exchange Commission, the office of the New York State attorney general, and the Wisconsin Department of Financial Institutions.[2] They accused Strong of something called market timing. But isn't timing markets precisely what a good investor is supposed to do? Buy at a time the market is low, sell at a time the market is high? Ah, but Strong's market timing was something different. Something that cost him his reputation, his job, and $60 million.

The First Among Fund Scandals

In the unholy pantheon of mutual fund scandals, market timing may be the last—or lowest—of sins.[3] When New York State Attorney General Eliot Spitzer hurled incendiary accusations at the mutual fund industry in his epochal press conference in September 2003, the scandal at the core of his allegations was market timing. Spitzer's charges sparked investigations by regulators, prosecutors, and plaintiffs into every cranny of this industry, and those investigations uncovered many of the other schemes that we have explored.[4] But the market-timing scandal, which implicated so many established investment advisers, is the ruse that most scorched the benign assumptions about the loyalty and good faith of those firms to whom Americans vouchsafed so many trillions of their hard-earned dollars.[5]

What had fund managers done to provoke such a firestorm? They used this scheme to prey upon their own customers. And, more worrisome, they did so by using a particularly harmful method of hunting: they offered their quarry safety, then allowed predators into the sanctuary. In this case, they offered investors something they advertised as a safe harbor from the dangers of market timing, a legal but harmful investing practice in mutual funds. Fund managers voluntarily and publicly adopted policies that purported to disallow market timing, which successfully attracted long-term investors to their funds. With those investors lured into place, the managers then actively collaborated with market-timing hedge funds to take money from those long-term, individual investors.

The Importance of Forward Pricing

The discussion of late trading, in chapter 7, introduced the unusual system that mutual funds use to price their fund shares. For largely historic reasons, fund shares are priced only once a day. Any investor who places an order to buy or to sell at 3:59 P.M. Eastern time or earlier will have his trade executed at the next price of fund shares, which will be determined as of 4:00 P.M. that day. Any investor who places an order at 4:00 P.M. or later will not have his trade executed that day but, rather, must wait until the following day, at which point he will receive the price calculated as of 4:00 P.M. that following day. In the business, this practice is known as *forward pricing*.[6]

As we saw with late trading, this focus on a specific moment in time creates a focal point for the attention of financial professionals. And like late trading, market timing also revolves around this 4:00 P.M. deadline. The original reasons for this method of accounting are understandable, but the consequences have proved extremely dangerous. Anything whose price is set just once a day but whose value fluctuates constantly will necessarily be inaccurate a great deal of the time. Like a stopped clock, the price of a mutual fund may be correct momentarily, but for much of the time the price is alarmingly wrong.

This divergence between value and price created opportunities for financial arbitrage that sophisticated hedge funds found irresistible in the early 2000s. By offering a variety of creative and lucrative payments to the managers of mutual funds, a number of hedge funds—such as Edward Stern's Canary Capital mentioned in chapter 7—enjoyed great profits by engaging in a particular species of speculation in mutual funds known as *time-zone arbitrage*.[7]

Time-Zone Arbitrage

Forward pricing may be understandable as a practical matter, particularly in an age of the abacus and slate. But it allows for distortions in the accurate pricing of certain funds.

Imagine a fund holding shares in the broad U.S. stock markets, whose price per share is calculated at $10 as of 4:00 P.M. on a particular day. If at 6:00 P.M. that day, the Federal Open Market Committee unexpectedly raises the federal funds rate, the $10 price would immediately become inaccurate. The value of U.S. equities in general will almost certainly fall upon bad news, strongly suggesting that the true price of this fund is something materially lower than, say, $10 per share. The $10 price would, therefore, no longer be accurate—in the parlance of the fund industry, it would be "stale."[8]

For the most part, stale prices may be lamentable, but they are not particularly harmful because all fund investors must wait another twenty-four hours to buy or to sell the fund. Anyone who wishes to buy or to sell upon hearing bad news simply operates in a slowed-down version of our hyperactive markets, and all investors find themselves in the same position vis-à-vis the stale price. But such parity and innocuousness is not always the case.

Consider, by contrast, a mutual fund that does not hold a portfolio of U.S. equities. Instead, the fund holds a portfolio of stocks that are traded on the Tokyo Stock Exchange. Because of the difference in operating hours between the U.S. stock markets, which govern the pricing of U.S. mutual funds, and the Tokyo Stock Exchange, which governs the pricing of this fund's portfolio securities, we now have an opportunity for time-zone arbitrage.[9]

The Tokyo Stock Exchange closes for the day at 1:00 A.M. Eastern Time in the United States, which is fourteen hours before an American mutual fund will next calculate its price. That is, the U.S. mutual fund will calculate its price at 4:00 P.M. Eastern time (when it is 5:00 A.M. the next day in Tokyo). How will the U.S. fund of Tokyo stocks calculate its price?

Typically, it will use the standard formula that we have already discussed: the fund manager multiplies the respective number of shares of each of the Japanese companies the fund holds by the corresponding price for each of those stocks. Note, though, that the prices of those Japanese companies have not moved in fourteen hours—since the closing bell of the Tokyo Stock Exchange.

Stale Prices

Now, consider the effect on those prices if something profoundly good or bad for the Japanese economy occurs during that long dormant spell. If a tsunami floods a nuclear reactor 141 miles northeast of Tokyo, let's say, we might safely assume that those closing prices of Tokyo stocks now vastly overstate their value.[10] Conversely, if the Japanese parliament unexpectedly passes a steep reduction in the tax rate on capital gains, one might assume that the values of those Japanese equities are now higher than their closing prices. In both scenarios, the Tokyo Stock Exchange is neither open nor able to incorporate those significant developments into the price of the Japanese equities. The only prices we have are the old, stale prices from when the Tokyo Stock Exchange closed hours earlier.

A U.S. mutual fund holding Tokyo stocks might, nevertheless, calculate its net asset value using the closing prices for those Japanese stocks, which as we know are now critically stale. In essence, the U.S. fund is offering its shares at a price that is trapped in the past. Any knowledgeable U.S. investor—and hedge funds certainly are knowledgeable—would be able to place an order to buy or to sell shares in the U.S. fund with almost total certainty that its price will immediately rise or fall afterwards. In essence, market-timing investors in these circumstances are arbitraging the inefficiencies in stock exchanges across different time zones.

If the news from Japan is bad, a market-timing investor could place an order to sell almost all her holdings in that U.S. fund and still receive the artificially high prices from before the tsunami. The investor would thus escape the fund before taking a hit from those certain losses. Conversely, if the news from Japan is excellent, a market-timing investor could place an order to buy a large stake in the U.S. fund and still receive the artificially low price from before the tax cut announcement. The U.S. fund's price will belatedly leap the next day when it incorporates the rise in Japanese stock prices on a reopened Tokyo Stock Exchange. So, if a market-timing buyer places a sell order the day after making a huge purchase, she could lock in those certain gains.

Two Complications for the Market-Timer

As lucrative as market timing can be, it remains something of a speculative venture. Even though a market timer could develop a powerful algorithm to guide its investment arbitrage and cultivate a pliant investment adviser to grant it timing privileges, every one of the timer's decisions to send millions of dollars in or out of a mutual fund still retains a fraction of a gamble.

Two practical impediments stand in the way of a committed market-timer. First, mutual funds are also managed by sophisticated financial experts who are, themselves, well aware of the perils of stale prices.[11] Although the use of closing prices is an easy and convenient means for calculating a mutual fund's net asset value, it certainly isn't the only option. As we have seen in chapter 6, federal law obliges fund managers to value their portfolio securities "fairly," which expressly permits (though it does not require) them in practice to shun closing prices if there is a good reason—such as a tsunami or a tax cut—to think those prices no longer reflect the fair value of the fund's holdings.

Indeed we already encountered the cottage industry of financial vendors that specialize in determining fair value for investments "for which market prices are not readily available,"[12] or in our examples, for which the only existing market prices no longer reflect an accurate value. So, a mutual fund may, therefore, be able to mitigate the problem of stale prices in a case as obvious as a major natural disaster or profound shift in fiscal policy.

We come now to the second problem for market-timers. Sitting around for weeks or months awaiting benevolent acts of God or whimsical legislation is no basis for a business plan. And if the most opportune of those arbitrage opportunities are also the most obvious to the boards and advisers of mutual funds—and therefore the most heavily defended against—then even sporadic opportunities might not be profitably exploited. How then are committed market-timers to earn their daily bread?

They need to figure out something that moves foreign stock exchanges in far-flung time zones with more regularity. If they could discover a constant stimulus that reliably produces predictable changes in those foreign markets, they could engage in market timing constantly, which would produce the regular stream of profits every successful business needs. As it happens, such a stimulus does exist, and the market-timing hedge funds have unearthed it. This stimulus also has the virtue of being subtle enough to avoid obvious detection and thus to be well defended by the boards of mutual funds.

So, what force reliably and regularly moves foreign stock markets? Well, we do. That is to say, the U.S. stock markets do.[13] With a remarkable degree of correlation, a rise in the U.S. stock markets prompts a rise in foreign stock exchanges, and U.S. declines trigger foreign losses. Although the correlation isn't perfect—it is about 0.6[14]—it has proved strong enough to produce reliable and lucrative results for institutional market-timers.

Any investor with the sophistication to scrutinize market-moving events in different time zones and the financial wherewithal to capitalize on them can make a great deal of money through this market-timing strategy. Indeed, hedge funds like Edward Stern's Canary Capital Partners thrived for years and generated gobsmacking profits using this strategy.

The Aggravations of Market Timing

Market timing as described thus far may sound a trifle mercenary, but it is perfectly legal. In fact, plenty of reputable economists believe that global financial markets work more efficiently when they are disciplined by arbitrage. Inasmuch as arbitrage involves taking advantage of price discrepancies, then it also ensures that those discrepancies will not last for long. As we have seen, market timing that exploits stale closing prices prompted rules permitting the use of algorithms that more accurately reflect the fair value of mutual fund holdings.

But like the Newtonian laws governing the conservation of matter, financial physics requires that money made by one party come at the expense of some other party. For a market-timer to swoop in to pocket profits or to dodge losses, someone else must necessarily lose those profits or eat those losses. And, in fact, this discomfort externalized by market timing lands on two other constituencies.

Harm to Other Investors

Long-term ordinary investors in a mutual fund are the ones who bear the losses avoided by market-timers and who sacrifice the profits diverted by market-timers.[15] To appreciate this dynamic, we first have to understand how a fund—or indeed, how any investment—puts its money to work.

Imagine if you had $100 to invest and you fortuitously selected an investment that doubled your money. Obviously, you would now have $200. But mutual funds never invest 100 percent of their money because they must keep a cash reserve on hand to pay out the redemptions of investors who want to leave the fund on any given day. If you retained $10 as a cash reserve in your wallet, then you would have been able to invest only $90 in your excellent investment, resulting in a total of $190: $90, doubled to $180, plus the $10 cash. In those circumstances, we would say that the $90 was put to work but the $10 cash was not. (In the investment business, this phenomenon is known as *cash drag*.)[16] Similarly, when market-timers invest their money in mutual funds, they do so only for extremely brief windows and not in time for their contributions to be put to work generating returns for the fund.

Consider what occurs when a market-timer invests a huge new chunk of cash after hearing about great news in Japan. If the fund began with $80 million in assets priced using stale Tokyo prices, and a market-timing hedge fund invested $20 million on the basis of positive Japanese economic news later that day, the hedge fund would then be entitled to one-fifth of the fund going forward. That is, in exchange for its $20 million investment in the mutual fund, the hedge fund would receive one-fifth of the mutual fund's outstanding fund shares:

$$\frac{\$20\,\text{million}}{\$80\,\text{million} + \$20\,\text{million}} = \frac{1}{5} = 20\%$$

The following day, the fund will incorporate the higher Japanese prices.

Let's stipulate that the fund does particularly well and gains $10 million in investment gains overnight owing to the higher prices in Japan. The total assets of the fund would now be $110 ($80 million + $20 million in new investments + $10 million in investment gains). So, if the hedge fund redeemed all its shares immediately, it would pocket $22 million (or 1/5th of that $110 million). A $2 million return on a $20 million investment is 10 percent—that would be one great night.

A spectacular return, undoubtedly, but now imagine if the hedge fund's investment was itself heavily leveraged, as hedge-fund assets typically are. Leverage in any financial transaction means that some minority of the assets used for a purchase are the buyer's own money while the rest are borrowed. A hedge fund's investors may contribute only a small percentage of the fund's overall assets, with the majority borrowed from a bank.

A typical home purchase is a similarly leveraged transaction, with homebuyers often putting down only 20 percent of the purchase price while borrowing the rest from a lender. Leverage magnifies investment gains, by both hedge funds and homebuyers. So, if the hedge fund uses a leverage ratio of 10:1, its $20 million investment would include only $2 million of its own funds and $18 million of borrowed funds. In such a case, the $2 million return in our hypothetical would constitute a 100 percent return on the fund's own $2 million investment (minus the costs of borrowing). Again, those returns are from only one transaction. These sorts of economics explain the spectacular success of market-timing hedge funds like Canary Capital.[17]

But let's focus now on the source of the market-timer's positive returns. The $10 million in investment gains that the mutual fund earned overnight in our example came only from the $80 million that was invested *prior* to the good news, not from any of the $20 million that the hedge fund invested *after* the good news. The hedge fund's new money just arrived at the mutual fund, leaving the mutual fund's portfolio manager no time to invest it in any underlying Japanese stocks.

So, the hedge fund has, in effect, skimmed off gains that were earned solely by the assets of the fund's long-term investors. If no hedge fund had arrived at the last minute, the mutual fund would have earned the same $10 million in gains that it did, but the gain would have been shared among only the previous investors—and those investors would have earned a 12.5 percent gain ($10 million / $80 million = 12.5 percent).

When the mutual fund's $10 million gain, however, has to be shared with the late-arriving hedge fund, the long-term investors enjoyed a gain of only 10 percent—($8 / $80 = 10 percent):

$110 fund: 1/5 or $22 million for the hedge fund

and

4/5 or $88 million for original investors

The hedge fund's $2 million in gains came out of the mutual fund's overall gains of $10 million, which were earned solely using the assets of the fund's long-term investors. The market-timing thus *diluted* the long-term investors' $10 million gain down to $8 million.

Without the market-timer's investment, the fund would still have earned $10 million in investment gains overnight, but those gains would have been shared only among the existing fund investors. In sum, the long-term investors in the mutual fund would have been materially better off had the fund's adviser not permitted the market-timer to invest.[18]

Harm to the Investment Adviser

Now, let's turn to the other victim of the pain caused by market timing. Perhaps fittingly, the other party who suffers headaches from intensive market timing in a mutual fund is the fund's own portfolio manager. Massive and rapid flows of money in and out of a mutual fund are extremely difficult for a portfolio manager to accommodate.[19]

Consider first a massive inflow of cash. In our example, the market-timer placed $20 million into an $80 million fund. As we have seen, only money that is invested makes money. Funds left in cash do nothing to generate gains. In fact, for a portfolio manager operating in a rising market, excessive cash is worse than nothing because it ruins the manager's grade point average.

In our example, the fund made $10 million on the strength of $80 million invested—the market-timer's additional $20 million joined the party too late to be invested. So, without the $20 million, the fund would have enjoyed a 12.5 percent return. But by adding another unused $20 million, the fund's overall return drops to 10 percent. Portfolio managers are often evaluated and compensated on the strength of their returns and clearly would like to earn the highest returns possible.

A related problem involves finding good investments to buy with such a large and unexpected chunk of cash. Although counterintuitive, sometimes there is such a thing as having too much money to invest. Portfolio managers may rely on a great strategy that involves, for example, investing in small start-up companies. But there are only so many start-ups and they need only so much cash, and thus a portfolio manager using such a strategy may not be able to invest a huge amount of money at a moment's notice. So, having unexpectedly large cash investments plunked down on one's fund can cause problems for managers and can easily depress the return rate of their funds.[20]

Now, let's consider what happens when a market-timer unexpectedly withdraws a massive amount of money. Here, the problem may be even more intense for a portfolio manager. If an investor pulls $20 million from a $100 million fund, the manager has only a few hours, at most, to raise the cash. Most prudent managers will retain 5 to 10 percent of their fund in cash in order to meet daily redemptions. If they keep more of the fund in cash, the fund will sacrifice returns because the cash will act as drag in a rising market.

But a market-timer may place a massive redemption order that wipes out all the fund's cash reserve and more. The portfolio manager will have no option but to sell some of the fund's investments to satisfy the market-timer's redemption request. Although managers buy and sell investments every day, most do so according to long-range and sophisticated plans that take account of seasonal economic trends, tax concerns, or other strategic considerations. Having to sell 10 percent or more of a fund at a moment's notice can cause headaches and trigger costs that will hurt the returns of the entire fund. The most obvious cost to these unplanned transactions will involve taxes. Capital gains that have been held for a short time are taxed at a higher rate than long-term capital gains. And a market-timer's order may trigger these short-term tax hits. At the same time, the portfolio manager may have to pay a broker-dealer higher commissions to execute last-minute, urgent transactions.

In short, rapid spikes of cash in and out of a fund are disruptive and generate higher transactions costs for the fund. The portfolio manager is the party who initially has to deal with these aggravations, but as is common in mutual funds, those costs will quickly be passed along to all the investors in the fund. Yet again, the boorish behavior of market-timers quickly becomes the financial problem of long-term investors.[21]

The Legality and Illegality of Market Timing

Because of these administrative and economic costs, many fund managers voluntarily converted market timing from a legal practice into an illegal one. In a state of nature, market timing is not illegal per se.[22] As a general principle of investing, many active investors unabashedly attempt to time their purchases and sales of securities. And inasmuch as markets are governed by cycles, many investors might reasonably attempt to time those cycles, also.

Indeed, when Eliot Spitzer and other prosecutors announced investigations into the illegal market timing of mutual funds, some confusion arose because of the perfectly innocuous connotations of the term in ordinary investing parlance. As the details of these inquiries in mutual funds emerged, however, pejorative implications attached themselves to the time-zone arbitrage we have been discussing. But, more pertinently, we learned that it was the investment advisers themselves who had converted legal market timing into an illegal practice.

How can private parties do that? Quite simply, as it happens, by imposing their own rules disallowing market timing in their funds. Once an investment manager prohibits market timing and publishes that proscription in the fund's legal prospectuses, any disregard of that policy is not only against the fund's private rules but now also a violation of federal securities laws. Operating a mutual fund in a way that violates its public prospectuses is illegal.

Many mutual fund managers voluntarily and publicly adopted anti–market-timing policies because they reasonably believed that long-term investors preferred to be insulated from the harmful costs of market timing in their funds.[23] But market timing can be an extremely lucrative practice for hedge funds. Eric Zitzewitz, professor of economics at Dartmouth College, has calculated that market-timers made profits of $4.9 billion each year at the expense of long-term investors.[24] So, not surprisingly, many hedge funds were willing to pay generously for the ability to continue doing it. And they found a number of mutual fund managers who were willing to violate their own policies, to harm their own long-term investors, and to incur the aggravation of market-timing transactions costs. For the right price.

In essence, hedge funds paid mutual fund managers to poach in the mutual fund's game reserves. By advertising their funds as anti-market timing, the fund managers successfully attracted long-term investors. But by then allowing market-timers to operate in those funds, the managers were granting hedge funds carte blanche for a turkey shoot.

Using Sticky Assets to Buy a Hunting License

The most obvious way to pay for this hunting privilege would simply be to hand over a check. But that kind of overt compensation is rare in the financial world. It smacks of brown paper bags filled with unmarked bills. Instead, the standard remuneration in market timing involved the creative use of that currency we saw before: "sticky assets."[25]

Investment advisers, as we have seen, are perpetually alive to keeping and attracting new assets under management as a way to maximize their revenues. As reported in *Fortune*, for instance, PIMCO granted "[Edward] Stern $100 million of timing capacity in three of its funds—and the right to make a staggering 48 in-and-out trades a year—in exchange for $25 million in sticky assets."[26] So, in return for permission to move millions rapidly in and out of certain mutual funds in an investment adviser's complex, the market-timing hedge fund offers to park other millions (in this case, $25 million) of "sticky" assets in other funds in the complex. Although the market-timed funds would bear all the costs of market timing—the long-term investment dilution and transactions costs we have just discussed—the fund manager would be compensated via the sticky assets. The only parties not compensated in this *quid pro quo* are the ordinary, long-term investors whose savings were invested in the market-timed funds.[27] They bear all the dilution and shared transactions costs of market timing without receiving any offsetting benefits.

Fund managers who collaborated in these arrangements thus betrayed the very investors whom they had promised to protect with their voluntary proscriptions against market timing. They accepted higher advisory fees in order to look the other way while their long-term investors were financially harmed. Had those fund managers never banned market timing in their funds, they might never have been guilty of anything illegal. Long-term investors might not have relied on their assurances of safety and no rules would have been broken. But once a fund's investment adviser publishes club rules in a formal fund prospectus, the adviser must follow those rules. The failure to do so is a violation of federal and state securities regulations.

The Impact of Market Timing

Jaded investors in our economy might not be surprised that some fund managers accepted bribes to violate their own rules, but very few people predicted the remarkably widespread collusion by so many of the investment industry's most famous names. Indeed, in the early 2000s, the mutual fund industry was basking in widespread praise from financial commentators who claimed that funds were managed so well compared to the dastardly executives of Enron, WorldCom, and the other operating companies engaging in accounting fraud.[28]

Nor would many have predicted the most extreme examples of market timing. Following the claims that Attorney General Spitzer announced at his press conference, the SEC roused itself belatedly to investigate the fund industry. That SEC investigation turned up a great deal of garden-variety market timing, but also a few truly remarkable cases. In accusations against Putnam Investment Management, for instance, the commission found that six of Putnam's own investment professionals had, in their personal accounts, market-timed Putnam's own funds.[29]

Similarly, in cease-and-desist proceedings against a midwestern investment adviser, the SEC alleged that the chairman and chief investment officer of the firm himself had market-timed his own funds.[30] Extraordinary. Why even fiddle with payoffs from hedge funds when one can simply siphon money directly from the investors in your own funds? What was that company? Strong Capital Management, Inc. of Wisconsin. Who was its chairman? Richard Strong.

Ultimately, dozens of fund complexes paid out billions of dollars to state and federal regulators to make investigations into market timing go away. And Richard Strong was banned from the securities industry for life.[31] But not before billions of other dollars were diverted away from individual investors and into the pockets of market-timers and the investment advisers who collaborated with them.

9

SELECTIVE DISCLOSURE

So long as Regulation FD openly permits selective disclosure by mutual funds that cost fund shareholders an estimated $5 billion a year, the New York Attorney General is entitled to describe the SEC as a "captured" agency.

—John C. Coffee Jr., *Professor of Law, Columbia Law School.*

In the summer of 1983, Hollywood inflicted upon us the third, almost indigestible installment of the original *Superman* films. Though the plot primarily concerns computer panic and sight gags, the movie opens with an intriguing financial scam. Richard Pryor, playing the role of Gus Gorman, a computer hacker, embezzles a fortune through a penny-shaving scheme.

We learn the premise of this subterfuge from a conversation in the WebsCo. corporate cafeteria between Gus Gorman and an anonymous co-worker as his expository foil. Gorman has just bemoaned the fact that taxes have reduced his paycheck to $143.80.

EXPOSITORY FOIL:Actually, it's probably more like $143.80-and-one-half-cent. There are always fractions left over in big corporations but they round it down to the lowest whole number.

GORMAN:What am I supposed to do with half a cent . . . buy a thorough-bred mouse? You mean everybody loses those fractions?

EXPOSITORY FOIL:They don't exactly lose them. You can't lose what you never got.

GORMAN:Then what happens to all those half-cents? The company gets it?

EXPOSITORY FOIL:No, not really. They can't be bothered to collect the half-cent from your paycheck any more than you could.

GORMAN:Then what happens to them?

EXPOSITORY FOIL:Well, they're just floating around out there. The computers know where.[1]

Cue the chimes of epiphany. Gorman proceeds to hack into the company's computer system (using the artful DOS command, "override all security") and directs all those half-cents into his personal account. His hacking talents bring him to the attention of the film's evil villain, Ross Webster, played by Robert Vaughn. Webster orders Gorman to compute dastardly deeds, such as an attack on Colombia's coffee crop and the creation of kryptonite, which prompts the eventual intervention of the man in tights and horrific film reviews.

Can the computer-literate really amass fortunes by shaving pennies from large flows of money? Indeed, they can—the entire high-frequency trading industry is built on that idea. But whose pennies do they shave? Yours, to a large extent, if you invest in a mutual fund. But can't fund advisers protect investors from those schemes? To some extent, but not when they are actively colluding with the penny shavers.

Insider Trading in Mutual Funds

No survey of dubious financial behavior could be complete without a discussion of insider trading, and mutual funds have their own equivalent in the practice of *selective disclosure*.[2] As with late trading, selective disclosure requires the intimate collaboration of fund insiders to perpetrate the scheme—the insiders are who selectively disclose nonpublic information to outsiders. The valuable information they disclose is, specifically, the exact holdings in the portfolio of a mutual fund. Such disclosure is deemed selective because the fund insiders reveal the information only to preferred clients, such as hedge funds, but not to the public at large.

How odd, one might think. What could be the use of a list of a fund's portfolio holdings, information which is already so widely reported?[3] First, let's note that portfolio holdings are not actually as widely reported as may appear. At least not completely or contemporaneously. Investment advisers do publish the largest ten investments in each of their fund's portfolios, but those lists omit what may be thousands of other investments in the portfolio, and the information is always published well in arrears, several months out of date.[4] At that point, the information is too dated to exploit.

To exploit? How, even if it were complete and current, could information such as this be exploited? A person—or rather, a sophisticated market trader—who knows precisely what investments a mutual fund holds at any moment can capitalize on that information by "front-running" the fund.[5]

Front Running

Front running is a time-dishonored scheme that stock traders have long employed to shave pennies from others in the market. To apply the practice in mutual funds, the front-runner must first discern a pattern in the way a fund adviser makes trades in the fund's portfolio. Like many professional money managers, the advisers of mutual funds often maintain internal targets for the composition of their portfolios' holdings. These advisers then regularly rebalance their portfolios to maintain those targets.

So, an investment adviser managing a fund that focuses on technology stocks, for example, might maintain a target of investing 5 percent of the fund's assets in shares of Facebook. As time passes, the market performance of Facebook or other holdings in the portfolio might move the fund's Facebook investments above or below that 5 percent target. With some regularity, then, the investment adviser will either buy or sell shares of Facebook to regain its preferred level of 5 percent. Recall that 5 percent of a massive mutual fund could in practice constitute tens or hundreds of millions of dollars in a public corporation's stock. So, these rebalancing trades by a mutual fund could, as a consequence, involve the purchase and sale of many millions of dollars of that stock.

For our aspiring front-runner, then, discerning a pattern in the trading habits of a mutual fund might involve closely following the fund's portfolio holdings over time.

On the other hand, a particularly obliging investment adviser could also simply provide the front-runner with the timing and the substance of the adviser's portfolio trades. That is, the adviser could selectively disclose that valuable information.

Then, when a front-runner has discerned a fund's pattern, she can plan her own trades accordingly. If the fund in our example has seen its Facebook holdings fall to 4 percent in the final days of a month, then the fund might with some predictability be planning to purchase a substantial block of more Facebook stock in the near future. And this is when the front-running occurs. Our front-runner can place her own order to buy Facebook shares just before the mutual fund does— that is, to front-run the fund.

Trading activity like this can also be inverted, of course: if the fund holds too large a Facebook position and will soon be selling, the front-runner could sell or short the Facebook stock before the fund makes its large trades.

The Impact of Front Running

Consider what will happen to the price of Facebook shares when an enormous mutual fund lumbers into the market to buy massive chunks of the stock.[6] A large enough order, all other things being equal, will almost certainly move the price of Facebook shares higher. Similarly, a very large order to sell could move the price of Facebook shares lower. If our front-runner has bought or shorted the stock ahead of these large movements, she will profit with very little risk.

But, one might reasonably wonder, how large could these profits be? Surely many of these variations in stock prices are minute. Indeed, they often are. But if the front-runner trades using leverage (by borrowing or buying on margin) or leveraged financial instruments (such as options or derivatives), she can profit handsomely even on very small variations in stock prices. As Gus Gorman teaches us, shaving enough fractions of pennies can lead to a fortune.

As always, we must ask—apart from any unseemliness, disloyalty, or illegality—what, if anything, is the concrete effect of this behavior on the savings of average mutual fund investors? And the answer here is the one we have seen so often: front running takes money away from them. When a front-runner buys or sells a stock just before a mutual fund does, the mutual fund will receive a less favorable price for the stock. So, if the front-runner and mutual fund are buying a stock in sequence, the purchases by the front-runner will drive up the cost for the mutual fund. And if they are both selling, the sales by the front-runner will drive down the proceeds for the mutual fund. In both cases, the front-runner's trades capture value from the mutual fund.

One might reasonably wonder whether the mutual fund is entitled to these proceeds. After all, every investor in the stock market is regularly affected by trades that occur just before hers. To the extent that front-runners have simply divined a mutual fund's trading pattern from public information, the proceeds are their reward for perspicacious investing. But when the foregoing, front-running trades are executed not by coincidence or the industry of others, but solely on the basis of privileged information, mutual fund investors have reason to be aggrieved. Agents of those fund investors have engaged in disloyal self-dealing to enrich themselves at a real cost to the investors.

But, are not the amounts of any price variations too small to worry about, particularly when apportioned down to the individual holder of fund shares? Perhaps not, when multiplied over years of saving and compounded decades into the future. As we have already seen when we examined the tiny percentages that investment advisers charge to large mutual funds, very small slivers of money can quickly amount to substantial sums.

But the atomistic level of the scheme contains its true genius. By front running mutual funds, a perpetrator can be sure that no individual victim feels too much pain, causes too much of a fuss, or bothers to try to stop the practice. Floyd Norris, of the *New York Times*, characterized the appeal and effectiveness of such a scheme: "If you want to steal a lot of money and get away with it, steal a little from a lot of people. They will probably never notice. If they do, they may not think it worth the effort to complain."[7]

The peril of our savings being bled through a thousand minuscule cuts is a recurring theme of investing via mutual funds.

Lest we ever grow complacent by the thought that the risks, the fees, or the losses are awfully small, the math of compounded interest helps illustrate the true danger. The Executive Office of the President of the United States released a report in February 2015 quantifying the cost of conflicted investment advice at about 12 percent of the value of a retiree's savings, for an aggregate cost of $17 billion each year.[8] And if statistics are not sufficiently compelling, let us bear in mind another popular illustration of the penny-shaving phenomenon.

Of more recent vintage than *Superman III* was the film *Office Space*, which built its plot around a similar scheme. In this movie, three cubicle-bound drones decide to rebel against their soul-crushing jobs by infecting the company's accounting system with a computer virus. Peter Gibbons, played by Ron Livingston, explains the software to Michael Bolton, played by David Herman.

> PETER GIBBONS:That virus you're always talking about, all right. The one that could rip off the company for a bunch of money. Well how does it work?
>
> MICHAEL BOLTON:What it does is, every time there's a bank transaction where interest is computed, and there are thousands a day, the computer ends up with these fractions of a cent, which it usually rounds off. What this does is it takes those little remainders and puts them into an account.[9]

Within days, the virus works too well, thanks to an errant decimal point, and steals several hundreds of thousands of dollars.

The Legality of Selective Disclosure

Whether it involves amounts that are small to the individual or massive in the aggregate, is abetting the front running of a mutual fund illegal? Certainly the SEC's avowed disapproval appears clear enough:

> We believe that the practice of selective disclosure leads to a loss of investor confidence in the integrity of our capital markets. Investors who see a security's price change dramatically and only later are given access to the information responsible for that move rightly question whether they are on a level playing field with market insiders.[10]

But, surprisingly, the legality of the question is not so clear.[11] In the context of operating companies, insider trading is governed largely by Regulation FD (for "Fair Disclosure"), which provides that if a public company "discloses material nonpublic information to certain persons," then "it must make public disclosure of that information."[12] So, a mutual fund that discloses its portfolio holdings to certain clients would, to comport with Regulation FD, also have to make those holdings known to the public. As we have seen, however, investment advisers engaged in selective disclosure of fund portfolio holdings have disclosed only selectively—to the adviser's preferred clients—and not to the public at large.[13]

But, crucially, Regulation FD does not apply to open-end mutual funds.[14] As John Coffee, one of America's leading corporate law scholars, has noted: "Put simply, the mutual fund industry received a carefully crafted immunity from selective disclosure that no other industry sector or class of issuers received."[15] Professor Coffee disapproves of the SEC's entire position on this practice, arguing that "the failure of the SEC to bring or even threaten insider trading charges is disturbing. It seems consistent with the critics' view that the SEC was 'captured' by the mutual fund industry."

But though Reg FD does not cover mutual funds, prosecutors can still punish obvious market manipulation in other ways. So, notwithstanding any real or perceived limitations on the ability of the SEC to bring charges for selective disclosure, Coffee has identified the wide array of tools—such as mail and wire fraud—that law enforcement officials could use to bring charges in these cases.[16]

But the SEC, in a subsequent rule release, had decided not to prohibit selective disclosure. Instead, the commission required only that fund advisers publish in their SAIs a written description of their policy on releasing information selectively. So, despite the SEC's rhetorical admonitions about advisers' refraining from perpetrating fraud or violating their fiduciary duties,[17] their rulemaking has been decidedly more tepid. Disclosure, once again, is the SEC's solution. But a rule that requires only confession is a rule that tacitly grants permission.

The information selectively disclosed can, as with so many of the other practices we have seen, constitute a valuable financial asset for investment advisers. An adviser can dispense information concerning portfolio holdings to attract or retain valuable clients. Many of the market-timing arrangements we saw in chapter 8 also involved selective disclosure, as market-timers could maximize their gains when they had particularized knowledge of the exact contents of the timed fund's portfolio.

Bank of America, perhaps not surprisingly, provided Edward Stern with "a peek at portfolio holdings."[18] And, as we have seen many times, anything that persuades clients to bring their business—and their sticky assets—into a mutual fund complex economically benefits the investment adviser through greater assets under management and greater revenues.

But as we also saw with market timing, advisers need not be so generous. They might conclude that portfolio information is not a bounty that has to be shared with their preferred clients. Not when the adviser's own employees might profitably exploit the information themselves. Recall that Richard Strong did not abet a hedge fund to market-time the Strong funds; he timed them himself. Advisers can do the same with their valuable information about a fund's holdings. Portfolio managers at an investment adviser, who of course know every detail about a fund's holdings and the fund's plans for future trades, are situated perfectly to cash in on their insider knowledge by front running a fund's trades themselves. Let us hope that investment advisers can resist this particular temptation.

PART III

ALTERNATIVE REMEDIES

Hey, if I were starting over from scratch today with what we know, I'd
blow up the existing structure and start over.
—Ted Benna, *"Father of the 401(k)"*

The alarming gauntlet of abuses through which we have just run in part II
could certainly cool an investor's ardor for entrusting all her savings to
mutual funds. But we must bear in mind that this murderers' row is not, nor is
it intended to be, fair proof that the mutual fund itself is irredeemably flawed.
No investment tool, no piece of technology, and perhaps no industry would
fare well when all its shabby behavior is revealed and recited in close order.

Lawmakers and regulators have made some attempts to address the
greatest vulnerabilities in funds, though to predictable resistance from the
financial industry. Certainly, we might have hoped for a touch more gallant
humility from a sector that so badly stumbled in 2008, but profits, bonuses,
and hauteur are back to record highs on Wall Street, as Trollope fore-
cast: "Throughout the world, the more wrong a man does, the more indig-
nant he is at wrong done to him." Nevertheless, as large and widespread as
some of these fund schemes have been, their impact on the overall millions
of investors and trillions of assets in mutual funds remains relatively small.

The horrific pictures shown in drivers-education courses are not
intended to shock teenagers back to their bicycles but, rather, to inspire
them to vigilance when they do drive cars. Similarly, these illustrations of
fund frailties are not intended to frighten investors into stashing their cash
under a mattress but, rather, to motivate them to tread carefully when they
do invest in mutual funds.

What might a cautious investor do to counter the array of vulnerabilities
in mutual funds? In part III we will examine several variations of funds and
fund-like alternatives that avoid some of the most dangerous elements we
have witnessed, while preserving the most powerful advantages of investing through funds.

10

401(K)S AND INDIVIDUAL
RETIREMENT ACCOUNTS

The 401(k) is a way for both your government and your employer to
disown you, and to leave your life savings to be raided by the financial-
services industry and its plethora of hidden and invidious fees.
—Felix Salmon, *"The Systemic Plight of Labor,"* 2013

In 2007, Lori Bilewicz from Milton, Massachusetts, prudently followed the
financial advice offered to many American employees—to her acute regret. Ms.
Bilewicz worked for a company based in Boston, and early in 2007, she began
participating in the company's 401(k) plan. Earlier chapters have discussed much
of what can hurt ordinary investors in a mutual fund. For many investors in our
country, the first line of defense is an employer-based, fiduciary-policed retirement account. When a sophisticated institution—charged with a legal duty to
make prudent choices for its workforce—selects the mutual funds in which its
employees can invest, will those individual investors be protected from the misadventures we have seen in the previous chapters? Lori Bilewicz, and many like
her, were not.

In corporate America today, almost every new job begins with a slog through
a blizzard of human resources forms. Like Ernest Shackleton trying to endure his
polar expedition, the newest members of our workforce encounter disorientation
and unceasing darkness on the first days of their career. At some point between
a tour of the cubicles and a lecture on how to unjam the printer, the typical corporate orientation will require incoming employees to sign—if not necessarily
to read or understand—dozens of documents. Somewhere deep in that stack of
pamphlets about obtaining health insurance, taking vacation days, and not burn-
ing popcorn in the office microwave will almost certainly be a few pages concerning the company's 401(k) plan.

This cryptically numbered financial tool has become a central brace in the
rickety scaffolding that supports America's trillions of dollars in retirement savings. What began in 1978 as "an arcane sub-paragraph in the U.S. tax code" won

the imprimatur of the Internal Revenue Service in a seminal 1981 ruling that "allowed workers to use tax-deferred salary money to build a retirement savings account."[1] Then, in less than four decades during which the traditional pension withered to insignificance, the 401(k) sucked in almost $5 trillion.

As described in this book's introduction, private businesses led this initiative to shift their employees—and the discomfiting burden of those employees' retirement costs—into defined-contribution accounts, such as 401(k)s, 403(b)s, 457s, and others. Still more Americans invest another $7.4 trillion through their Individual Retirement Accounts (IRAs). With pensions dwindling, and individual accounts exploding, our national way of saving has undergone an astonishing conversion. In just a single decade from 2004 to 2014, assets in 401(k)s almost doubled, from $2.2 trillion to $4.3 trillion. Within America's defined-contribution plans, the most popular investment option is the mutual fund, and these funds hold $3.8 trillion, or 56 percent of those assets. Similarly, in IRAs, mutual funds hold $3.6 trillion, or 48 percent of the total.

For employees, the promise of the 401(k)—and its sibling plans that have sprouted from other sections in the U.S. tax code—is immense. These accounts can, potentially, allow Americans to partake of the best attributes of mutual fund investments while protecting them from the worst. Not only do the plans provide their users with a tax-advantaged—and therefore economically preferable—means of investing, but they also present what, in theory, is a prudent menu of funds hand-picked by legal fiduciaries. Yet, as with every host that pulses with money, 401(k)s and IRAs are vulnerable to the predations of determined fiscal leeches.

The Operation of Individual Investment Accounts

At companies throughout the United States, 401(k) materials bear the name or authorship of the outside vendor that provides these financial services to employers.[2] As protagonists—and occasional antagonists—in earlier chapters, many of those providers should now be familiar: Fidelity Investments, Vanguard Group, and TIAA-CREF are among the biggest and most prominent vendors of defined-contribution plans and IRAs. Often, the firms that advise mutual funds also provide the 401(k) plans to U.S. corporations. As we shall see, the similarities between managing mutual funds and administering 401(k) plans are legion—but the differences are critical.

Though the details of 401(k) plans vary widely from employer to employer,[3] most share a troika of central features. The first is a need for users of a plan to enroll—that is, each new employee must decide whether or not to create his or her own 401(k) account. The second is a need for the employee to specify contributions; having enrolled, each new 401(k) holder must instruct the payroll department to divert a particular amount of his or her salary into the new account.

The third is a need to select investment options; once the cash begins flowing into the new 401(k), the employee must choose which specific investments (mutual funds, usually) his or her money will be invested in. Here, then, are three simple steps ordinary Americans can take to begin saving effectively for decades to come; nevertheless, distressing numbers of Americans routinely stumble over at least one of these liminal steps.

For those employees who successfully negotiate their way into a 401(k) plan, what will they find awaiting them? A 401(k) plan typically consists of a specific menu of mutual funds, annuities, or other investments into which the employees can direct their savings. The plan's *administrator*—which can be the employer, the outside vendor, or both—is legally responsible for choosing this selection of investments, and for doing so prudently.[4]

In the largest 200 defined-contribution plans, the average number of funds on the menu is twenty-two.[5] In 90 percent of 401(k) plans, the funds on the list come from a variety of fund families. Only in 10 percent of plans does a single investment adviser manage all the funds on the 401(k) menu.[6] The sentiment behind this diversification of offerings is the idea that employers should provide their employees with the "best-of-breed investments" from across the entire universe of funds and investment advisers.[7]

Yet 401(k) offerings do not always look like this; indeed, some menus can be radically different. Consider, for instance, the plan offered to Lori Bilewicz in Boston. Her plan offered 160 funds, not twenty-two, and every one of those funds was managed by the same investment adviser, Fidelity Investments. Bilewicz initially invested in fourteen of these funds, but over time, grew aggrieved with what she perceived as problems with the offerings in her employer's menu. The 160 funds, she believed, constituted "a bewildering array of overlapping and redundant investment choices."[8]

The funds were also unnecessarily expensive, with over 88 percent of them being actively managed rather than less expensive index funds. Unhappy with these problems and the high number of choices yet limited quality of all these funds managed by a single adviser, Bilewicz withdrew her entire account balance in July 2011.[9]

Then, in March 2013, she sued both the plan adviser and her employer's investment committee "responsible for selecting, evaluating, monitoring, and maintaining the Plan's investment options." This lawsuit by Ms. Bilewicz created quite a furor among employers and plan administrators, who wondered what it portended for their responsibilities and legal duties to the employees in their own 401(k) plans. And though it came amid a wave of litigation by employees distressed at the choices made on their behalf by their employers, the Bilewicz case was truly remarkable.

Before we explore the implications of these lawsuits, let us first consider the variety of benefits that these plans can confer on their users.

Benefits of Defined-Contribution Plans

Though private employers may originally have been the motivating force behind the expansion of defined-contribution plans, plenty of American employees have come to embrace them. The chief financial benefits of 401(k)—and 403(b), and 457—plans are their preferential tax treatment under our Internal Revenue Code and their often-generous augmentation by employers.

Another commonly cited benefit is the combination of autonomy and control they confer on their holders—though whether that particular attribute is indeed a true boon is a highly debatable proposition.

A final characteristic of these plans, which is indeed an improvement over pensions, is their portability—that is, the ability of the users to carry their retirement savings in a defined contribution with them when they leave an employer. This portability is due to the fact that an employee's defined contributions—other than in 457 plans, curiously—are deemed to be the property of the employee. This trait also preserves those assets from an employer's bankruptcy. Pensions, fatally, never enjoyed this status and were regularly plundered in corporate bankruptcies.

Tax Advantages

All payroll contributions that we, as employees, direct into our 401(k) accounts are deducted from our salaries prior to the withholding of taxes. This use of pre-tax income is a powerful enhancement to our ability to save. Indeed, the permission to save and invest portions of our salary before the Internal Revenue Service gnaws on them is a momentous subsidy from the United States to its working employees. Indeed, this tax treatment effectively adds substantial amounts of money to the accounts of employees over the length of their careers. Even though assets in 401(k) plans are taxed when employees eventually withdraw them from their accounts, the potential forty-year postponement of that reckoning is a considerable boon.

First, the time value of money counsels, as it always does, in favor of accelerating income and postponing payments. A dollar today is almost always worth more than a dollar a year from now, to say nothing of forty years from now. So, taxes paid forty years from now will cost far less than an equivalent amount of taxes paid today. Though our 401(k) system does not eliminate taxes entirely, its lengthy postponement of taxes is financially equivalent to a significant reduction in the taxes we ultimately do pay. The fewer taxes paid, of course, means the greater the monetary corpus an employee can save.

Second, the power of compounded interest works even more magically upon a larger initial corpus. So, by contributing larger, untaxed amounts early in the life of a 401(k) account, an employee can accelerate the process by which that nest egg grows. Consider, as a simplified example, two savings accounts at a bank that pays the round, if fanciful, amount of 5 percent interest per year. Into one account, we contribute $10,000; into the other, we contribute what would be left after $10,000 is taxed at a personal income rate of 30 percent, or $7,000. If we leave those two contributions untouched to compound for forty years, the two accounts would come to hold, respectively, $32,620 and $22,834. Our initial $3,000 difference has over time swollen to a difference of almost $10,000. Tax savings plus compounding thus yields tremendous results.

Third, the rules of 401(k) plans contemplate withdrawals when the employee has entered retirement. Though plan participants are permitted to withdraw their savings earlier, federal law imposes punitive fees for doing so. Medical emergencies, evictions, or funeral expenses might justify such withdrawals (and, in some circumstances, may not trigger the penalty tax) but whimsy would not be a good reason. Andy Spade famously tapped his 401(k) early to finance the empire of accessories masterminded by his far more famous wife, Kate. But such brilliant, or perhaps fortuitous, withdrawals are far rarer than ill-judged and financially ruinous early withdrawals. Premature speculation and 401(k) savings are a messy combination.[10]

Given these pragmatic constraints and, indeed, the intended design of the 401(k) system, those who withdraw money from their 401(k) accounts are almost always retirees. That is, they are individuals who are no longer receiving a salary. And, though exceptions do exist, older people withdrawing money from 401(k)s will usually find themselves in a lower tax bracket than they inhabited as salary-earning members of the U.S. workforce. A lower tax bracket, of course, means that the amounts withdrawn from 401(k)s will be taxed at a lower rate than they would have been as funds disbursed via paycheck.

Employer Matches

Apart from federal tax policy, the most common way in which assets of 401(k) plans are augmented is through matches by employers. Many, though by no means all, employers match or exceed their employees' contributions to defined-contribution accounts. Up to a limit of a few percentage points of an employee's salary, for instance, an employer might contribute a sum equivalent to what the employee does.

So, for a person who makes $100,000, an employer might match up to 5 percent. In such a case, if the employee contributed $5,000 to the 401(k), the employer would kick in $5,000 of its own dollars. In effect, these employers are giving their employees free money for participating in the company's plan. If the employee, instead, contributed only $4,000, the employer would do likewise, and the employee would leave $1,000 of employer loot unclaimed.

Employers establish these plans for their employees—and choose to offer matching contributions—not out of charity or largesse but for the same reason they offer everything else in the usual array of benefits, be they health insurance, soda-stocked fridges, or Ping-Pong tables. They are hoping to hire talented employees in what is often a competitive market for labor in the United States. As economist Justin Wolfers puts it: "Employers don't raise wages because they want to; they raise wages because they have to."[11] And defined-contributions plans have flourished remarkably in recent decades.

Employee Control

Though 401(k) plans are offered by employers and administered by investment advisory firms, employees are the parties primarily responsible for managing their own 401(k) accounts. Employees, for the most part, must take the initial steps to enroll and contribute to their retirement plan. Then, once they have accumulated assets to invest, they face their gravest responsibility: they must determine how best to allocate their savings among the options available in their 401(k) plan.

Typically, the plan's administrator maintains a website by which employees can access their personal 401(k) accounts. These websites list the plan's menu of investment options, as well as the account holder's balance and transaction activity. Employees can use the website to monitor their investment returns, to alter their investment choices, and to withdraw their savings, just as they might with an ordinary investment account at Merrill Lynch, E*Trade, or Charles Schwab.

Some commentators herald this individual control as empowerment, a form of fiscal autonomy for American citizens. Others lament it as the crumbly base of an untenable arch bearing the weight of our citizens' future economic welfare. Our examination of the promise and perils of 401(k)s will allow you to form your own conclusion.

Portability

For whatever their bygone glory, pension plans suffered notoriously from one enormous handicap: they weren't portable. That is, any remunerative entitlements an employee might have earned over years of service to a particular employer could be lost in an instant if that employee moved to a new job or stopped working too early. The effects of this policy were profound, both in handcuffing employees to unpleasant and unwanted situations and in severely penalizing employees forced to move for reasons not of their choosing.

In this regard, then, the 401(k) has been an unvarnished improvement. Though participation in a 401(k) account may be tied to a particular job, the savings in a 401(k) plan will never be locked in. Any employee who wishes to leave a job can easily walk out with her 401(k) savings, including everything contributed by the employer and the investment returns thereon. Typically, the employee "rolls over" the contents of her 401(k) (which is tied to a particular employer) to an IRA (which is not). This rollover process must be managed carefully to preserve the favorable tax treatment of the savings—and to avoid triggering crippling tax penalties—but firms that offer IRA accounts are particularly skilled at negotiating the rules to welcome new assets.

Individual Retirement Accounts

Very similar to 401(k) plans—yet holding an even richer lode of assets—are Individual Retirement Accounts (IRAs). Currently, IRAs hold $7.4 trillion, of which $3.6 trillion are invested in mutual funds.[12] Indeed, because 401(k) plans and IRAs share so much in common, they are often discussed as a single concept, and are often lumped together into an undifferentiated pile with 403(b) and 457 plans. Through both 401(k)s and IRAs, investors can make pre-tax contributions to an account that they themselves manage, and both are usually administered by the same fund families we have already encountered. The chart in figure 10.1 reveals the remarkable growth of both 401(k)s and IRAs in recent years, with IRAs maintaining a significant lead.

But their differences are important to note. First, 401(k) (and 403(b) and 457) accounts are available only to employees through a retirement plan sponsored by their employers. IRAs, by contrast, are available to anyone who cares to

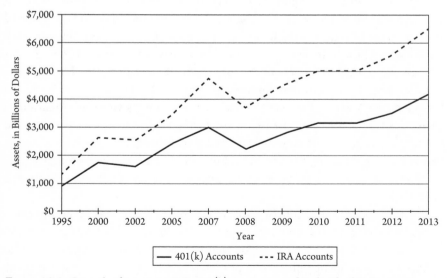

Figure 10.1 Growth of Assets in U.S. 401(k) Accounts and Individual Retirement Accounts.

open an account. One need simply respond to the bevy of advertisements from the usual suspects by calling or logging on. But because IRAs are not connected to employment, no employer exists to make matching contributions.

Related economic disparities are that the annual limit on an employee's contributions to a 401(k) is currently $18,000, while the limit for an IRA is $5,500, and IRA contributions are restricted largely to after-tax earnings. So, while IRAs are more ubiquitous, they are also somewhat more limited in their financial prowess. One occasionally hears of IRAs bulging with balances of millions of dollars, but those situations usually involve executives at hedge funds or private equity funds who have contributed to their IRA shares in their spectacularly successful investments.[13]

The Fiduciary Standard versus the Suitability Standard

A more important distinction between these two types of retirement accounts relates to the financial entities that administer them and their respective legal duties. With 401(k)s, federal law imposes on plan administrators—that is, the employers and the fund advisers they hire—a fiduciary duty to act prudently and to monitor each plan's investment offerings.[14] With IRAs, by contrast, the financial entities providing the accounts may operate unencumbered by such legal responsibility to act in the investor's best interest. Indeed, this schism in the legal duties of firms who manage the many trillions of dollars in retirement accounts has greatly disconcerted academics, regulators, and, most recently, the president of the United States.

This curious divide originated from a bifurcation of two of America's leading financial intermediaries. On the one hand are our old friends, registered investment advisers, whose focus has always been to provide clients with advice about how to invest their money. As we have seen, advisers charge fees that are percentages of assets under management and, under the law, they are regulated by the Investment Advisers Act of 1940.[15] On the other hand are broker-dealers, whose financial bailiwick in olden days was the execution of securities trades for their clients. In brokering such trades, brokers received orders from their clients and they charged those clients a commission for each trade. As a legal matter, brokers are regulated by the Securities Exchange Act of 1934 and rules promulgated by Financial Industry Regulatory Authority (FINRA).[16]

These historical and regulatory distinctions explain how the two groups came to operate under two different legal regimes. Specifically, only investment advisers are obliged to act as fiduciaries for their clients. In the dusty tomes of Anglo-American jurisprudence, the status of fiduciary carries with rhetoric requiring almost religious self-sacrifice. As one of the most famous legal opinions in American corporate law preaches, fiduciary obligations are among "the highest known to the law,"[17] requiring "not honesty alone, but the punctilio of an honor the most sensitive" from fiduciaries who are "in a position in which thought of self [is] to be renounced, however hard the abnegation."[18]

Brokers, by contrast, are subject merely to a standard under which they may recommend only investments that are "suitable" for their clients, according to factors such as the clients' age, other investments, financial situation, tax status, and so forth.[19] This suitability standard, in practice, by no means requires any renunciation of the self. On the contrary, broker-dealers routinely embrace the self, recommending investments that "generate more profits for the brokers (or their firms) at the customers' expense."[20]

But distinctions between the services of advisers and brokers have broken down in recent years and, in practice, the twain have very nearly met. The change has largely been one-sided, with brokers migrating well beyond their traditional execution of orders by offering their clients expansive advice on how to invest. In addition, "many brokers have begun to charge asset-based fees and now market themselves as financial advisers, not stockbrokers; still they continue to avoid regulation under the Advisers Act."[21] In sum, brokers would like to enjoy the profits of acting as investment advisers without having to endure their fiduciary obligations.

The law is littered with this phenomenon of regulatory arbitrage. Two groups begin by doing different things subject to quite reasonably different legal regimes. Then one group discovers the advantage of acting like the other, without the burden of the other's legal obligations. Airbnb and similar services offer lodging without having to obtain hotel licenses. Hedge funds offer loans without having to comply with banking law's capital reserve requirements. Jenny McCarthy offers vaccination advice without having to attend medical school.

At times, we the people may deem this evolution to be a healthy innovation for our society. Yay, Uber! But sometimes we conclude that the imbalance may be both unfair to the overregulated party and potentially dangerous to a deceived public. Hostelries will feel disadvantaged by having to pay more for legal compliance than their Airbnb rival; and guests may mistakenly believe that all their lodging options are held to the same legal standards of safety. With investment advice, advisers argue that brokers are advantaged by their unfairly low "suitability standard"; indeed, the White House agreed and recently released a report expressing concern that brokers and their weaker standard inflict concrete harm on investors.

So long as savings are in a 401(k) plan, they are protected by the fiduciary standard. But when those monies are rolled over into an IRA, they become especially vulnerable. Many IRAs are provided by broker-dealers, who are free to provide conflicted advice, such as to invest in financial products that provide larger revenue-sharing payments to the broker.[22] A recent report by the President's

Council of Economic Advisers noted that savers who receive this conflicted advice earn a return of roughly one percentage point less each year than they do under a fiduciary standard. In 2012, rollovers from 401(k)s to IRAs exceeded $300 billion, and economists expect that number "to increase steadily in the coming years."[23] The White House report estimated that conflicted advice costs investors $17 billion each year.

Solutions to Regulatory Arbitrage

Incidences of regulatory arbitrage may be fairly common, but so too are their solutions. They are often straightforward and come in at least three varieties. They include prohibiting the behavior, regulating both parties to the higher standard (leveling up), or regulating both to the lower standard (leveling down).

Thus, a city might ban Airbnb, might require Airbnb to comply with hotel standards, or might eliminate regulations for hotels. In our land of investments, little energy has been expended toward either barring brokers from providing investment advice or leveling down by eliminating the fiduciary standard for investment advisers. Instead, the debate focuses primarily on whether to level up by imposing a "uniform fiduciary standard" on all parties. Perhaps unsurprisingly, advisers are pushing for this change, while brokers are fighting it savagely.

The Department of Labor has attempted for years to expand the fiduciary standard to brokers, without much success. In 2011, the department proposed—and then promptly rescinded—its first attempt to promulgate rules in this area. The brokerage industry deemed them too aggressive. Then in 2015, it tried again, proposing rules that would revise the law to extend fiduciary obligations to brokers providing advice on savings held in retirement accounts, be they 401(k)s or IRAs. The department's claim is that these rules would save investors $40 billion over a decade by eliminating conflicted advice.

Once again, the brokerage industry has contested the rules, arguing that they will not lower but, in fact, raise costs for investors. Unlike 2011, this time the Department of Labor has the public support of the White House, which may help these rules survive the lengthy process of regulatory enactment.

Though the brokerage industry has preserved its regulatory preference so far, it faces battle on a widening front. The push for a fiduciary standard is spilling beyond retirement savings, which labor laws govern and the Department of Labor regulates. Now, proponents of the fiduciary standard are pushing its adoption in the wider field of all investment, which the securities laws govern and the SEC regulates. The head of the SEC, Mary Jo White, has stated publicly that she would like her agency to promulgate a uniform fiduciary standard.[24],[25]

Potential Problems with Retirement Accounts

In conceptual terms, a 401(k) plan serves as yet another layer of intermediation between investors and investments. Once upon a time, most Americans who wished to invest in public companies would do so by directly buying particular stocks or bonds. As mutual funds grew in popularity, Americans increasingly bought shares in those funds, which in turn acquired portfolios of securities in public companies.[26] And now, with the rise of 401(k) plans, more than 50 million Americans direct their savings first into a 401(k) account, through which they then predominantly select mutual funds, which in turn invest in the securities of public companies. So, in effect, two layers of counselors now stand between investors and their ultimate investments: first, the employers and plan administrators charged with overseeing 401(k) accounts; second, the investment advisers who manage mutual funds.

All that extra intermediation could, of course, provide more cordons of security around the precious savings of ordinary Americans. Structurally, 401(k) plans happen to fall within the protection of one of America's most famous, sprawling, and brooding legal omnipresences: ERISA.[27] The purpose of ERISA is to serve as a huge, malevolent force that frightens the financial industry into behaving itself. More technically, the Employee Retirement Income Security Act of 1974 established heightened regulatory and fiduciary obligations for financial intermediaries who handle retirement savings, such as the money in 401(k) plans and pensions. ERISA requires, for instance, that the selection of investments included in a 401(k) plan be "prudent."[28] So, when our 401(k) system works well, these additional security measures protect and nurture the growth of individual savings.

But, as we might also now suspect, extra layers of intermediation also introduce extra mouths to feed. As a relatively benign matter, any financial company that provides 401(k) plans, oversees the plans' companion websites and banks of telephone operators, and generates regular statements for account holders is going to expect, quite reasonably, remuneration for its pains. Accordingly, 401(k) plans often come with administrative fees assessed on the accounts of their participants, which will come as a surprise to the 70 percent of plan participants who think their 401(k) is free.[29]

As a more malign matter, however, 401(k) plan administrators face temptations very similar to those that have bewitched so many mutual fund managers. If 401(k)s are a wildly popular on-ramp to mutual fund investments, toll booths can be placed just as easily at the start of a freeway as in the middle of one. So, if an administrator—like the unscrupulous investment advisers discussed in earlier chapters—determined to filch plan assets, it would find in 401(k) accounts today a rich trove of almost $5 trillion.

Investor Irrationality

What can go wrong with 401(k) accounts? Almost everything, at any stage in the process. As shown in the discussion of fees that advisers of mutual funds charge, a system that puts every individual in charge of investment decisions places a great deal of weight on the rationality of those individuals. And the use, misuse, and disuse of 401(k) accounts have proved picture windows into the financial psyche of the ordinary investor.

Consider, for instance, the fact that large numbers of new employees do not enroll in 401(k) plans when they begin a job. And of those who do, large numbers do not specify any contributions to their accounts. In both these cases, no money is being saved. But do these data suggest investor irrationality?[30]

Not necessarily. One can imagine many reasons not to enroll or to contribute to a 401(k) account. After all, new employees include many young people, who may already be yoked to a cartload of student debt. After paying for a new suit, a used futon, and a gross of ramen noodles, a young employee may simply have no money left to save. Why squirrel away money for your seventies if you're starving today?

Or, some have made the calculation that the money is better spent in the present. Consider the wisdom of *Superman III*'s Gus Gorman, our sage of financial management, about the taxes withheld from his paycheck:

> GORMAN: Hey, what is this?
>
> EXPOSITORY FOIL: First paycheck?
>
> GORMAN: It's the first rip-off man, I'm supposed to get $225 a week, right? This says $143.80, how I'm supposed to live on that? Look at this, state tax, federal tax, Social Security tax.
>
> EXPOSITORY FOIL: So, you're still getting some money when you hit sixty-five.
>
> GORMAN: So, I'm getting money when I hit sixty-five? I want mine now, when I can enjoy it, while I'm young. I want to get down, boogie. Boogie, boogie.[31]

By themselves, then, examples of employees declining to make use of their 401(k) plans cast no aspersions on those employees' mental faculties.

But what about those matching payments by employers? Recall that in many 401(k) plans the employer agrees to contribute its own money to the employee's account in equal amounts up to a predetermined threshold. By declining to enroll or contribute in those circumstances, an employee would now not just be failing to save but also be squandering gifts of additional cash. Would that be irrational? Again, the employee's perfectly rational explanation might be that $1,000 today is worth $2,000—and all gains compounded thereupon—several decades hence.

Of course, the larger the mismatch between these sums, the harder this position will be to maintain.

Consider, for instance, a wild disparity. What if the employee were not willing to save $1 today for $1 million in twenty years? At some point, one might reasonably question the employee's decision. That is, his rationality. When the mismatch is sufficiently large, the employee should pursue extreme measures to take the vastly larger, if long-deferred payout. To secure a million bucks in twenty years for the price of $1 today, a rational actor would look very hard for some way to not spend that $1, or to borrow it, or to beg or steal it. Again, some circumstances might truly make saving anything today impossible: a medical emergency, a tax bill, a physical inability to eat any more ramen. Still, when the amounts forgone in the future are sufficiently huge, a rational response is to adjust one's behavior in the now.

And let's grapple with reality for a moment: not every new employee who fails to enroll or to contribute to a 401(k) plan is doing so after carefully calculating her current need for cash, the potential effect of long-term compounding, and the myriad other factors stitched into the fabric of this complicated decision. Many are just sick of forms. Or don't know what a 401(k) is all about. Or are busy watching something on HBO.

But when pressed, some of those who recuse themselves might nevertheless cling to a diffuse if perfectly rational explanation: the legal constraints of the 401(k) structure are the problem. One may decline to save $18,000 or $18 today because the money is so hard to get back out of a 401(k) without severe penalties. Who knows what emergency or calamity might occur tomorrow? This problem of being locked into a 401(k) in an uncertain world is real. But it is also limited.

Consider a plan in which the employer contributes $1,000 if the employee does the same. Assume the employee takes advantage of the program and thereby accrues a 401(k) balance of $2,000. Now, if an emergency occurs and she needs her original $1,000, what can she do? She could withdraw her funds early and suffer a penalty for doing so. But that penalty would "only" be approximately $800 (a 10 percent withdrawal penalty of $200, plus 30 percent in approximate state and federal taxes). An appallingly punitive amount, to be sure, but the employee would nevertheless receive $1,200. That is, even when confronted with an emergency need for her money, the employee is still better off enrolling, contributing, and taking advantage of the employer's match than declining to save her $1,000.

And, remember, she never really had the choice of taking all of her $1,000 because that salary will come to her only after the withholding of taxes. At our hypothetical rate of 30 percent, she would have received only $700. So, yes, the penalty for early withdrawal is certainly significant, but an employer's matching contributions might more than compensate for it.

And, remember, too, that employees can often also take out a loan against their 401(k) balances—that they then repay to themselves—which is another way to reap the financial advantages of these plans with even fewer penalties. Finally, in truly dire emergencies such as becoming disabled or incurring a large medical debt, an employee may be able to withdraw sums from a 401(k) without paying any penalties.

But what about all the time and energy involved in establishing and maintaining these accounts? Might not an employee be rationally apathetic and justify her estrangement from the 401(k) on the basis that it's just not worth her time? Indeed, the economic literature well recognizes the transactions costs of searching, monitoring, and switching investments. But it also is quick to quantify them. So, if a person claims that the administrative aggro is just too big a headache, we can test that proposition. A 401(k) plan with employer matching might grow to be worth many thousands of dollars in the future, so one will need to place a high dollar value, indeed, on one's billable time to justify refusing to establish an account.

A Policy of Paternalism?

This question whether people are neglecting investment accounts for rational or irrational reasons is an important one. If our citizens are rejecting 401(k)s in large numbers after they conduct careful analyses of the present and future costs and benefits, then potential regulators have a challenge to justify any governmental intrusion into those citizens' decisions. If, on the other hand, the citizenry are allowing their accounts to fall into desuetude out of ignorance, distraction, or other irrational reasons, then these behavioral impediments provide a justification for regulators to intervene.

Proof of irrationality is a very difficult thing to produce, as our foregoing list of excuses and explanations for not pursuing an account has shown. Is our investor acting irrationally or is he reasonably accelerating income to when he needs it most, reasonably protecting himself from unknown financial shocks, or reasonably choosing to allocate his time and attention to other tasks? Happily, some data do exist to answer at least some of these questions.

Consider an example from the United Kingdom, where some pension plans are paid entirely by the employer. All the employee need do is enroll. Just lift a Biro and sign that HR form. But, no, almost one out of every two eligible employees in this situation fails to sign up. As Cass Sunstein and Richard Thaler describe this phenomenon in *Nudge*, "This is equivalent to not bothering to cash your paycheck."[32] But might the employees need the money now? No, they make no contributions to the plan, so there is no money now. But might they fear for a financial emergency? Repeat, there is no money to be had now. But might they have better uses for their time? If so, then their time must be worth thousands of pounds an hour . . . a much higher hourly rate than the kind of person who needs an employer-sponsored retirement plan. The only persuasive explanation is the obvious one: many people make poor financial decisions that cause themselves real financial harm.

Let us consider now that hardy band of employees who do manage to push through the enrollment process: those who do establish a 401(k) account and even specify how much of their paycheck they would like contributed to it. What then happens to their money? Distressingly, in many cases, nothing. Or, rather, the fiscal equivalent.

When money flows into a 401(k) account, the plan administrator directs those sums into whatever investments from the plan's menu the account holder has elected. But what if the owner hasn't made any elections? That is, after pushing through the paperwork thus far, she has fallen at this new hurdle. In that case, the contributions most often accumulate as cash. Or, in some cases, as savings in a money market fund. But, our neglectful friend might counter, "cash is still something . . . so, my choice (or lack thereof) is still saving." Yes, undoubtedly holding cash is saving, but the problem is that it's almost certainly saving far too little.

Stashing money under a mattress is also saving. And saving is only a portion of the rationale for using a retirement account. As time passes, inflation acts as a corrosive force upon cash, slowly but powerfully eating into its purchasing power. Two bits might have bought you a shave and haircut in World War I, but twenty-five cents wouldn't pay for a smear of lather today.

Similarly, a series of maximal 401(k) contributions over a forty-year career would certainly amount to a decent corpus: $720,000 using current limits, to be precise. But consider the effect of inflation. The inflation rate fluctuates continually, averaging more than 3 percent over the past century. If we assume a consistent rate of 2.5 percent, inflation would inexorably ravage our cash. The $18,000 we contribute today would drop in purchasing power to almost $14,000 within ten years; then below $11,000 after another decade; and all the way down to $6,703 after forty years. Holding cash in an inflationary environment is like standing still on a moving walkway in reverse, forever receding into the distance.

To avoid our savings from dwindling away in this manner, we need to harness the power of investments. The reason retirement plans offer an array of mutual funds, rather than simply a metal box with a sturdy lock, is that our savings must increase to keep up with inflation. Indeed, to support a healthy retirement, our savings should outpace the inflation rate. So, if a plan participant enrolls and contributes, but leaves her savings in cash for forty years, she will discover an appalling surprise in her account when she retires: not quite bread crumbs and a lump of moldy cheese, but almost certainly a sum inadequate to cover the future's higher costs of living longer.

But if we do assume—or even if we just worry—that many people's decisions not to enroll, not to contribute, or not to invest in a 401(k) account are irrational, what could be done about it? Well, we could change the default settings in these accounts. That is, we could permit employers to enroll all their employees automatically in a 401(k) account. We could also permit those employers to contribute a percentage of those employees' salaries into those accounts. And we could permit those 401(k) plans to invest those contributions in something more productive than merely cash or a money market account. Indeed, with the Pension Protection Act of 2006, Congress allowed employers to make precisely these choices. The law required that default investments needed to be low risk; the ideal choice would be something like a broad-based, passively managed index fund, but a popular choice is a target-date fund. Since the adoption of this law not quite a decade ago, the effect upon 401(k) savings has been dramatic.

Under the old regime, an employee's lapse at any of these three stages could severely handicap her future wealth. But if an employer adopts the new law's rules, an employee who does nothing may still find herself pursuing a prudent and modest, if not particularly aggressive, investment strategy. But how can the government and employers justify putting people in accounts without their permission, harvesting their salary without their permissions, or exposing those savings to investment risk without their permission? In a few ways.

First, by citing the alarming statistics on the large numbers of people who do not save anything for their future. Second, by permitting everyone to change these settings. Any employee aggrieved by one of these "default" decisions can simply reverse it without penalty: she can change the investment elections, change the amount of contributions, or even close her account.

For those of us who do find ourselves in charge of a 401(k) account—as a matter of will or by default—additional concerns await us, however.

Bad Investment Options

What if the array of menu choices in a 401(k) plan is a poor one? Recall that the employee's responsibility in a 401(k) is to select a mix of investments from the menu chosen by the plan's administrators. If the administrators have assembled a menu chock full of poor choices, then the employee's options are necessarily going to be hobbled. As one example, recall that Lori Bilewicz lamented that, in her 401(k) account, the employer offered too many choices of mutual funds and that those choices were too expensive.

In the 401(k) plans of many companies, the menu of options can be remarkably poor in a variety of ways. Not only might the mutual funds be expensive, as Ms. Bilewicz alleged, but the employer might have included the entirely wrong class of shares. As we have already seen, investment advisers regularly offer an array of share classes in the same fund. One of the most common distinctions in share classes is between retail shares and institutional shares. That is, shares offered to ordinary investors off the street versus shares offered to large organizations that bring in large amounts of assets. As we have also seen, the fees associated with institutional share classes are far lower than retail shares.

If a company, such as Boeing perhaps, offered a 401(k) plan in which all the mutual fund options were retail classes, its employees should be perplexed. A corporation as large as Boeing, with many thousands of employees and many millions or billions of dollars in its 401(k) plan, should clearly have the economic clout to gain admittance to the very best class of fund shares at the very lowest fees. Yet a surprising number of employers choose to include in their 401(k) menus classes of fund shares that carry prices no better than their individual employees could obtain if they walked in off the street.

Another problem with the fund offerings in a 401(k) might be the revenue-sharing arrangements between the investment adviser and the employer. We know that many investment advisers are willing to use the assets in a mutual fund to reward those institutions that help the fund to sell its shares. In the open market, those institutions are typically broker-dealers. But in 401(k)s, the entities chiefly responsible for the success and sale of mutual fund shares are the employers who choose to include particular funds in their 401(k) menu.

Again, consider a company such as Walmart, with its enormous workforce and their huge mountain of retirement savings.[33] If the Walmart 401(k) plan contains only one or two dozen investment options, the odds are extremely good that each of those investment options is going to enjoy a large inflow of investments, merely through the steady contributions of savings by Walmart's employees. And since many employees are reluctant to manage or change their 401(k) settings with much regularity, once an employee selects a fund in his 401(k) account, the fund can remain an election for years or decades of future contributions.

For a mutual fund, getting onto a 401(k) menu can be as lucrative as getting onto a broker's preferred fund list. We shouldn't be at all surprised, then, to learn that fund advisers are willing to reward their gatekeepers generously for this access. Of course, every dollar of reward paid out of a mutual fund to a 401(k) plan administrator comes directly out of the savings of employees—that is, from the savings of people for whom the fund adviser and administrator are supposedly legal fiduciaries.

Before we try to solve this problem of poor investment choices in a 401(k) plan, let's consider how that inferior array might have come to be chosen. Really, only two explanations make sense. The poor array of choices is a result either of incompetence or of disloyalty. That is, either the plan administrators don't know what they're doing or they know very well what they're doing, which is attempting to enrich themselves at their employees' expense.

Expertise

Let's start with the innocent explanation. Perhaps a 401(k) plan's menu comprises poor choices because the plan's administrator simply doesn't know what a good mix of choices should look like. Though America has many, perhaps a few thousand, large corporations with sophisticated human resources and legal departments, our country has many thousands more companies that are far smaller operations. Certainly a junior manager in the HR department of a local business has a wide variety of responsibilities, from tracking sick days to finding health insurance. We should not be too surprised, then, if that manager has neither the expertise nor the training to master portfolio theory and fund returns, too.

But don't employers usually acquire the services of an external administrator to provide the company's plan? And shouldn't that outside administrator possess the requisite expertise? Yes, employers do, and yes, the service providers should. But that brings us to another explanation for poor menu choices.

Before we explore this darker material, let's pause to revisit the bright shining rope ladder that Judge Easterbrook offered in chapter 4 as an escape from problems with mutual funds: exit. "An adviser can't make money from its captive fund," he opined, "if high fees drive investors away."[34] Within the walls of a 401(k), captive employees can invest only in the funds chosen by the plan's administrators. So, one corollary to Easterbrook's koan is that an adviser can make money from captive funds if investors have no way to escape high fees.

Disloyalty

So, what might explain why the menu of a 401(k) plan is riddled with poor options? One explanation is that poor options are often expensive options—just as Ms. Bilewicz claimed in her lawsuit—and that higher fees will lead to greater returns for the investment adviser. As we have seen with revenue-sharing payments before, an adviser might be willing to reward the employer for agreeing to these poor menu choices. This explanation is certainly a tad disheartening, but one that our explorations of adviser infidelity in part II might support.

Whatever the specific arrangements between the employer and vendor of a 401(k) plan, data certainly suggest that these plans offer a distressingly expensive array of investment options. In 2015, a study by Ian Ayres of Yale Law School and Quinn Curtis of the University of Virginia Law School argued that fees and menu restrictions in 401(k) plans "lead to a cost of seventy-eight basis points in excess of index funds."[35] And "fees are so high" in 16 percent of the plans they analyzed, "they consume the tax benefits of investing in a 401(k) for a young employee."[36] The implications of these findings are distressing, as they demonstrate how high fees can inflict a punishing drag on savings in mutual funds.

Litigating 401(k) Fees

In recent years, plaintiffs have launched a hail of lawsuits that attempt to hold employers and outside providers liable for offering poor investment choices in 401(k) plans. Much of this litigation has been brought under ERISA, and it alleges that the plan administrators violated their fiduciary duty to offer prudent invest-ment choices. The plaintiffs argue that the inclusion of mutual funds with high fees or the choice of unnecessarily expensive classes of fund shares is imprudent, particularly when inexpensive funds and share classes—with equivalent perfor-mance at lower prices—are so widely available. The plaintiffs in these lawsuits have, to an impressive extent, failed. Few of them have actually won at trial or on appeal, and indeed some have lost very prominent cases against large employers such as John Deere and Walmart.

In *Hecker v. Deere*, Dennis Hecker and several of his fellow employees sued their employer, John Deere, as well as the trustee of John Deere's 401(k) plans, Fidelity Investments. Hecker and his fellow plaintiffs alleged that Deere and Fidelity vio-lated their duties under ERISA by providing investment options with excessive fees and failing to disclose revenue-sharing arrangements between Fidelity and John Deere. Jeremy Braden brought similar charges against Walmart, arguing that the ten mutual fund options in the company's 401(k) plan—all retail—were imprudently high priced given the economic power of the plan's $11 billion in assets.[37] While a court of appeals in *Braden* held that the small number of options in Walmart's plan supported the plaintiff's claim, a different court of appeals in *Hecker* ruled in favor of the defendants, notwithstanding their choice of high-priced funds.

The successful tactic for defendants in the *Hecker* case has come to be known as the *large-menu defense*.[38] The judicial adoption of this defense is troubling, so let us take a moment to examine it. In essence, the employers and plan ven-dors point out that, with a bit of rooting around on the 401(k) plan website, an employee can select investments other than the preferred menu. And since the employee's choice is not just a dozen or two mutual funds but, rather, thou-sands of other funds and securities, the employer has made a "prudent" array of investments available. A number of courts, operating somewhat on intuition rather than empirical data, have accepted this slightly sophisticated notion of "if some is good, more is better."

But there are two problems. First, recall that an important reason ERISA imposes a fiduciary duty on financial intermediaries that handle retirement assets is that the universe of investment options is wide and wild. What average employ-ees, investing their life savings, need is a sophisticated financial intermediary with the competence and care to intercede on their behalf. By winnowing down the overwhelming choice of investments available in the wild, an ERISA fiduciary offers prudent choices to its intended beneficiaries. By adopting the large-menu defense, courts are instead rewarding defendants who abdicate this duty.

Second, large menus are pernicious to investors. Academic studies have dem-onstrated that offering more choices to consumers such as investors can have a stultifying effect. As anyone who has been paralyzed by a restaurant's 300-item menu can attest, too many choices can often be more harmful than too few.

One study has shown that for every ten additional choices included on a menu, participation drops by 2 percent. According to the study, the average plan with thirty options had a participation rate of 70 percent, but when those options were increased to fifty-six, the participation fell to 61 percent.[39] Yet the overriding goal of our defined contribution plans is to encourage participation, so the encouragement of large menus in them may be distressingly counterproductive.

Not all plaintiffs have been stymied by the large-menu defense—a few have enjoyed success. First, many have negotiated large settlements prior to any verdict. Second, and more important, the threat of lawsuits already appears to have had a salutary effect on sloppy 401(k) plans.

As the footsteps of these lawsuits have tread across the HR departments of America, many employers and administrators have embraced "voluntary" changes to the choices in their 401(k) plans. Participants in great numbers of 401(k) plans have recently received notices from their plan administrators announcing the change of investment options in their plan from, typically, retail to institutional share classes.

Though employees should certainly be grateful for the change, they might reasonably be curious also. Why, they might ask, weren't their savings already invested in those more favorable share classes? And how much better might their investments have done had they been?

So, even without many favorable verdicts for their efforts, plaintiffs in 401(k) litigation may nevertheless have won benefits for many other employees in the United States. But what of Ms. Bilewicz and the lawsuit she brought against her employer? Opposing counsel representing Fidelity, the adviser of all the fund's in Bilewicz's 401(k), naturally harrumphed that her lawsuit was "entirely without merit." Then on a holiday weekend—Fourth of July, 2014—when news goes to die, Fidelity released the announcement it wanted no one to hear. Fidelity had settled this case and one other for $12 million. News reports noted that some "industry watchers said the move by Fidelity surprised them because the huge firm has vigorously defended itself in similar cases."[40]

Given the large number of these cases against Fidelity and other plan administrators, what made this one so special? The answer had to do with Ms. Bilewicz's occupation. We haven't yet discussed what she did for a living. Unlike the employees who brought those other lawsuits, who perhaps sold retail at Walmart or built tractors at John Deere, Ms. Bilewicz and her fellow plaintiffs worked at a company that had a certain degree of expertise in mutual funds. So, they knew enough to recognize a good mutual fund investment from a bad one.

The place she worked was a company called Fidelity Investments. Bilewicz and her fellow plaintiffs—some of the people who knew Fidelity's mutual funds better than anyone else—concluded that Fidelity's offerings in Fidelity's own 401(k) plan were so imprudent that they warranted a lawsuit. No wonder Fidelity wanted this case settled so quickly.

The lesson for the rest of us is clear. None of us in a 401(k) plan can assume that the "prudent" choices made on our behalf are prudent at all. Investing successfully in a defined contribution plan, like all investment, requires diligence and vigilance. But the financial advantages can easily reward our efforts.

11

TARGET-DATE FUNDS

Set It and Regret It? Target-date funds in the crosshairs.
—Consumer Reports, *2009*

For everyone who held investments in the year 2008, September was the cruelest in a long train of abusive months. The fifteenth was not the ides, but it was fateful nonetheless as America's long-tottering subprime foolishness at last collapsed when Lehman Brothers declared bankruptcy. After lurching about for months, this venerable—or at least really old—investment bank finally crumpled like a boorish party guest, pulling down the tablecloth of global finance with it. Stock markets plummeted, portfolios crashed to smithereens, and trillions in investments turned to ash all across the planet.[1]

Though investors everywhere cowered in loathing and fear, not all believed themselves vulnerable to the vicissitudes of this once-in-a-century cataclysm. In a few complacent corners of the financial community, some investors sheltered within instruments they thought capable of weathering the storm. Indeed, inside a few citadels and fortresses, some hedge-fund moguls contrived even to win billion-dollar fortunes by placing some of the greatest trades ever,[2] usually big shorts, on the falling market.[3]

Mutual funds, of course, are far more limited in their ability to take advantage of short selling and derivative investments that might have protected them in the downturn.[4] So, the net asset values of many funds plunged as precipitously as the equity zeppelins to which their portfolios were tethered. A few mutual funds, however, claimed to be different. These happy few boasted that they, too, were built as sanctuaries in financial storms. They were target-date funds. Their boasts, alas, were unavailing.

Target-date funds are designed to provide their investors with an ever-evolving portfolio that automatically shifts over the decades from an aggressive emphasis (so useful to building a nest egg) to a more cautious approach (so useful to preserving it). Their targets are the years in which their investors hope to retire. Many investors who held target funds dated 2010 in September 2008 assumed their portfolios had almost entirely fled the reckless ambitions of youth to nestle in the calm senescence of old age. But they were very wrong.

The First Target-Date Funds

Only fifteen years before, in March 1994, the first target-date funds came onto the market under the management of Wells Fargo and Barclays Global Investors.[5] These two firms recognized and attempted to solve a chronic problem with mutual fund investing: the inattention of fund investors. Indeed, the target-date fund can, when used carefully, solve one of the most intractable problems with personal investing.

As shown in the examination of investors' clumsy use of 401(k) plans, people have found all sorts of obstacles to blunder over when managing their savings. An investor may neglect to enroll in a 401(k) account, to contribute funds to the plan, or to select investments for the cash he does save. And even if an investor does successfully negotiate this steeplechase, yet more obstacles lurk in the years and decades ahead.

Consider a dutiful young member of the workforce who does everything conscientiously to set her mutual fund investments on course. If she has, indeed, been prudent, she will have chosen a relatively aggressive mix of equity-heavy funds to capitalize on during the forty years she has to build up her investment returns. The conventional advice for youthful investors is to indulge in just such a healthy dose of higher-risk investments. If this strategy yields success, then these investors will enjoy compounded growth for decades to come. If, on the other hand, the risky investments produce failure, then the investors will have decades to recover from the early setbacks.

But the appropriate mix of investments for a twenty-something is surely not equally salutary for an employee on the cusp of retirement. At that stage of one's career and life, an investor wants to curtail risk and preserve all the savings she has amassed. Imminent retirees are, of course, about to lose their regular stream of salary and find themselves needing to draw upon whatever savings they have amassed to live. Here, then, is still another profound challenge for anyone using mutual funds to save for the *longue durée*: how can we change the mix of our investments to match our tolerance for risk as we grow older?

Our Ever-Changing Tolerance for Risk

An investor's mix of funds needs to change as she grows older. The computation for this change is not particularly difficult; in fact, the investing community bandies about an old chestnut as a guide for allocating investments: 100 minus your age = your appropriate percentage of equity investments[6] (the balance of investments, quoth the conventional wisdom, should be in bonds or cash). Like all rules of thumb, this one is subject to plenty of critiques, quibbles, and regional variations.

Yet this simple function does effectively convey a largely uncontroversial tenet of investing: investors should grow less aggressive as they grow older. For a twenty-year-old investor, our rule would counsel investing 80 percent of his assets in equities; but by the time he reached seventy years of age, his equity holdings should have dropped to 30 percent. Whether or not those percentages are precise or ideal in any platonic sense, this crude rule does convey the received advice to transition gradually from risk taking to risk avoiding over the course of one's career in personal investing.

The essence of the rule relies on the inherent nature of stocks versus bonds. Stocks are a more volatile means of investing that have the ability to produce greater gains and, of course, correspondingly greater losses. Bonds and other debt, on the other hand, provide the alternative bargain of greater predictability with fewer risks and correspondingly fewer possible gains. By gradually shifting one's savings away from riskier equities to more predictable debt as one approaches retirement, the conventional thinking goes, an investor shifts from attempting to inflate a portfolio toward attempting to preserve that portfolio.

The last thing anyone wants is for a lifetime of savings to vanish in a fit of ill-timed market volatility on the eve of retirement.

The Problem with Ordinary Mutual Funds

Prior to 2004, almost all mutual funds proclaimed their own single, immutable investment policy.[7] A fund might track the S&P 500 index, for instance, or a basket of Japanese technology stocks, or emerging market bonds. But whatever policy the fund professed, that policy was largely intended to remain constant over time. That index fund, then, would still be attempting to track the S&P 500 just as faithfully thirty years into the future as it would today. Creating variation in the complexion of an investor's overall savings portfolio was thus the obligation of the investor herself.

The investor was the requisite agent of change who bore the duty to reallocate her own portfolio to manage any process of lowering risk over time. As we might well suspect, however, such a careful, regular, and conscientious calibration of fund holdings is a rather fanciful expectation to place on ordinary investors. We should not be surprised to learn that many investors chose one of two alternative—and equally unhelpful—approaches instead.

Churning and Ignoring

Generally, individual investors tend either to churn or to ignore. That is, investors may, on the one hand, get a little too involved with their portfolios and fiddle with them all day long.[8] If this happens, the investors regularly suffer from mistiming the market and racking up high transactions costs that swamp any investment gains. Or, on the other hand, investors never pay much attention to their portfolios and let their investment elections languish unchanged for years, or even decades. Settings that may have been chosen prudently for a young adult remain in place and grow ever more imprudent as the investor approaches retirement.

So, just as some 401(k) holders might awake from Van Winkle slumbers to discover that decades of their savings have languished uselessly in a money market account, many others may be hazarding the opposite problem. They could awake to find that their precious nest egg was rising and plunging on the waves of outrageous fortune in risky equity funds, even on the eve of retirement.

The Success of Target-Date Funds: Rotisserie Chicken

Wells Fargo and Barclays sought to solve this problem with their target-date funds. And though their concept is still very young—just barely old enough to order a beer in most states—it has been wildly successful. Target-date funds enjoyed an explosive debut, swilling an astonishing $741 billion in assets during the past twenty-one years. In that short time, target-date funds have grown particularly attractive to investors saving for retirement: 89 percent of their assets are held in IRAs or 401(k)s, a percentage that has risen rapidly. As of year-end 2013, target-date funds had accumulated 15 percent of all 401(k) assets, and that percentage, too, is sure to rise.[9]

Some of the remarkable success of target-date funds may be due to the exertions of one of America's best-known entrepreneurs and salesmen. This fellow doesn't peddle mutual funds or, indeed, any financial instruments. His most famous invention, beloved of insomniacs across America, is a small metal box that purports to rotate and heat protein faster and more cheaply than archaic methods of food preparation, such as ovens. Best of all, the inclusion of an ingenious chronological device—known as a "timer"—on each Ronco Rotisserie switches the machine off when the meat is "done." Miraculous!

Infomercials are truly peculiar phenomena. There's something profoundly bizarre about watching a man pretend to shush an audience he has paid to cheer him wildly. But infomercials are also undeniably effective. Ron Popeil appears to have grown rich—based on his million-dollar claims in Ronco's recent bankruptcy, anyway—and his taglines have certainly grown famous.

Americans everywhere recognize the exhortation—bellowed antiphonally by Popeil and his planted audience—to "set it and forget it." The timer's magical properties apparently liberate America's worried masses from whatever anxieties have been keeping us awake at night. Knowing that our lobster tails and pork loins will come to a stop before rotating themselves to cinder, we consumers are now free to forget them and thus liberated to return to gawping at late-night infomercials.

Target-date funds are almost invariably described using Ronco's "set it and forget it" tagline. They aim to update themselves constantly to remain prudent at all stages of their investors' savings career—and thereby to be a one-stop destination for an investor's savings. The investment advisers that offer target-date funds typically include years in their titles that correspond to the years in which the intended investor will retire. Vanguard, for instance, currently offers eleven such funds, each named a Target Retirement Fund and each containing a year in its name, ranging from 2010 through 2060 in five-year increments. The idea is that a person who turns thirty years of age in 2015 and who plans to retire thirty-five years later, at age sixty-five, would choose the Target Retirement 2055 fund.[10] (The investors in those funds can, like any other fund investor, withdraw their savings whenever they want.)

Throughout those decades, the fund itself—and not the investor—makes the prudent adjustments from holding primarily equity investments to primarily fixed-income investments as the target date approaches. This change in allocations over time is known as the fund's *glide path*. When depicted graphically, as in figure 11.1, the declining percentage of equities vaguely suggests the gentle approach of an airplane coming in for a soft and safe landing.[11]

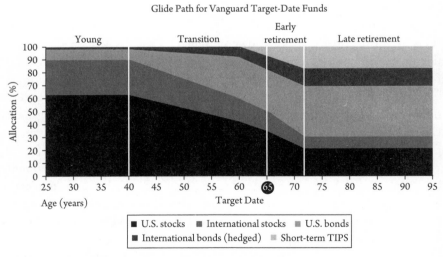

Figure 11.1 Glide Path for Vanguard Target Date Funds.

Funds of Funds

Target-date funds are typically structured as funds of funds. That is, the target-date fund holds investments only in other mutual funds, rather than in the securities of operating companies. So, while a typical mutual fund might feature a portfolio of stocks or bonds issued by hundreds or thousands of different corporations, a target-date fund might invest in a mere handful of other mutual funds.[12] Indeed, the most rudimentary approach would be for a target-date fund to invest in just two other funds: an equity fund and a bond fund. Simply by adjusting the balance of these two holdings, a portfolio manager of the target-date fund could modulate the fund's overall risk profile.

Thirty-five years before the target date, for instance, the fund's manager might allot 70 percent of the portfolio to the underlying equity fund and only 30 percent to the underlying bond fund. Then, with each passing quarter or year, the portfolio manager could redeem a portion of the equity fund and acquire a dash more of the bond fund, reducing risk as the target date neared.

In practice, target-date funds are not quite this basic. Vanguard's 2055 fund, for instance, invests in four other funds: one U.S. and one international equity fund, and one U.S. and one international bond fund.[13] Fidelity's Freedom 2050 fund invests in as many as twenty-five other funds.[14] In those target-date funds, then, portfolio managers choreograph a more complex balance of ingredients in their quest to reduce risk gradually and gracefully.

The Appeal of Target-Date Funds to Ordinary Investors

The evolution of increasing risk-aversion comes built in to target-date funds themselves. They are the Ronco Rotisseries of the mutual fund world. Investors simply elect the appropriately dated fund from the array in their retirement accounts, then forget it for a few decades. Each fund in the array evolves on a slightly different schedule, and investors can pick whichever one is closest to their intended retirement date. The appeal is easy to see. These funds take from investors a heavy and enduring burden: to rebalance their portfolio from riskier equity investments to more conservative bond investments over decades. When they work correctly, target-date funds take care of these changes themselves.

A target-date fund may be a very good option for the average individual investor. Indeed, the Department of Labor has designated target-date funds as appropriate Qualified Default Investment Alternatives (QDIAs) under the Pension Protection Act of 2006. QDIAs are funds that a 401(k) plan fiduciary may choose as default investment for plan participants who fail to make their own election for the investment of assets in their accounts. Because many investors fail to make their own elections—or, having done so, fail to change them—funds chosen as a QDIAs often receive a strong and steady flow of new investment.[15]

Gaining this highly prized status helped target-date funds enjoy their explosive growth. In the decade prior to 2006, target-date funds had amassed just $71 billion; in the decade since then, that number has risen tenfold to $741 billion. Many investors in these funds seem delighted to "set it and forget it": a recent report by Vanguard, which manages an enormous portion of savings in target-date funds, found that the average number of trades investors make in and out of these funds each year is one.[16]

Missing the Target

But this statistical success by no means suggests that target-date funds are free from peril. Indeed, because they have grown in popularity so quickly, their flaws may both be still hidden and when manifest, likely to affect large numbers of ordinary investors disproportionately.

A few early problems crept to the surface in the aftermath of the 2008 financial crisis.[17] If this were a Hollywood horror film, our scene would open in an ominously quiet and dark apartment. Down a long corridor sits the front door, at the base littered with an unremarkable pile of junk mail. The rattle of a key in the lock and a blithe humming announces the arrival of our silver-haired protagonist. Pushing the door open, he juggles his keys and latte in one hand as he crouches to sweep up the junk mail with the other. But one letter in particular catches his eye, and he slices it open with his key. With an insouciant sip of his drink, he pauses to peruse the document within.

The humming then stops, swallowed by a sharp gasp. The latte crashes to the floor, leaving a splash highly evocative of blood spatter. And our hero produces a soul-piercing howl. The camera pans down to follow the pages he has dropped as they float to the floor. They come to rest in a gory puddle of coffee and soy milk. Amid the sounds of our hero's gulping sobs—and just before the coffee soaks through the carpet—we catch a glimpse of the monthly performance report of his 401(k) account, dated October 2008. Crimson figures announce the fiscal bloodbath: minus 40 percent! Fade to black.

Now, of course, no one should be surprised that investors lost money in September 2008—when markets fall off cliffs, money gets lost. But the hero of our story, and lots of people in real life, had some reason to expect otherwise. They were investors in target-date funds. And not just any target date funds; funds with imminent target dates. As the *New York Times* reported: "People in their 60s and late 50s with funds dated 2010 and 2015 were flabbergasted that their accounts had lost a quarter of their value, on average, as calculated by Morningstar, the fund research service."[18] Such a collapse might, indeed, have been surprising.

A fund just a mere two years away from its target date ought to have almost completed its glide path. And a fund that had shifted almost entirely away from risky equities and into safer fixed-income investments should have been largely insulated from the turmoil of 2008's collapsing stock markets. So, what could account for these precipitous failures on the eve of the target date? Wasn't the whole idea of these funds that they would, by this point, have transitioned automatically to safer investments?

The *Times* noted both the explanation and a further curiosity: "More surprising was that these funds typically had about half their holdings in stocks, and most of them did not significantly reduce that percentage until the investors were in their 70s or older."[19] These vertiginously high levels of equity investments certainly explain how the funds manage to lose such huge amounts. But what could possibly account for such a dysfunctional glide path? These target-date funds did not appear to glide in for a smooth landing; they seemed instead to crash into a mountainside. And for investors two years away from their retirement, losing a quarter of their life's savings was catastrophic. All of a sudden, retirement for many investors just glided off into the sunset.

Explanations or Exonerations

A variety of explanations can account for these unexpectedly aggressive target-date funds, some benign, some malignant. Let's begin with the exculpatory stories.

Consider what it means to retire as an American today. The average age at which Americans retire is now sixty-two years, having crept up from fifty-nine years over the past decade. But what has changed more dramatically in recent years is not the age at which Americans stop working but the age at which Americans stop living. In just the past generation, the life expectancy of Americans has lengthened by almost a decade. So, the average person who retires at sixty-two today is expected to live more than another two decades.

More specifically, sixty-two-year-old men in this country have another 19.81 years of life expectancy; women of that age have another 22.65 years of life expectancy.[20] This two-decade period is how long the average American is going to have to live without receiving additional income from salary. Bridging this lengthening retirement highlights the difference between target-date funds whose target is to get investors *to* the date versus those whose target is to get investors *through* that date.

"To" Funds

Let us imagine what might happen, first, with a strictly construed target-date fund—that is, a target-date fund that attempts to carry its investors only *to* their retirement date. The glide path of such a fund would, upon reaching the target year, have leveled off into a safe, flat line of cash or cashlike investments, such as money market funds. All traces of investment—and its attendant risks—would be gone. The fund itself would then just be an inconvenient checking account. In essence, the fund's managers would be saying to their investors, "Congratulations on completing your career; collect your gold watch and come get your cash— we're done here."

That approach might be prudent or even appealing in a world in which inves- tors tended to live for just another few years after retiring. They could collect their lump sum, book a few cruises, and enjoy their rewards.

"Through" Funds

When people have twenty years to live, though, a stagnant wad of cash is not going to get the job done. Even those who have amassed relatively large war chests are unlikely to be able to dig into them for such a long time. Instead, prudent investors—and prudent portfolio managers of target-date funds—may conclude that generating the assets a retiree will need to pay for two decades of retire- ment requires more. More investing, to be precise. A target-date fund might thus attempt to carry its investors *through* their retirement date and closer toward the real finishing line. For those funds, a more appropriate glide path is one that main- tains a more aggressive position in equities, even through the date in the name of the fund.

So, were you retiring in 2010 but planning to live until 2030? In 2008, you might very well have needed a fund that still held a sizable position in equities to generate enough investment returns to bridge that lengthy gap. But if a calamity does strike equity investments, as happened in 2008, the fund will understand- ably suffer daunting losses. This explanation may not do much to calm the horror of those who faced enormous losses on the cusp of their retirement, but it is at least innocent and well intentioned.

The moral of this story is that investors must pay close attention to whether their target-date funds are *to* or *through* funds—their glide-path charts should reveal the answer.[21] Of course, that degree of attentiveness is a lot to ask of some inves- tors. Many investors may not realize that glide paths differ across different fund families, nor may they be fluent in deciphering those unfamiliar glide-path charts. So, once again we reprise our Easterbrook versus Posner disagreement about the capabilities of the investing public: Easterbrook's economic model suggests that investors know perfectly well what their glide paths will be, or should neverthe-less be charged with that knowledge; Posner's model is far less sanguine.

Consider again for whom target-date funds are intended: investors who have specifically selected a device that handles the more challenging aspects of invest-ing. For that population, a glide path may be an impenetrable disclosure device. And once we have encouraged, enticed, or even defaulted investors into funds that they can set and forget, it seems cheeky, at best, to demand they conduct a sophisticated analysis of the variable asset-allocation models over forty-year time horizons. Investors who are comfortable calibrating optimal risk settings decades into the future probably do not need a target-date fund. A professional chef doesn't need a Ronco rotisserie; those of us who do will be unhappy to find a lump of scorched brisket spinning around in it. And we're unlikely to be com-forted to hear that we should have consulted charts somewhere in the manual.

One solution to this problem is for target-date funds to standardize their glide paths.[22] Freedom-loving capitalists everywhere do not, in general, like to be told to standardize things; that edict smacks of lockstep regulation, while nonstan-dardized innovation is the free-market way. Although regulators such as the SEC could impose standardization externally, so too could the industry itself. Consider the status of target-date funds: the federal government has blessed them as QDIAs and, as defaults, they receive huge streams of money from the most unsophisticated investors. Tying a modest dose of investor protection to that default status would not be an unfair bargain nor a crushing burden.

Misbalancing Fund Portfolios Toward Higher Fees

Now, let us consider a less charitable interpretation of why target-date funds per-formed so badly in the 2008 crisis. What's another reason a fund's adviser might have kept a disproportionately high level of the fund's assets invested in equities? Because doing so is more financially lucrative for the manager. Let's see how.

First, let us recall how beneficial the inflow of new assets is to investment advis-ers, particularly through a spigot that investors tend not to shut off.

Second, let us note again the underlying funds in which our target-date funds are investing. With our Vanguard example, we saw that they can be broad-based equity or bond funds. With Fidelity, they also include another score of more spe-cialized funds. But one thing that those underlying funds almost always have in common is that they are funds managed by the same investment adviser. So, our Vanguard target-date fund invests in four underlying Vanguard equity and bond funds; and the Fidelity target-date fund invests in almost two dozen other Fidelity funds.

Those investment advisers could thus be generating advisory fees at two levels: from investors in their target-date fund and from investors in their underlying funds.

This structure may be understandable and predictable, but it is by no means necessary. An adviser could create a target-date fund and then go hunting for the very best funds in the world to add to its portfolio, irrespective of who those funds' advisers might be. This best-of-breed approach would be ideal for investors, since they could find all-star investment options in one shop. But we should not be surprised that advisers tend to prefer keeping the assets—and thus the fees—all in the family.

Now, let us note the well-worn fact that different funds charge different fees. More pertinently, equity funds and bond funds charge different fees. Guess which ones charge more? In 2008, the average equity fund charged 83 basis points; the average bond fund charged 61 basis points.[23] A target-date fund that kept more of its assets in equities than in bonds would, therefore, generate more revenue in advisory fees. An adviser would not necessarily have to violate a stated investment policy to reach this goal; the adviser could simply announce a glide path that is particularly aggressive and thus more inclined to hold greater amounts of equities. Loyally following an overaggressive glide path would not violate the adviser's disclosure documents. A manager can, therefore, overweight equities either by ignoring a prudent glide path or by adopting an imprudent one.

Risks Yet to Mature

The 2008 crash may have provoked target-date funds to bite their investors but perhaps, like dogs, every financial innovation should be allowed one bite. Perhaps, too, we might assume that the spate of congressional hearings, regulatory inquiries, and associated hand-wringing that followed the alarming performance of some target-date funds has effectively mitigated the worst of their nefarious management. But we should not.

Even if the mistakes or missteps of 2008 never haunt us again, target-date funds still carry future risks that accompany their manifold benefits. At least three other potential problems should make us cautious about them.

Learned Docility

Driverless cars, we are told, are our inescapable destiny. Let us consider, for a moment, their blend of risk and reward. Cars in America already have rear-cameras, blind-spot alerts, and self-parking ability; once we evict gormless humans from the driver's seat, we can also look forward to smoothly flowing, rationally ordered, accident-less traffic. The benefits of these innovations are Stepfordian wonders! But will they not just as surely bring their own detriments?

Technology that infantilizes its users carries the potential to incapacitate those users. Teenagers today might still enjoy sporting the mechanic's uniform of white tee-shirt and blue jeans as they did in the 1960s, but very few have any idea what to do when the central processing unit under the hood of their cars malfunctions. When was the last time anybody fixed a television or memorized a telephone number? Matriculating high-schoolers can barely write with a pen anymore.

If target-date funds sufficiently lull an entire generation of investors into not having to worry about how markets work, then many investors may not bother to learn. The sales pitch for these funds is, in essence, "We know you lot are awful at managing money—just trust us and we'll take care of everything." But we've known for a long time that doling out tasty fillets instead of teaching people how to fish isn't the wisest of policies. One cannot simply throw fish at the problem. Lobotomizing our investing public may thus expose unsophisticated customers to the abuses of ill-intentioned advisers.

If the average number of trades in a Vanguard account has dropped to one per year, then we need to be worried.[24] Keeping unnecessary churning in retirement accounts to a minimum is a lovely goal, but an average of one trade per year is evidence that lots of people are close to sleep. And one trade is the *average*; for every hyperactive, pajama-clad day trader clicking through a hundred moves in his 401(k) plan, we have ninety-nine people doing absolute nothing in their accounts. We should be wary of any policy prescription that sounds like, "Just take this little pill and go to sleep."

Dangerous Admixtures

Another problem with target-date funds is that they are intended to serve as a complete portfolio for their investors. But surely that's a convenience, not a problem, isn't it? Keeping every penny in a single fund sounds far simpler than watching over a brood of investments. Indeed, it might be—if a single adviser could be trusted and if investors had the requisite discipline.

When we diversify our investments, we do so to reduce the risk of our exposure to failing enterprises. But not only can stocks and bonds fail; so, too, can investment advisers. If we place every penny we own into a single mutual fund, we will be devastated if that fund turns out to be, for instance, the Reserve Primary Fund. Sure, that fund ended up losing only a little after breaking the buck—but its failure illustrates the risk. And litigation froze the fund for over a year.

For those investors disciplined enough to pour their entire savings into a single target-date fund, yes, this attribute is convenient. But many investors today have some of their savings in a target-date fund and the rest in an incoherent mess of other funds. Target-date funds, though, are meant to act like multivitamins: a single pill with carefully measured doses of all the underlying investments. When people pair a multivitamin with doses of other medicaments, they risk dangerous overdoses.

What If Bonds Are Not Safe?

A third potential issue is that the entire theoretical foundation of target-date funds may rest on a dangerous fault line. The premise is that bonds are safe. Glide paths move investors away from "risky" equities to "safe" debt. And if debt is safe, then that's great. But what if debt isn't safe?[25]

What if we have just enjoyed a long, bullish phase for debt instruments? If a bearish correction, or a black swan,[26] or some other animal unfriendly to investors strikes fixed-income investments, then target-date funds could be savaged. And, ironically, the longer the debt appears safe, the more complacent investors will become. And the more damaging any eventual reckoning will be. Plenty of sophisticated investors are skeptical of the enduring safety of bonds, so the warnings are already in the public domain.

"Solving" our reliance on debt instruments as safe harbors is not going to be easy. Much of our investing infrastructure—including almost all target-date funds—is built on this idea. Individual investors are not, of course, able to alter the glide path of target-date funds, but their choices can influence what advisers offer. In this, as in so much of what can potentially go wrong with investing, the answer may be more enlightened vigilance.

The words of Ron Popeil—or perhaps his legal team—in the owner's manual for his rotisserie offer wisdom for investors everywhere: "Please don't take 'Set It and Forget it'® literally. Always use caution and check on your Rotisserie from time to time."[27]

12

EXCHANGE-TRADED FUNDS

Many things going on in exchange traded funds are bordering on insanity.

—John C. Bogle, *Founder, The Vanguard Group, 2007*

On January 22, 1993, the investment adviser State Street Global Advisors introduced a new investment product: something very like a mutual fund, with all its diversification and ease of redemption, but also with a few striking differences.[1] They called their offering a Standard & Poor's Depositary Receipts fund and claimed that it offered their investors exposure to the S&P 500 index, just like a regular index mutual fund. But that is where the similarity to mutual funds ended.

The most notable differences begin with where these new shares appeared, which was on the floor of the American Stock Exchange. Investors in mutual funds can buy shares directly from the investment adviser, through a brokerage firm, through a 401(k) account or IRA, or via any number of other channels. But for all their ubiquity in our financial system, the one place shares of mutual funds do not haunt is a stock market. Yet, here were these new shares of an instrument that purported to be just like a mutual fund and the shares were listed on a stock exchange. And, like everything else listed on an exchange, they traded.

State Street Global Advisors called their new invention an *exchange-traded fund*, or ETF. The ETF lays claim to many benefits over a regular mutual fund, but its chief attribute is the one captured in its name: the fact that its shares can be traded on an exchange, just like ordinary stock. That characteristic means that there is a different pricing scheme from that of regular mutual funds. Rather than being priced once a day, after the 4:00 P.M. close of markets, ETFs instead trade on stock exchanges all day long.

Recall that one of the oldest and oddest vestigial traits of mutual funds is the way they are priced: once a day, and no more. So, no matter how much the stock market might oscillate all day long, mutual funds wait for the markets to close, then publish a single price at which all investors may buy and redeem fund shares. How un-American! Our financial system has in recent years relentlessly shaved the time between stock trades from seconds to microseconds to milliseconds, but not for mutual funds. For mutual funds, the minimum delay now—as it was in 1940—is twenty-four hours. How positively prehistoric. Or, perhaps, how remarkably prudent.[2]

Though exchange tradability is a feature that certainly gives ETFs greater flexibility and precision than mutual funds, one must wonder of how much use it is to someone planning to save for years, or decades, ahead. Nobody celebrates the minute at which the *Mayflower* departed Rotherhithe or arrived in America. Indeed, some observers believe that, far from an improvement, exchange tradability is actually a detriment to ordinary investors. Hyper-tradability might tempt investors to day-trade, with all the predictably disastrous results that accompany pajama-clad financial decisions.[3]

The structure that allows ETFs to trade more quickly does, however, imbue them with certain attributes that can be of use to long-term investors. Their potential for low fees and tax advantages, for instance, can make them preferable to mutual funds with similar investment profiles. Indeed, ETFs have been extremely successful new investment instruments, having grown over the past twenty years from nothing to more than $2 trillion.[4]

Much of this explosive growth has come from sophisticated institutional investors, such as hedge funds, rather than from individual investors. And, in many respects, ETFs are to mutual funds as scalpels are to butter knives. In the hands of experts, they can perform with far more precision and efficiency. But in the hands of amateurs, they can slice their holders to bloody ribbons.

Trading Funds on a Stock Exchange

This book's exploration of late trading and market timing began with the unique pricing system that mutual funds use. What was most notable about that pricing system were the striking and clunky historical legacies of the 1940s. With only rudimentary calculating power at their disposal, investment advisers would have found the task of determining the net asset value of a mutual fund almost impossible during the trading day. The constant fluctuation of the value of investments in a fund's portfolio posed an enormous challenge. The mathematics may have been straightforward, but the computational power was absent.

Today, of course, we enjoy computing power in abundance. A five-year-old's flashing sneakers mighty contain a chip powerful enough to handle the calculations. Anyone with a smartphone can track the prices of a fund's portfolio securities as they fluctuate on stock markets. ETFs are, at their heart, an attempt to update mutual funds to the present, when we can easily keep up with all the second-by-second changes in the value of a fund's portfolio holdings. The technical challenges of figuring out what the net asset value of a mutual fund's share is at any given moment is not difficult. And we will soon see just how ETFs have solved that problem. A bigger challenge arises from investments that require more than mere arithmetic.

Illiquid Investments

What if the fund in question, perchance, holds investments for which market quotations are not readily available?[5] These investments might be illiquid securities, for example, or shares in private companies. The process for pricing those investments in a regular mutual fund is often overseen by a committee of the board of trustees, which must determine a fair value, after considering a variety of prudent factors. But such a deliberative process would, of course, be incompatible with a fund that is trading rapidly throughout the business day. How could any group of humans, no matter how brilliant, dedicated, or well compensated, accurately price a piece of real estate every few seconds?

Index Investing

So, the quick and dirty solution for ETFs is to exclude those sorts of investments. Instead, ETFs began—and largely continue—by tracking an index.[6] Indices have a venerable position in American investing, and their importance to mutual funds has already been shown. The discussion of fees in chapter 4 noted that mutual funds typically attempt either to outperform the market or merely to track an index. Funds in the first category are called *actively managed* because their portfolio managers actively buy and sell investments according to their own particular recipes for financial success. Funds in the second category are called *index funds,* and their managers passively follow algorithms that keep pace with particular indices of U.S. or foreign stocks.

What are stock indices? An index is something like a barometer or thermometer, according to your preferred metaphor, that reveals the weather or health of publicly traded companies. The most famous indices are the Dow Jones Industrial Average and the Standard & Poor's 500, and they are regularly reported as a quick way to inform the public about the general performance of our stock markets.

Another metaphor for indices is as grade point averages for the companies they comprise. So, the Dow Jones index mathematically reflects the performance of the thirty stocks it covers. And with five hundred stocks, the S&P 500 is considered by many to be a bellwether for the overall U.S. stock market. Since its predecessor's inception in 1928, this index has risen an average of approximately 10 percent each year. Perhaps not surprisingly, many ordinary investors are content simply to invest their money in a way that tracks one of these major indices. They can do so through index mutual funds and ETFs.

For the operation of ETFs, the most important attribute of a stock index is that the securities in the index carry prices for which market quotations readily exist. Each of the world's major indices does comprise publicly traded securities, though not necessarily ones traded within the United States. In order for ETFs to trade all day long, their users must be able to look up the prices of its index securities at any given instant.

As we delve into the operational mechanics of ETFs, we should try to bear in mind whether these technical innovations succeed in creating a better tool for investment. Of course, a comparative like *better* demands that we know for whom and for what investment purpose these new tools funds are intended. What we may discover is that ETFs are extremely popular and quite suitable for sophisticated institutional investors, such as hedge funds, but perhaps a lot less so for ordinary, individual investors.

How ETFs Work

ETFs are intricate but also very elegant. Certainly the operations of ETFs appear more complicated than those of ordinary mutual funds. But one simple fuel, abundant in our economy, ensures that ETFs run smoothly: human greed. More specifically, ETFs require arbitrage to work properly, and arbitrage runs on the desire by humans to buy low and sell high—quickly, relentlessly.

Let's consider again the chief attributes of an ETF. First, to be exchange tradable, a fund must by definition be able to trade all day long. To do that, we know an ETF must track only securities that are, themselves, publicly traded with regular prices constantly available. Second, if an ETF purports to track an index—as they almost all do—then it must do so accurately. That is, the price of the ETF must reflect the price of its corresponding index at all times, with every blip up or down of that index throughout a volatile day on the market. So, an S&P 500 ETF, for instance, must perform just as the S&P 500 does, minute by minute, second by second.

In practice, however, this requirement for perfection is actually quite difficult to achieve. Like every system, our economic markets suffer from friction, which imposes logistical challenges on any instrument attempting to track another perfectly. Any delay or other impediment will impose a drag on the security that is attempting to mimic another. Since a stock index is simply a conceptual GPA, we cannot invest directly in it. Instead, we must invest in the ETF that attempts to track the index. But if the ETF is slow and fails to keep pace with the index, then like a film with its audio out of sync it will not serve as a compelling facsimile.

The ETF Casino

So, how do ETFs attempt to solve these issues? They use a system that is not at all intuitive. The world of ETFs is similar in many respects to that of mutual funds, but also askew in a few important ways. Investment advisers of ETFs, for instance, are known as *sponsors*. And sponsors launch their ETFs by issuing shares, but in a very different way from mutual funds.

Creation Units

ETF sponsors do not issue individual shares to individual investors, as we have seen with mutual funds. Rather, the sponsor issues only massive blocks—often of 50,000 shares—known as *creation units*. And the only permitted buyers of these creation units are institutional entities that have entered into agreements to become *authorized participants* (APs) in the ETF.[7]

Conceptually, it may be helpful to think of these ETF shares akin to casino chips. That is, they represent monetary value, but they are not money itself. No one in a casino would confuse chips for cash. And although chips can be converted into cash, they are not greenbacks, nor are they legal tender on the street. They are an arbitrary currency that the house has created. And, if it wished to, the house could assign an arbitrary value to its chips—$3.34 per chip, say. Our challenge is to figure out how the value of shares in an ETF maps onto an actual stock index.

If our institutional AP acquires 50,000 shares in an ETF that claims to track the S&P 500 index, the AP will expect the value of those fund shares to mimic what the S&P 500 index is actually doing. If the S&P 500 index rises 2.79 percent on a given day, the ETF shares must do so also. With ETFs, of course, we no longer think in terms of days, we think in terms of seconds. So, if the S&P 500 index ticks up a few basis points at three seconds past 10:02 A.M., the ETF shares must do the same instanter.

Baskets of Index Stocks

Let's return to the initial transaction, in which the AP acquires 50,000 fund shares from the ETF. What wasn't mentioned is what the AP paid for those shares. The answer is not the big wad of cash one might expect but, instead, a basket of shares in the underlying index. Again, if the example ETF is one tracking the S&P 500 index, then the AP must buy its creation units with a big collection of actual shares of companies included in the S&P 500 index.

But now, really, this transaction appears to be some mysterious species of bartering: a basket of stocks for a roll of casino chips? This bizarre back-alley trading doesn't seem to make any sense. Why, for instance, would a large institution bother with this ordeal? Any buyer who can acquire a basket of thousands of stocks that replicate an index obviously has no need of shares in an ETF that is also trying to mimic that index. By assembling the basket, the buyer would have already created its own homemade replica of the index, so why proceed further? Why bother with the hassles and transaction costs of acquiring the ETF shares, which are just an inferior proxy of the index?

And, more pertinently, how does this strange swap constitute a money-making venture, either for the selling ETF or for the buying institutional AP?

The answer to several of these questions is that the AP is not buying the ETF shares for itself. A large financial institution, indeed, is not likely to need these ETF shares. But everything we have seen so far has merely involved the construction of infrastructure behind the scenes between large and sophisticated financial institutions: ETF sponsors and major broker-dealers. If we were discussing the distribution of dollar bills, we would in effect have looked so far only at the U.S. mint's operations; we would still have yet to get to the ATMs and ordinary Americans. The AP in our story buys ETF shares—our casino chips—only to sell to other, individual investors who do need them. Ordinary, average investors who have neither the time nor the resources to acquire the extensive and expensive list of stocks in an entire index.

Inventing a Currency for Retail Investors

So, the business model for the APs in this system is to buy ETF shares wholesale, then to resell them retail. Since these shares must be accurate, the APs cannot mark up the price of fund shares. But they can tack on a surcharge. And since most APs are financial broker-dealers, they are quite accustomed to charging brokerage fees to investors who use their services to buy and sell shares.

The world of investment funds has long existed to capitalize on this proposition. Average investors would like diversity but cannot afford to assemble it by themselves, so they will pay for the convenience and management that accompanies small slices of diverse investment pools, such as mutual funds and now ETFs. But when we've seen this phenomenon before, the fund has sold its shares directly to retail investors. Why do we need the intervention of APs in this new system? We need them because they provide the machinery that powers the second-by-second system to track the index. With a regular mutual fund, the daily pricing system is so slow that the fund itself can manage the process itself at the end of each day. But now that we want to trade shares all day long, we need to harness the expertise of large institutional players familiar with our stock markets.

Consider what might happen if an ETF sold its shares directly to the public. Every second or so, the ETF would have to announce the price of its shares to willing investors. But what if the ETF got sloppy or slow? The price of its shares would start to diverge from the index, and investors would get upset at the inaccuracy. And there would be very little individual investors could do about those inaccuracies. Except, of course, to stop buying ETF shares.

The Power of Arbitrage

But let's see what happens within the system that ETF sponsors have constructed. We now have two currencies that purport to be worth the same amount: the ETF shares and the underlying index. Furthermore, the sponsor of the ETF has contractually obliged itself to treat those two currencies the same.

We saw that the ETF gives APs a creation unit of 50,000 fund shares in exchange for a basket of stocks in the index the ETF tracks. What we did not see, but which is also true, is that the ETF must also honor the transaction in reverse. That is, in exchange for any creation unit of 50,000 ETF shares that an AP may present, the ETF sponsor must return a basket of the index stocks. The sponsor thus stands upon the fulcrum linking the artificial ETF currency and the real stock index. This system that treats fund shares and index stocks as equivalent creates a wonderful opportunity for arbitrage.[8]

Arbitrage carries the whiff of financial speculation and economic carrion. Indeed, arbitrage was a favored tool of everyone's favorite Hungarian currency-destroyer, George Soros.[9] But arbitrage is also capable of creating salutary social effects. Arbitrageurs who buy goods cheaply in one country to sell in another country generate both gains for people who work in the manufacturing country and savings for those who live in the buying country. Indeed, when arbitrage works well, it can be extremely effective at narrowing or even eliminating price discrepancies.

Disciplining Divergence

Let's consider what would happen if shares in an ETF that tracks the S&P 500 began to trade at values higher than the actual stock in the S&P 500. Large financial institutions with the money and technology to act quickly and on a massive scale could buy enormous amounts of the real stocks in the S&P 500 companies. They could then present baskets of those stocks to the ETF sponsor and receive in exchange large blocks of the ETF shares. By then selling those ETF shares on the stock exchange, the financial institution would receive a small profit.

Now consider the opposite, if the ETF shares began to trade for less than the actual S&P 500 stocks. In this scenario, our large financial institutions could buy big blocks of the ETF shares relatively cheaply on the stock exchange. They could then present those ETF shares to the ETF sponsor and receive in exchange baskets of real S&P 500 stocks. By then selling those real S&P 500 stocks on the stock market, they would once again reap a small profit. Here, then, is the second way in which institutional APs can make money by trading in ETF shares. Though the margins from these arbitrage trades may be very slight, they can still be highly profitable. First, an AP can employ leverage to magnify even small gains. Second, APs can use high-frequency trading technology to make these trades every few milliseconds all day long.[10]

But let us also note the external benefits of this arbitrage by the APs. If the ETF shares and S&P 500 shares begin to diverge, institutions will buy the cheaper one and sell the more expensive one. Elementary economics—and demonstrable market forces—teach us that buying tends to raise prices and selling tends to lower them. That is to say, the happy side effect of any arbitrage activity will be to bring the ETF prices back in line with the index. ETFs thus harness the greed of arbitrageurs to provide a highly accurate index fund that can trade reliably all day long.

Tracking Error

The catch, however, is that ETFs are never perfectly accurate. They all suffer from a certain degree of "tracking error" between the price of their shares and the value of the underlying index. Sponsors disclose the extent to which their ETFs diverge from their indices on charts in the prospectuses for ETFs. Interestingly, the tracking errors across different ETFs almost always share a notable trait.

Though we have seen that ETF shares could trade above or below their index, depending on the market forces prevailing at any given second, the tracking error in ETF prospectuses always seems to be an error in the same direction. ETFs tend to err by always being worth a little less than their indices, never by being worth a little more. How odd.[11]

Not really, of course. ETFs suffer from a constant source of friction that pulls their share value down under all market conditions. ETF sponsors, like all advisers to investment funds, impose fees on the assets they manage to enjoy a profitable role as the indispensable intermediary in this system. So, every ETF share ends up being worth just a tiny bit less than the underlying index. ETF sponsors don't gamble in the arbitrage game. They are more like the owners of the casino, making chips and creating the game. They don't look out at the tables and wish they were gambling—they know it's more reliably profitable just to take a small cut of all the action.

This business of being a financial intermediary is not terribly burdensome for the ETF sponsor. Unlike their mutual fund counterparts, they do not need to interact with the investing public, only with a small universe of sophisticated institutions. The process of tracking an index is also almost entirely automated, with computers guiding almost every aspect of the trading, which helps its profitability.

The Benefits of ETFs

But now let us consider what we have wrought. With considerable effort, we have essentially created an instrument identical to an old-fashioned index mutual fund except for the fact that this new ETF can be traded every second of the day. Is exchange-tradability a meaningful benefit?

America would seem to think so, if the economic success of ETFs is our guide. Since that winter morning in 1993, ETFs have enjoyed explosive growth, gobbling up almost $2 trillion in assets today.[12] Surely, these numbers suggest that ETFs are the change we have been waiting for; don't they? Well, let's take a closer look. The standard advice for anyone who is saving for the long term is to buy and hold investments and not to churn through expensive and futile trades. How, then, could it possibly help to have purchased an S&P 500 ETF at 10:02 A.M. versus at 1:53 P.M.? Certainly, one price might be better than the other, particularly if we happen to be talking about a historically volatile day. But over decades? Worrying about second-by-second pricing precision as part of a forty-year investing horizon seems goofy, or at least irrelevant. But some argue that rapid pricing deserves worse than indifference.

Exchange tradability is not just a harmless bell or whistle affixed to an old idea if that exchange tradability provokes harmful behavior. Jack Bogle argues that ETFs appeal to the baser instincts of ordinary investors.[13] If these funds can be traded quickly, he fears, then they will be. Once we move away from the idea that investors, particularly lay investors, are rational actors, we must acknowledge our fallibilities. Presenting investors with instruments that carry the temptation to trade them may be a poor idea. Day trading is not just gambling, it's gambling with a $10 fee on every bet: just like everything else that trades on an exchange, ETF shares carry brokerage commissions.

Is it a good idea to give a student driver a 662 horsepower Ford Mustang GT500? The driver might, of course, use that jet engine to amble along our civic byways prudently. Yet the temptation to depress the pedal and unleash the ponies might be extremely tempting. And the results, of course, would be truly unsavory. So, if ETFs are a tool for expert investors, such as hedge funds hoping to equitize cash or hedge a position, then we might be agnostic. But to the extent they are offered to ordinary investors, we should be skeptics.

So, what other attributes of ETFs might weigh in their favor? The list is quite impressive, but as we'll see, some of these putative benefits come with certain drawbacks, particularly in the hands of amateur investors.

Heightened Liquidity

Perhaps the true superiority of ETFs over mutual funds is not the ability to trade in and out of their shares all day long. Perhaps, instead, it is the ability to redeem ETFs instantly, before bad news strikes.

Certainly, an investor can sell her ETF shares at 10:00 A.M. rather than having to wait until the end of the business day. So, if a few hours are critical in a cratering stock market, then perhaps ETFs do have the advantage. But, of course, both ETFs and mutual funds typically settle on a T+3 schedule, so the seller will probably have to wait a few days for the proceeds to arrive, in either case. And, again, if our focus is on long-term investors who are saving over decades, timing differences of this precision seem largely inapplicable to the broader project.

Fees

One of the strongest arguments in favor of the use of ETFs is their low cost. Like any fund that attempts simply to mimic an index, including index mutual funds, ETFs generally avoid the additional costs of paying human managers to manage the portfolio actively. So, with a plain-vanilla ETF, which tracks a common index, the sponsor should incur and impose comparatively few expenses.

The only daily operations for the ETF sponsor would involve processing the transactions that convert baskets of securities into fund shares and back again. And those trades are almost certainly automated by a computer algorithm. Because almost every ETF tracks an index and does not interact with retail investors, its average expense ratio is far lower than those of average mutual funds. And over long-term, forty-year investment horizons, low fees are perhaps the single most important variable. If an investor could select low-fee ETFs while resisting the temptation to trade them rapidly, then such a portfolio could do very well.[14]

As it happens, one of the larger costs associated with ETFs actually has very little to do with their daily operations. Financial firms do not have to pay much for the computers they use, the electricity they consume, or the Russian Ph.D.s they hire to program their algorithms. What they do have to pay for is the use of an index. The S&P 500 ETF is not owned or operated by Standard & Poor's Financial Services LLC. Rather, State Street Global Advisors sponsors the fund and simply licenses the use of the S&P 500 name. Many investors want to track the S&P 500—no one wants to invest in something called the X&Y 499, even if it happened to be virtually identical.[15]

Name recognition has been important to the success of ETFs. S&P 500 ETFs, in particular, have been highly successful. The biggest ETF, with more than $170 billion in assets under management, is the SPDR ETF that tracks the S&P 500 index. And ETFs sponsored by BlackRock and Vanguard that also track the S&P 500 index are numbers two and eight, respectively, on the list of the ten biggest ETFs.[16]

Securities Lending

ETFs do have an interesting way to offset both tracking error and their operational expenses. Because they receive large baskets of securities from the APs with whom they do business, an ETF carries a massive inventory of securities. These securities need not simply reside in a bank vault somewhere; they can be put to use. By whom?

In our capital markets, sophisticated investors have a regular need to borrow securities and many are willing to pay to do so. Anyone who is bearish on a publicly traded stock, for instance, who believes that the stock is going to decline, and who would like to invest money on that supposition may choose to take a short position. To do so, that investor will need to borrow the stock, often from a lender such as a large investment fund or ETF.

Shorting a stock, like all good investing, involves buying low and selling high. Just not in the usual order. Instead, a covered short involves first borrowing shares of a stock and selling them, then waiting for the price of that stock to fall. If and when it does, the investor can buy new shares at a cheaper price and return them to the lender. So, by selling high, then buying low, an investor can capitalize on the decline in a stock's price.[17]

An ETF sponsor can lend out stocks from its considerable inventory to other market participants who wish to short those stocks. Like any lender, the sponsor can, of course, charge for the loan of these shares. So, investors can short, sponsors can make money, and supposedly everyone can win. But some ETF sponsors have been accused of being remiss in sharing the proceeds from their securities-lending programs with their ETFs for the benefit of investors in those ETFs.[18]

This line of revenue should enable an ETF sponsor to boost their returns, to off-set their management fees, and thereby to minimize any tracking error. Sponsors do have one, somewhat surprisingly principled reason for not reinvesting more of these proceeds into their ETFs. If, perchance, the sponsor boosted the fund by pouring too much money back in, then the shares of the ETF could end up being worth more than the index it is tracking (at least until the difference was eliminated by arbitrage). What an outrage!

Perhaps not for ordinary investors, but many institutional investors could be upset. Any investor who is shorting an ETF is counting on its shares declining in value. If they instead rose because of artificial injections of revenue from the sponsor, the shorter would be furious.[19] This phenomenon—coupled with the economic importance of institutional investors to ETFs—explains why ETF sponsors focus not on juicing their performance but in providing extremely accurate performance.

Tax Treatment

Wherever two or more market participants are gathered, a third is always among them. The U.S. Treasury, of course, inserts itself into our financial transactions to collect taxes.

In their early years, ETFs generated a great deal of early enthusiasm when commentators suspected their unique structure might escape tax liabilities. Because APs trade baskets of securities for fund shares—and do not buy or sell them for cash—some thought the realization event for a tax obligation was absent from the transaction. Upon closer examination, however, the magnitude of the ETF's ability to avoid taxes appears to have been greatly exaggerated. Although ETFs do, on average, carry lower tax burdens than comparable mutual funds, the difference is not quite as attractive as originally thought.[20]

Investing Flexibility

Because shares of ETFs float on stock exchanges, investors can treat them like any other security traded on an exchange. Investors can, if they wish, for example, short an ETF. As we have seen, shorting a stock is a maneuver that attempts to capture gains from the decline in a stock's price. But a critical difference separates long positions from short positions.

If you buy a share of Google for $100 in the hope that it will rise—a long position—you can be mistaken. The stock could fall, perhaps even precipitously. But there is a limit to how badly things can turn out. If Google goes bankrupt, you would lose $100 per share. Gut wrenching, no doubt, but a known and quantifiable risk. If, on the other hand, you took a short position on Google when it was trading for $100, what could be the maximum possible loss? These days, Google is trading for more than $500 per share. The horrible decision to short at $100 would inflict a $400 per share loss. But there is no limit to how much a stock price can rise. The possible loss from a short position is therefore infinite, and potentially catastrophic. And that makes shorting securities far riskier than taking long positions. If we wonder whether ETFs are a reasonable substitute for mutual funds, this difference is important.

A number of ETFs also employ leverage to magnify their gains. Leverage, of course, has the power to magnify losses also, which can make them particularly dangerous for ordinary investors. Leveraged ETFs often advertise their degree of leverage with a multiplier in their name: 2x or 3x, for instance.

Some ETFs also combine leverage with inversions to produce truly bizarre results. In a minus-3x leveraged ETF, for instance, when the index goes down 1 percent, the ETF shares are meant to go up 3 percent. Once again, though, if the index moves in an unfriendly way, investors can be hurt badly and quickly. In this example, if the index rose 1 percent, the ETF shares would drop 3 percent. Leverage does magnify gains, but it also allows investors to damage their savings with bad decisions even more quickly.[21] To smudge things even more, some of these ETFs do not perform as advertised, particularly in volatile markets, producing even more unpredictable results.

Another attribute of exchange-traded securities, such as ETF shares, is that they can be acquired on margin. Margin is essentially another form of leverage, as the margin comes in the form of a loan from the brokerage house. And, once again, leverage such as margin raises the stakes for the investor.

To recapitulate these musings, note that an individual investor could, should she wish, short a leveraged ETF on margin. What a toxic brew! The magnitude of possible losses is enormous, and they could come at high velocity.

In a mutual fund, a dollar invested is certainly a dollar that can be lost. But ETFs permit the stacking of explicit leverage on top of implicit leverage in inherently risky market bets. These sorts of risks are largely antithetical to investors whose avowed goal is to save over many years for their future livelihood.

The Drawbacks of ETFs

We have seen that some of the foregoing benefits of ETFs come with potential detriments in the hands of some investors. ETFs carry an additional set of attributes that may be drawbacks in the hands of most investors.

Tracking Error

Most ETFs suffer from a degree of divergence between the performance of their shares and the performance of the index the ETF is attempting to mimic. This divergence is known as *tracking error*. In ordinary market conditions, tracking error rarely amounts to more than a marginal bookkeeping variance, but in periods of market volatility, it can expand to a significant disparity.

If the Dow Jones index were to fall 300 points in few hours, for instance, the arbitrage mechanism upon which ETFs rely for accuracy can fail. The institutional arbitrageurs who provide the buying and selling pressure that keep ETF shares and indices in line with one another may prefer, in disconcertingly volatile markets, not to buy or sell. When the bottom falls out of the market, many market participants prefer to withdraw from the market and freeze their positions. But ETFs rely upon a constant flow of arbitrage in order to keep their price tied to the index.

An oscillating market with regular ups and downs is good for arbitrage, as it provides the gaps that provide arbitrageurs with opportunities for profit. But a wildly oscillating market is not. Too much volatility frightens investors into holding on to their parachutes and avoiding risk altogether. So, in the moments of greatest market stress, ETFs have a habit of not working the way they should.[22]

Obscure Indices

As we have seen, ETFs like to track indices. But how many indices are there? More than you might think. In addition to classics such as the Dow Jones, the S&P 500, and the Wilshire 5000, there are dozens of others you may not have heard about, focusing on particular regions and even specific countries: for instance, the MSCI EAFE (for stocks in Europe, Australasia, and the Far East), the FTSE Euromid (mid-sized European stocks), and the CAC 40 (forty of the larger French companies). An expansive list of indices might include a few hundred.

But currently there are almost 1,500 ETFs in our market. So, what are the sponsors of these ETFs doing? In some cases, they are duplicating existing ETFs—which is why we have a variety of S&P 500 ETFs. In other cases, the sponsors are creating their own indices. Consider, for example, the HealthShares Dermatology and Wound Care ETF, which closed soon after it began. This ETF purported to track an index of companies in that particular niche. But how many companies might reasonably be included in such an index? Not many. A narrow index contradicts one of the core tenets of ETFs: diversification. When an index is so narrow and specialized, the poor performance of just a few companies can harm the entire ETF.

As ETFs have colonized and exhausted the supply of reasonable indices, they have expanded into unreasonable ones. And those kinds of ETFs are narrow, risky, and poor choices for retail investors.

Actively Managed ETFs

One of the newest developments by sponsors has been the creation of actively managed ETFs. Active management, whether in an ordinary mutual fund or an ETF, is an effort to beat the market. And though advisers are chronically abysmal at accomplishing this feat, they nevertheless are loath to make public what they believe are their magic formulas for doing so. Actively managed ETFs, then, are something of an oxymoron.

That is, they purport to combine the market-beating possibilities of active management, which demands secrecy, with the exchange tradability of ETFs, whose arbitrage requires the disclosure of portfolio holdings. So, the sponsors of these funds do not want to make their recipes public, but APs in ETFs must know what basket of stocks to buy to trade in for ETF shares. How could one possibly buy a basket of stocks when the full contents are not disclosed?

The somewhat discomfiting solution is that these ETFs are almost entirely index, with a Tabasco dash of active management. The sponsor thus asks for a basket that comprises 95 percent shares and 5 percent cash. The sponsor then uses the cash for undisclosed portfolio acquisitions, with the idea being that wise choices will give the ETF a boost over its more pedestrian, fully indexed equivalent.

The SEC—and the investing public—has largely been unimpressed by these innovations.[23] To the extent these ETFs attract retirement savings with their promise of better returns, they may be more useless than silly.[24]

An Overview of ETFs

So, what are ordinary investors to make of ETFs? Their booming assets suggest something of popular endorsement. But their $2 trillion are, to a surprisingly large extent, assets of sophisticated private funds who use ETFs to equitize cash or to hedge against other, short-term market positions. Indeed, such institutional investors account for more than 50 percent of all assets in ETFs.[25]

Amateur investors are at great peril swimming in the same ETF waters as professionals, but with some prudent restraint, anyone can take advantage of the benefits of ETFs. The ETFs do tend to be cheaper than mutual funds, largely because index investing is cheaper than active management, and well-managed ETFs do also enjoy some tax benefits. By choosing from a few responsible ETFs, in lieu of their mutual fund analogs, and treating them as mutual funds by not trading them rapidly, an investor might be financially better off after forty years. The challenge is to avoid the temptation to trade an ETF rapidly or to partake of their more exotic and dangerous variants.

13

MONEY MARKET FUNDS

> But more than five years after the Reserve Primary Fund broke the buck, money market funds have so far been able to block significant changes to the status quo. This is a glaring vulnerability, and it would be unforgivable to fail to address it before post-crisis amnesia sets in completely.
>
> —Timothy Geithner, *Stress Test*, 2014

Imagine you are the mayor of a small town with a curious sinkhole problem. In the middle of your busiest sidewalk, a new hole has opened. The hole isn't terribly large nor particularly lethal, but it does have the nasty habit of swallowing stray pedestrians. While you work to arrange the permits, funds, and contractors necessary to repair the hole, you must choose a temporary measure to protect your citizens from this hazard. As a regulator, do you decide to (a) do nothing or (b) surround the hole with orange cones and yellow tape?

Doing nothing has the virtue of being cheap and easy to administer. You can also justify this choice with a soupçon of neoclassical economic theory: the rational acts of your citizens, whose well-ordered preferences will surely include a desire to preserve themselves from obvious harm, should lead them to skirt the sinkhole.

The other option—of warning citizens with temporary but permeable barriers—is neither free nor foolproof. You will have to pay for the cones and the time of city workers to place them carefully around the sinkhole, and some number of skateboarders and texters is likely to plunge in regardless. You can justify this more cautious approach with a behavioral economic analysis, which attempts to anticipate the cognitive limitations of your more foolish townsfolk and urges measures to preserve them from their worst selves.

Now what about a third option? Option (c) would be to cover the hole with a thin tarpaulin painted to look like a stretch of sidewalk.

But that's preposterous. Disguising the peril as a safe patch of ground is surely the worst possible response. Even leaving the hole gaping would be better—at least some pedestrians might then notice and avoid the danger. No policymaker would go out of his way to deceive people into thinking something that's dangerous is safe. Would they?

In the world of investment funds, the SEC may already have done so. About thirty years ago, federal regulators adopted rules that camouflage some of the risks presented by money market funds.[1] Indeed, the disguise has been sufficiently successful to persuade many Americans that money market funds are as safe as federally insured bank accounts.

The Centrality of Money Market Funds

The SEC granted permission to investment advisers to use special accounting rules that disguise the volatility of money market funds. Those rules helped to suggest that these funds may be sleepy and harmless. By 2008, we had collectively entrusted a record high of nearly $4 trillion to them.[2] Yet, money market funds are—and have always been—investment funds with the same fluctuating portfolios as all the other funds we have explored. And if their portfolios decline, they are perfectly capable of losing money.

In September 2008, we at last fell into the hole. In the midst of an epochal financial crisis, the risks of money market funds became manifest, and their inopportune failure gave our entire economy a life-threatening heart attack. To restart these funds—and to ensure the credit they provided to corporate America began circulating again—the Treasury Department produced an expensive defibrillator. The Temporary Guarantee Program for Money Market Funds guaranteed the share price of all these funds up to $50 billion.[3]

Today, huge numbers of investors still rely on money market funds and invest more than $2.6 trillion in them.[4] The administrators of retirement plans routinely designate money market funds as a default setting in our IRAs and 401(k) accounts. That status as a qualified default—and their use by investment advisers as a cash equivalent—means that these funds often serve as a central waystation through which large volumes of our contributions and exchanges flow.

Indeed, so safe is the reputation of money market funds that many investors may think of them as something contrary to an investment—that is, as a refuge beyond the reach of threatening financial conditions. When storms roil the markets, we may believe that redeeming our mutual fund holdings and moving the savings into a money market fund is as safe as ducking into our own fiscal panic room. But a closer examination of their origin and operations reveals some vulnerabilities. Before we can be so sanguine about treating these funds as our ultimate financial redoubt, we must look closely at their failures and at their alternatives.

Money market funds promise extremely low returns in exchange for what was—until 2008—thought to be equally low risk. The underlying securities in which money market funds invest are among the most highly rated government and corporate debts, which markets and ratings agencies have traditionally considered extremely safe investments.[5] But money market funds teach a crucial lesson that is valuable for the entire American system of capitalism.

When glamorous and dangerous financial instruments such as hedge funds fail in an economic crisis, no one should be terribly surprised. Hedge funds, after all, unabashedly embrace high risk for high return. But when more pedestrian investments fail, we have great cause for alarm. In his memoir of the 2008 financial crisis, former Treasury Secretary Hank Paulson recounts that only when he learned of the failure of a money market fund did he realize we were facing an economic abyss.[6]

The Origin of Money Market Funds

Many ordinary investors believe that their savings in money market accounts are just like deposits in bank accounts: guaranteed some sort of interest rate (even if minimal), federally insured against loss, and safe. They're wrong on all three counts. But the confusion is understandable, perhaps even intentional. The money market industry has worked hard for many years to smudge the distinctions between bank accounts and money market funds.

Though bank accounts have been with us for centuries, the history of money market funds is surprisingly brief. Because they are so simple and unambitious, one might assume they date to the earliest years of collective investment, just as the simplest organisms in the fossil record are the oldest. But, in fact, money market funds originated only in 1971.[7]

At the time, a very important federal rule governed the interest paid on bank accounts. For many years, bankers enjoyed life under the rule—Regulation Q—as it fostered the notion of their lives that Ogden Nash satirized:

> Most bankers dwell in marble halls,
> Which they get to dwell in
> Because they encourage deposits and discourage withdrawals.

Regulation Q, which the Federal Reserve had promulgated pursuant to Section 11 of the Banking Act of 1933, imposed ceilings on both checking and savings accounts. It barred the payment of any interest in checking accounts and authorized the Federal Reserve to determine the interest rates paid by banks in savings accounts. One purpose of this rule was to vitiate the danger of banks from competing with one another by ratcheting up their promised interest rates and then reaching for those high yields by investing deposits recklessly. Some legislators believed that is the behavior that caused a rash of bank failures in the 1930s. By the 1970s, one significant consequence of Regulation Q was that banks could, under certain conditions, pay customers artificially low interest rates while padding their own profits.[8]

Let's consider 1979 for perhaps the starkest example of banks' ability to take advantage of the Regulation Q ceiling. That year, the three-month Treasury bill paid a return greater than 12 percent, but the Federal Reserve never allowed the Regulation Q ceiling to rise above 6 percent. So, by investing their depositors' money in T-bills, banks could collect at 12 percent and pay out only at 6 percent, pocketing the substantial spread in guaranteed profits.

In Charles Dickens's *David Copperfield*, Mr. Micawber offers a very simple formula for contentment: "Annual income twenty pounds, annual expenditure nineteen and six, result happiness." America's banks embraced Micawber's advice, and Regulation Q provided them with a far, far better margin of contentment.

But in a world of choices and a market that is at least moderately efficient, such a precarious arrangement was destined to topple.

In 1970, Bruce R. Bent and Henry B. R. Brown, of the investment advisory firm Reserve Management Company, Inc., launched a new mutual fund that they called the Primary Fund. Their idea was to create a mutual fund that was just as safe as a bank account but that also provided a slightly better return for its investors. The Reserve Primary Fund became the country's first money market fund.

The Safety of Money Market Funds

Because mutual funds are governed by the federal securities laws, but not the federal banking laws, Regulation Q and its limit on interest rates did not apply to the Reserve Primary Fund. Nor did it apply to the several other, similar funds that advisers launched throughout the 1970s. As a family, these money market funds claimed to be as safe as bank accounts but notably more remunerative for their investors. Their interest rates were more attractive than those of bank accounts—and attract they did. Millions of dollars flowed into these new funds.

But were they as safe as bank accounts? In addition to Regulation Q, federal laws impose several other rules on banks, many of which attempt to ensure the safety of deposits. Capital requirements, for instance, force banks to hold a certain percentage of assets in reserve against potential demands from their depositors. But mutual funds are not required to hold anything in reserve, though they are also not leveraged as bank holdings often are. Banks are also required to pay insurance premiums on their deposits to underwrite coverage by the Federal Deposit Insurance Company. But mutual funds do not have to carry that insurance or to pay for it, so their holdings are not covered by it. How, then, could Bent and Brown claim that their Reserve Primary Fund was so safe?

They adopted a policy of assembling the fund's portfolio using some of the safest investments available in our financial markets. A safe investment is, of course, one with low risk. Every risk of an unhappy investment is—like each Russian family—unhappy in its own way. Risk can come from the length of an investment (the longer, the riskier), the nature of the investment (equity is riskier than debt), and the credit-worthiness of the entity issuing the security.

As an initial sorting mechanism, we can roughly divide the world of issuers into the municipal and the corporate—that is, into governments and companies. And within those categories, we can then rate their riskiness relative to one another. Just as credit bureaus like TransUnion, Experian, and Equifax assign each of us individually a FICO score that attempts to assess our personal creditworthiness, so too do the Nationally Recognized Statistical Rating Organizations (better known as the ratings agencies of Standard and Poor's, Moody's, and Fitch) grade the creditworthiness of municipal and corporate issuers.

Sitting at the head of the class is the U.S. government. The ratings agencies almost universally rate U.S. debt as AAA, their highest score, as a reflection of America's economic prowess and excellent history of repaying its debt. But, as every student knows, letter grades can be highly subjective. Indeed, the U.S. grade wobbled a bit in the aftermath of the financial crisis, when Standard and Poor downgraded the United States to AA+ for the first time in history. But America's normally stellar marks can be confirmed by a more objective measurement. The financial markets, which reflect the particularized assessments of millions of separate firms and individuals from around the world, also assess the creditworthiness of issuers. And while the markets can often be wrong, they are rarely susceptible to the jingoism of American exceptionalism. They use a compellingly objective system of their own to assign numerical grades: an interest rate.

In the financial markets today, investors are willing to lend money to the U. S. government in exchange for a very low rate of return; indeed, the lowest of any borrower anywhere. A loan's interest rate is essentially a barometer that reflects how afeard the market is of a particular investment. If we compare two loans identical in duration and size, but differing by the country doing the borrowing, we can see this principle in action. To induce investors to lend it money, the country of Burkina Faso must pay those lenders a far higher interest rate than must the United States. Investors simply will not give their money to a country with a riskier economy without receiving financial compensation to assume that risk. Conversely, the U.S. debt pays a lower interest rate because investors assess the United States to be a safer creditor and more likely to repay the loan.

The same phenomenon applies to corporations. Those companies that the market believes to be more creditworthy—because they are more profitable, more stable, better managed, or more devoted to repaying their debts—will, in general, receive higher credit ratings and pay lower interest rates. But because companies do not have the economic power and stability of sovereign nations, they typically pay a slightly higher interest rate for the money they borrow than countries do. And, indeed, the process repeats itself at the level of individuals: the most creditworthy among us may receive the lowest rates on our mortgages. But individual rates are not nearly as low as those paid by solid countries or corporations.

So, when Bent and Brown went looking to build a portfolio for their money market fund that was both safe and profitable, they sought out the most highly rated corporate issuers. And within that universe, they chose the safest kind of investments—that is, loans that are very short term. Debt always gets repaid before equity, and shorter-term loans are safer than longer-term ones. (If you lent ten dollars to a friend, would you rather try to collect it tomorrow . . . or thirty years from now?)

Why wouldn't a money market fund choose government issuers to be sure the portfolio is truly as safe as possible? Some do. But others recognize that a loan that is almost perfectly safe is also an investment that will pay almost nothing in interest. In order for some funds to compete with bank accounts or other money market funds, they take a modicum of greater risk to generate a higher yield. The "prime" in those funds' names is a term of art in the investment world that indicates the fund invests in corporate, as opposed to governmental, issuers.

As it happens, many of the most highly rated companies in the world borrow, a lot, for very short periods. So, money market funds like the Reserve Primary Fund could use its investors' assets to build a portfolio of safe investments with an attractive yield.

Recall that when the Reserve Primary Fund was in its infancy, banks were enjoying life under the fixed rates and certain profits of Regulation Q. Regulation Q, however, is one of our society's illustrations of how a regulation can boomerang on its beneficiaries. The banking industry, which enjoyed many decades of indolent luxury under the interest-rate ceiling may ultimately have proved too clever for itself. When the Reserve Primary Fund and its fellow money market funds appeared, investors pulled money from bank accounts to invest in the new funds, and banks could not raise their interest rates high enough to stop those investors from leaving.

The Accounting Rules of Money Market Funds

Still, the investment advisers of money market funds thought they could make their new funds even more compelling. The problem with a money market fund, as with all investment funds, is that they don't really look like bank accounts. After all, even a very safe and stable portfolio in an investment fund will nevertheless fluctuate by tiny amounts every day. A bank account doesn't do that. If you put $100 into a bank account (and somehow escape their punitive fees for a small deposit), you will never see less than that amount in your balance. But a $100 investment in even the safest mutual fund may tick up to $100.02 one day and down to $99.99 the next. Such tiny undulations are hardly a big deal, but they are a perpetual reminder that your savings are bobbing around on the potentially volatile waves of the financial markets.

In such a world, there was no escaping the sense that money market funds were not as safe as bank accounts. And that impression was precisely what fund advisers wanted investors to confuse. So advisers—individually at first, then collectively—petitioned the SEC for a special dispensation from ordinary fund accounting rules. As we have seen, a fund must ordinarily mark the value of its portfolio using readily available market quotations.

Consider a simplified money market fund that holds a single $100 dollar IOU, payable in thirty days, from a highly rated company. At the close of each of the intervening days between when the loan was made and when it is to be repaid, the market quotation for such a loan might fluctuate minutely based on factors such as the condition of the borrower's finances and the market's overall health. Those fluctuating prices will, of course, cause our fund's net asset value also to fluctuate.

But, argued the advisers of money market funds, why bother to note these tiny variations? Would it not be so much simpler and tidier to mark the IOU as $100 on every day of its duration? In fact, bargained the advisers, to ensure that these variations are minute, we will promise to construct a portfolio of only the safest loans of the shortest duration to the soundest borrowers. The SEC relented.

The SEC promulgated a new regulation—Rule 2a-7[9]—specifically for money market funds. So long as a fund holds a particularly conservative portfolio (consistent with parameters that constrain the length of the loan and the creditworthiness of the lender), then the fund can drop the usual mark-to-market accounting in favor of the stable NAV of "amortized cost accounting." If something particularly bad happens in the portfolio, the rule provided, an adviser will have to let its investors know. But, in the meantime, investments can be held at a consistent, albeit artificial, dollar amount.

Though this rule change might seem like niggling minutiae of interest only to the green-eyeshade set, it had a profound impact in the real world. A stable dollar value in money market funds then allowed those funds to offer services anathema to ordinary investment funds. Since the assets are stable, there is no fear that someone will withdraw more money than he holds in a fund. Thus investors could, for instance, now write checks on their money market funds and withdraw cash from them using an ATM card. To investors in these funds, such benefits were highly visible and extremely redolent of bank accounts.

The detriments, however, were far less obvious. The removal of the fluctuating NAV eliminated a subtle but constant reminder that these funds were investment funds and they carried the real potential for loss. And though they now looked an awful lot like bank accounts, they most decidedly were not. They did not, after all, carry FDIC insurance. So, in the event of a serious problem, investors would not be made whole. Of course, advisers appreciated not having to pay that insurance; it allowed them to offer yields higher than bank accounts or to pocket the difference. This heady admixture of bankiness without the burdens proved wonderful for money market funds and, of course, their advisers: they drew in billions, then trillions of dollars, much of it from bank accounts.

But by allowing money market funds to use an accounting method that intentionally smoothed over the volatility of their investments, the SEC granted the advisory industry a regulatory subsidy that disguised the danger of these investments. Sooner or later, someone was going to step on this flimsy sheet and fall into the hole beneath.

Breaking the Buck

From time to time, money market funds encountered some difficulties. Even though Rule 2a-7 obliged advisers to invest only in conservative loans, sometimes even those loans can go awry. If the loans were truly riskless, after all, they would pay zero interest; and every loan in the portfolio of a money market fund pays interest.

Rule 2a-7 also requires advisers to monitor the *true NAV*—known as the "shadow NAV"—of their money market funds and to tell the world if this true NAV and the stable NAV ever differ by more than half of 1 percent. When a loan in the fund's portfolio goes bad, the true NAV can drop significantly below the stable NAV. A money market fund whose value falls outside of this margin—and that therefore cannot repay 100 cents on the dollars—is said to have "broken the buck."

In the first thirty-seven years of their existence, only one money market fund did break the buck. This small municipal fund ran into trouble when some of its investments failed, but the loss was minor and the rarity of the event was hailed as proof of the safety of these funds.[10] What many investors did not know was that on more than a dozen occasions, money market funds would have broken the buck but for bailouts by the funds' investment advisers. When portfolio loans went bad and jeopardized a fund's NAV, these advisers poured enough money into the funds to avoid breaking the buck. These near-misses never made headlines, however, and the sense that money market funds were secure persisted. Then something truly awful happened.

The Credit Crisis

In this century's early aughts, Americans soothed their losses from the dotcom implosion by morbidly gorging on mortgages and all manner of financially engineered variations thereon. The feasters-in-chief were large investment banks, which made huge profits on packaging mortgage-backed securities like collateralized debt obligations and CDOs-squared. By 2008, the collapse of our national, real-estate–based Ponzi scheme was manifest to all—though not to our ratings agencies. The credit rating of short-term debt owed by Lehman Brothers, as just one example, was AAA on January 1, 2008. And it stayed at that stratospheric level throughout the mudslide of bad news that slewed down upon our economy in the spring and summer of 2008. In fact, Lehman's paper held a AAA rating all the way to September 14, 2008.

The following day, Lehman filed for bankruptcy.[11]

Mourn as we might the demise of this 158-year-old investment bank, the real relevance of its decline and fall is the money it owed at the time of its death. One chunk of the loans on which Lehman defaulted was the $785 million it had borrowed from a money market fund.[12]

The Market for Commercial Paper

But why would a company with $600 billion in assets need to borrow anything in the first place? As it happens, large businesses regularly take out large short-term loans. But surely enterprises so flush with assets of their own could conjure the money they need from their own coffers? Indeed, they could. But to do so, they would have to guess how much they needed and they might guess wrong.

Consider the treasurer of a large corporation such as Exxon. At the beginning of each month, the treasurer knows that she must have enough cash available at the end of the month to pay the salary of all the company's employees. Last month's payroll was $49 million. So, the treasurer could set aside $49 million of corporate assets and let them sit idle for thirty days. But if there has been any variability in payroll, then a cautious treasurer might set aside a little more, perhaps $55 million. Seems like a prudent choice. So, why don't corporate treasurers do this?

The problem is the *opportunity cost*. From Exxon's perspective, that $55 million could have been put to work during those thirty days. Corporations, like investment funds, use their assets to generate returns. Chief executive officers, like portfolio managers, are not paid to leave money sitting in a bank account. Perhaps the money could have been used to extract more oil and thus to earn higher profits for the company. Investors in Exxon will not be cheered to learn that potential profits went uncollected because of timid cash management.

Happily, the American financial system provides a solution to this problem: the commercial paper market. The money market is a highly liquid pool of money that reputable borrowers can tap for large amounts at cheap prices on short notice. This ready stream of cash makes life for corporate treasurers so much easier by eliminating their need to predict the future. If a corporate treasurer reserves too much corporate money to pay bills, then those assets remain idle and unprofitable; if she reserves too little, she'll have to borrow money in any event. Indeed, for some corporations, the cost of borrowing in the money market is lower than the additional profits they can generate from their assets. With its low costs and high liquidity, the money market lubricates the U.S. economy and allows our corporations to run more efficiently and at a higher tempo.

But from where does all the money in the money market come? From lenders looking to make safe, short-term, low-interest loans. That is, from money market mutual funds, of course. In fact, the $785 million that Lehman Brothers borrowed had been lent by just such a fund: one called the Reserve Primary Fund.

Yes, with a poetic echo rare in the prosaic world of finance, the weak foundations of money market funds failed in the very first of their kind. When Lehman declared bankruptcy, much of its $785 million loan looked like it might have turned to dust and become worthless to the Reserve Primary Fund. On September 15, 2008, that fund managed a total of $62 billion, so even the complete destruction of Lehman's $785 million loan would have constituted a loss of about 1.3 percent of the fund's portfolio.[13] Not much of a hit, one might think, and the NAV of an ordinary mutual fund would simply have ticked down the following day. But $785 million certainly was too large a loss for the fund's adviser to cover out of its own pocket and more than enough to break the buck at that time. Many months later, after the unwinding of Lehman, this loan did generate partial returns to the fund—but only long after its buck was broken.

The Run on Money Market Funds

But in September 2008, the U.S. treasury secretary wasn't getting vertigo at the prospect of a few investors facing a minor haircut. The problem for the Reserve Primary Fund was the implication of its broken buck. First, recall that the special accounting technique of money market funds—amortized cost accounting—had created an artificial sense of certainty for those funds' investors. While ordinary mutual funds have values that float up and down, money market funds have values that are either normal or broken. So, just the incredibly rare announcement that the fund had broken the buck caused alarm. But more damaging was what the announcement triggered—every financier's greatest fear: a run.

In an ordinary mutual fund that has lost 1.3 percent of its NAV, a redeeming investor will receive 98.7 percent of the fund's previous value. But money market funds are different. They promise redemptions of 100 cents on the dollar. So, those investors in the fund who recognized the implications of Lehman's bankruptcy the fastest—sophisticated institutional investors with a close eye on the financial markets—were also the first to redeem their shares in the fund.[14] Really? Why panic over a 1.3 percent loss? First, because they might have to cover that 1.3 percent loss if the fund cannot, and 1.3 percent can be a painful hit if applied to a large enough number. Second, because they know that in a fund that promises 100 cents on the dollar—just as in a bank account—the 1.3 percent loss won't stay that small for long.

What happens to a $785 million loss in a $62 billion fund as the fund shrinks from mass redemptions? As money pours out of the fund, the $785 million loss becomes, relatively, a larger and larger hole in the fund. In a $62 billion fund, $785 million is a 1.3 percent hole; but in a $31 billion fund, it is a 2.5 percent hole. In a $10 billion fund, it is a 7.9 percent hole. In a $1 billion fund, it is a 78.5 percent hole.

Just as investors shoved past Jimmy Stewart in *It's a Wonderful Life* to get to the teller window, what may begin as a minor loss quickly balloons. Eventually, the last investors to redeem will get nothing. Since every investor knows this peril of a run, each is best served by redeeming immediately. Except, of course, that mass redemptions guarantee huge losses for someone. Individual rationality causes collective irrationality. And the problem wouldn't stop with just the Reserve Primary Fund.

After all, investors might fear, perhaps other money market funds held Lehman loans. And with other financial giants cracking under the weight of all that subprime garbage on their books, perhaps another bank would soon declare bankruptcy, triggering a run on any other funds that held its debt. The run on the Reserve Primary Fund threatened to trigger a run on the hundreds of other money market funds.

But this contagion needn't be a calamity, a sober witness might conclude. If calmer heads could prevail, we could simply stop all redemptions and divvy up the losses pro rata. That is, to prevent a run, we could treat money market funds the same way we treat other mutual funds. Ultimately, this is what happened in the Reserve Primary Fund. Except it took complicated, expensive litigation and well over a year to untangle the fund.[15] In the heat of a money market meltdown, Hank Paulson needed quicker solutions.

Systemic Risk

Hank Paulson was not terribly worried about the losses being suffered by either fund investors or fund advisers. Both of those populations, after all, voluntarily chose to hazard their money in risk-bearing investments. For Paulson and our federal regulators, the greater and more sympathetic risk was the existential threat to our broader economy.

When all our money market funds froze their activities during the credit crisis, so as to avoid making any Lehman-like investments, the fount of our money market coughed dry. Then all the ordinary, operating companies in our economy that lustily drank from money market funds found themselves gasping for liquidity at a parched watering hole.

If one cannot easily muster sympathy for Exxon or General Electric, spare a thought for their employees—including the secretaries, security guards, and janitors—whose paychecks were just days away from bouncing. The failure of money market funds very quickly shifted our financial crisis from billionaires losing their bonuses to ordinary workers going without their salaries. That tectonic shift opened the abyss into which Paulson peered with horror.

And it's what prompted him and other financial regulators to enact their billion-dollar program to buttress our money market funds. By guaranteeing these funds up to $50 billion, the Treasury Department threw up a wall of money to ward off additional runs.[16] But levees of cash are not a long-term solution to the vulnerabilities of money market funds.

The Regulatory Response

As America clambered out of the massive crater of the 2008 financial crisis, some contended that there hadn't really been a problem with money market funds. Yes, one had cracked under unusual strain, but it had ultimately lost only a small percentage and everything else had been fine. But those who had stood closest to the brink of the financial apocalypse disagreed.

The SEC's very first set of new rules after the crisis addressed problems with money market funds. In January 2010, the SEC passed new regulations requiring money market funds to hold even shorter-term loans with even higher scores from ratings agencies.[17] To many observers, though, these changes were striking for their lack of ambition and even for their counterproductivity.

First, critics wondered why the SEC was willing to rely on ratings agencies once again. One of the very few problems in the crisis upon which almost all postmortems agreed was that the ratings agencies had been unremitting fiascos.[18] Their inflated ratings on Lehman's loans had been catastrophically inaccurate, to say nothing of their preposterous AAA ratings for much of the subprime sewage. Second, shortening the length of loans may reduce their risk, in general, but shorter loans also come due faster. And, in a crisis, those quicker maturities could accelerate defaults.

Though the fund industry may have been content to accept these minor modifications, many critics wanted more serious changes to money market funds. Some of those critics happened to be the more irredentist members of the banking industry who, ever since the 1970s, have been attempting to recover their Alsace-Lorraine—the deposits they lost to money market funds. The aftermath of the breaking of the buck has featured these two financial elephants—the fund industry and the banking industry—stomping around in a mammoth legislative tussle. Ordinary investors will have to live with their resolution of the matter, and hope not to get crushed beneath their feet.

The biggest issue in the debate has been whether to eliminate the use of Rule 2a-7's special accounting rules. Without amortized cost accounting, funds would have to use a floating NAV, like all other mutual funds. The fund industry protested that a floating NAV would eliminate many conveniences—such as ATM withdrawals and check writing—without offering any corresponding benefits. Under normal circumstances, a floating NAV may not appear to float very much at all because its fluctuations may only rarely amount to more than fraction of a cent.

Banks and other proponents of the floating NAV, on the other hand, contend that the mere fact of occasional changes, even if rare and small, will reinforce the idea that money market funds are not bank accounts, but investments capable of losing money. A floating NAV may also mitigate the threat of a run, inasmuch as every investor will receive a proportional amount of the loss. Running loses its appeal when there is no prize for getting to the fund first.

The SEC's latest decision has been to split money market funds into two categories: institutional and retail. Institutional funds, in which large investors save their money, must use a floating NAV to forestall the threat of runs. Retail funds may retain their amortized cost method of accounting.

Overview

Perhaps the SEC's rules will at last fill this hole in the ground. But the recent history of money market funds should chasten ordinary investors. If these funds are the "safe" ones, the ones held out as the equivalent of cash, and they could fail at such a critical moment, we must always be vigilant. Should we continue to use them? Certainly, inasmuch as they are so central to investing in mutual funds generally and we have little choice.

But there are a few alternatives. Perhaps none that would be a place of perfect safety in a financial Armageddon. But the surest refuge may not be in the world's largest or oldest corporations; it is more likely to be in instruments backed by the full faith and credit of the United States of America. A financial crisis serious enough to ruin the U.S. government will probably raise greater existential concerns than the details of a future retirement. Though that may be a dour way to embrace Treasury bills and the funds that invest in them, we must consider the worst outcomes when we build our castle keep.

PART IV

CURES

Whether in taking out a student loan, buying a house or saving for retirement, people are being asked to make decisions that are difficult even if they have graduate training in finance and economics. Throwing the financially illiterate into that maelstrom is like taking students currently enrolled in driver's education and asking them to compete in the Indianapolis 500.

—Richard H. Thaler, *New York Times*, 2013

So, what are we to do with our system for saving? As a nation, we have arrived at an arrangement that drops individuals into the ocean of global finance and offers them a single raft: the mutual fund. Despite their reputation as simple—even plodding—investments, mutual funds have a tendency to leak our vital monetary sustenance. The leaks can come slowly and steadily, through fees, or more quickly and alarmingly through schemes of unethical advisers.

More recent financial innovations—such as 401(k)s, target-date funds, ETFs, and money market funds—certainly have the potential to plug and even to overcome these leaks. But they carry hazards of their own. Investors need a healthy dose of financial literacy to capitalize on these possible solutions without doing more harm to their personal wealth. Investors also need greater structural clout to offset the economic strength of financial firms with whom they do business, so that the overall wager of our investment system is more balanced.

Indeed, we must consider possible changes that would improve our societal relationship with these funds. The foregoing chapters of this book have foreshadowed aplenty the challenge of improving funds. We have witnessed the enthusiasm and creativity some misbehaving advisers devoted to their creative arsenal of ruses for extracting money from investors. Entrenched institutions will hardly stand aside for reforms that save investors money at the institutions' expense. And even without the opposition of entrenched interests, policies to improve personal wealth and societal security will be complicated and difficult to enact. Still, we must try.

14

A HEALTHIER USE OF MUTUAL FUNDS

> That's one of the strangest ironies of this story: after decades in which the ideology of the Western world was personally and economically individualistic, we've suddenly been hit by a crisis which shows in the starkest terms that whether we like it or not—and there are large parts of it that you would have to be crazy to like—we're all in this together.
> —John Lanchester, *Why Everyone Owes Everyone and No One Can Pay*, 2010

How America saves is a question both personal and political. The personal consequences to each of us of saving enough money—or of falling short—are obvious and direct. No politician or governmental agency will ever care more about our personal finances than we will. Yet if we prove individually hopeless at this project, our collective failure may prove sufficiently calamitous to imperil the national commonwealth.[1] This menace of this risk swells as ten thousand more Americans retire each day.

We as a society have hazarded this peril by experimenting with an unproven means of saving for the future. The extinction of pensions[2] and the rising hegemony of defined-contribution accounts have devolved the responsibility for our future wealth to each of us personally. For the most part, however, we are a nation of investing amateurs. In our atomistic new investing paradigm, some of us may do well; some almost certainly will not.

So, let us confront an important question for the future of our country: if, as many financial experts predict, large numbers of Americans are going to do a poor job of saving, investing, and managing money over the coming decades, what might the failure of our experiment look like?

When millions of senior citizens reach for their savings, only to find their financial cupboard is bare, will our government launch a massive and expensive program to bail out that vulnerable—and politically active—segment of our society? In recent years, many Americans have been astonished by the magnitude of governmental bailouts for powerful financial institutions. Still, those bailouts came anyway. Might a profound failure of our defined-contribution system prompt a similarly expensive, after-the-fact governmental rescue?

Or, on the other hand, will we as a society look upon empty savings accounts the same way we look upon empty bank accounts, empty pockets, and empty hands—by looking away? Life in a fabulously wealthy nation with dramatic wealth inequality, such as the United States, requires lots of looking away. The poor have ever been with us—and those with impoverished savings accounts may soon be, too.

One of those two responses has the virtue of requiring absolutely no preparation, so long as we can tolerate the whimpering poverty of large numbers of our fellow citizens.[3] But that is its only virtue. So, let us prepare instead for the other possibility, in which the deficiencies of our current system ultimately threaten another financial bailout that would draw heavily upon the public fisc.

Many proposals for improving our current system focus on two related ideas: enhancing the default settings for our investments, and increasing the amount we save. These initiatives are linked, and both are commendable.[4] The more prudent the default settings in our individual accounts are, the more money we are likely to save. The more money we can save through those accounts and mutual funds, the greater our buffer against future financial peril. Yet these proposals are incomplete. For even if we do succeed in pouring more money into mutual funds, much of that money will miscarry.

We do not address burglary by filling our safes with more money. We do not fix leaking buckets simply by adding more water. We must make other improvements also.

The Impediments

Though we have explored many faults and foibles of investment funds, two particularly important impediments stand in the way of reforming how we save: the financial literacy of our citizens, and the structural imbalances in our system.

Before we grapple with those problems, let us first acknowledge another powerful, if ironic, barrier to change: the recent rise in our investing wealth. In the half-dozen years following January 2009, when our stock markets had crumpled from the punch of the 2008 financial crisis, the Standard & Poor's 500 index increased by 250 percent. That incredible market rally lifted balances in millions of 401(k)s and IRAs to glorious new heights. And perhaps also ensured that nothing much will be done to improve our system anytime soon.

Individually, when our balances soar in bullish markets, we can very easily assume that our funds are performing beautifully and that we are using them correctly. How could this complacency be wrong—the proof is right there in the profits? We rarely ask, lest we think ourselves too greedy or inadequate, "How much better might we have done?" A rising market can thus hide the blemishes of fund fees and structural defects beneath a soothing compress of investment gains.

Collectively, our political will to change rules or to punish malefactors also tends to dissipate amidst the bonhomie of record highs for the Dow Jones. But as the protagonist of every medieval folk tale and children's story knows, the time to prepare for winter is when the sun is shining.[5]

Financial Literacy

The first impediment to better savings is our own technical inadequacy. Our new paradigm of saving may have appointed Americans to be the chief financial officers of their economic future, but that's a role many may not have wanted, nor one for which many have trained. Whether we care to admit it—and most of us would prefer not to—we must improve our own facility with personal finance. When we discover where to tread and where to avoid, we can improve our ability to enjoy the considerable benefits of mutual funds while shunning their dangers.[6]

So, how can we learn to use mutual funds as prudently as possible?

For an answer, let us look once more to our automotive metaphor. Over the past hundred years, America adapted to a startling new technology completely different in velocity and power from what came before. And the risk of error has been lethal. So, how have we coped with the car?

In all sobriety, we must begin by acknowledging that many of us haven't. Though the fatality rate is far lower than it once was, many, many thousands of Americans still die every year on our roads. When offered the supremely convenient and liberating joys of the automobile, we have demonstrated an impressive tolerance for failure. So, lest anyone assume that Americans simply will not stand for the occasional 401(k) going broke, be warned. We can put up with a lot.

Financial Licenses

So, how have we come to educate ourselves about the prudent use of our new automotive technology? We require lessons and we require licenses. The lessons are both theoretical and practical. New drivers must study the rulebook and perhaps the occasional gruesome video to learn the principles, regulations, and consequences of what they are about to undertake. Beginners must also learn how to use the machines themselves, often under the tutelage of driving instructors. Finally, learners are not legally permitted to take to the roads until they obtain a license by passing tests of written and driving competence.

When it comes to our life savings, on the other hand, we require none of these steps. But, in some measure, we should. For certain investments, I propose a modest licensing regime: we should require individuals who wish to invest savings held in tax-advantaged accounts using investments outside of the default settings to first obtain a license to do so. To obtain the license, individual investors should have to take lessons and to pass a test. Only then should they be permitted to invest outside of the default investments selected by plan administrators and to redirect their investments into riskier funds.

Investors who fail the test or decline to take it can, via those default investments, still enjoy automatic enrollment in an individual account, automatic contributions into that account, and automatic investments into the Department of Labor's Qualified Default Investment Alternatives, such as target-date funds and other broad-based index funds. Indeed, for many investors, such an approach is a comparatively prudent way to husband their savings.

Many questions—and perhaps a few execrations—about this proposal may immediately surge to mind.

The Propriety of Governmental Involvement

First, how dare the government interpose a barrier between a citizen and her own savings? This concern is certainly the most serious, as it raises both principled objections about state involvement and practical concerns about governmental efficacy.

Let's start with the intellectual objection that requiring a license to manage one's own money is an impermissible restraint upon—and perhaps even a governmental taking of—a citizen's private property. The right to squander your own money is God given. Or, at least, your own problem and none of the government's business.

To some extent, this objection is eighty years too late, inasmuch as the Social Security Act was passed in 1935 and already imposes heavy mandates about how we save. But with respect to this proposal specifically, note that the license would not apply to general savings. A person could, under the proposal, do anything whatsoever with the money she brings home after taxes.

Rather, the proposal applies only to funds voluntarily placed into tax-advantaged accounts such as IRAs, 401(k)s, and the other plans that enjoy preferential tax treatment. No one is compelled to participate in these plans. And our government need not offer a tax boon on the savings in those accounts. Americans enjoy many constitutional rights, but the right to save money in a tax-advantaged account is not among them. If our elected representatives, in Congress assembled, choose to stay our sovereign's hand from collecting taxes in certain programs, they could certainly impose requirements on the individuals who choose to participate in those programs.

Indeed, they already do. Citizens who choose to participate in these plans have to abide by numerous rules governing the amount they can contribute, the amount and timing of their withdrawals, their ability to borrow from their own savings, and on and on. As it does in many, many other contexts, our federal government could easily and constitutionally condition our use of these accounts upon our meeting a few other requirements. And those requirements could include our obtaining a financial license.

Consider all the other circumstances in which we require a license: to drive, to fly a plane, to perform a manicure. In some cases, we even require licenses for constitutionally protected behavior such as owning a gun. A license is something our society can and often does require for all manner of behavior.

The justification for governmental involvement in those cases, however, is that those behaviors all involve possible harm to others. And, one might argue, the only harm involved with investing is to the individual who squanders his own money. This libertarian argument is that consenting adults should be free to harm themselves if doing so harms no one else. Squandering your life savings, however, is not just your problem. We have good reason to expect that many Americans will do poorly in our defined contribution system and that large-scale failure will inflict greater demands on societal resources. People with no money of their own will need help from existing governmental programs and may, in a sufficiently dire failure, demand entirely new public bailouts in future.

The costs of supporting those who cannot financially support themselves already fall upon the government, and therefore upon the public at large. And with a failure of our defined contribution system, the burden would increase dramatically. The proposed financial licenses would apply only within existing federal programs and would require citizens to spend no money of their own. The licensing regime would also not apply to the investment options that the Department of Labor allows—and plan administrators select—to serve as default investments.

Still, one might contend, savings are different. Licensing the use of our own property seems like an affront to natural justice and is, perhaps, akin to licensing the right to have children or to get married. The government should abstain from interfering with these sorts of natural rights. As it happens, we do license marriage. But, it's true, we don't require licenses to have babies, even though bad parents can inflict considerable harm upon individuals and society.

Investing in a 401(k) account, however, is not a natural, biological function. Neither is investing generally, but this proposal would not affect investing generally. Under the proposal, citizens would remain free to do anything they wish with their own money that they bring home. This proposal would simply install a turnstile on a government-built path to substantial tax breaks.

Why require the license only for tax-advantaged accounts? Because the nexus between the governmental benefit and the governmental restriction is particularly tight. Because the existence of those tax-advantaged accounts has been a contributing factor in our societal embrace of a system that makes individuals responsible for their own savings. And because those accounts contain many trillions of the dollars that we hope are going to pay for our golden years.

Recall also that this proposal applies only when an individual wishes to depart from default investment settings. So, if an employer defaults its employees into a target-date fund, and the employee is happy with that choice, no license is necessary. If anyone wants to boycott the licensing regime, she can do so—and her money would perform perfectly well in sound default settings.

Notice, though, that a licensing regime on this sort of non-default, free-range investing will also enhance our ability to strengthen the default options. A large number of experts on savings argue that Americans need to invest larger proportions of their salaries in investment funds. Some also argue that those defaults should be made more aggressive in order to build a larger corpus of savings.[7] We can be more adventuresome with our default settings when we know that investors who depart from those settings are financially competent. Or are at least licensed as such.

The Effectiveness of Licensing

Now, we come to a second objection, concerning not the propriety but the efficacy of the proposal: why do we think lessons and licensing would do any good? Notice that this argument (that the proposal is anemic) is in some tension with the first (that the proposal is overbearing). Still, different critics may prefer different criticisms, and bad regulation can be worse than none at all. In any event, lawyers will unabashedly make both arguments.

Let's start with the administrability of lessons and licensing. How could lessons and tests be given to so many millions of Americans? Well, quite easily and cheaply. Employers already interact with their employees to establish these tax-advantaged accounts during the hiring and orientation process for new employees. The only additional step would be for employers also to provide those new employees with a link to a website that administers the requisite lessons and licensing process. Many federal agencies already offer an uncoordinated array of materials on financial literacy. The lessons could be provided through an online process, similar to the highly popular massive open online courses (MOOCs) that many universities already offer to millions of users. Costs of such a regime could be funded either from the government's existing financial literacy budgets or from a financial industry eager for customers to invest in more expensive actively managed funds. Whatever the costs of the program, they would likely be outweighed by the benefits of a more sophisticated investing public making fewer investing errors.

The actual effort to improve Americans' numeracy might be more of a substantive challenge. Financial literacy is a subject in which Americans could certainly stand to improve, even though many books, websites, and video lectures currently abound as resources.[8] As we just noted, major governmental entities already expend public monies on this project. But previous efforts to improve financial literacy have a mixed record, which Richard Thaler summarizes as follows: "Over all, financial education is laudable, but not particularly helpful."[9]

Thaler nevertheless argues for continued efforts and experimentation: "If we try enough approaches, and evaluate what works, we may improve such programs' effectiveness."[10] He and other experts in this field highlight ideas such as "just-in-time education," in which lessons are provided close in time to when people need the information, and the dissemination of simple rules of thumb.

Both such techniques could easily be incorporated into financial lessons conjoined to the process of enrolling in tax-advantaged accounts. The information would be just in time, coming right when the users are about to make their own investment elections. And the information could easily offer rules of thumb about fund decisions. Indeed, Thaler's own examples include a pair: "invest as much as possible in your 401(k) plan" and "save 15 percent of your income."[11] For a universe of people about to invest in mutual funds, many more targeted guidelines could emphasize the benefit of low fees, index investing, and dollar-cost averaging.

We could quibble about the precise content of these lessons, but a curriculum offered to tens of millions of Americans would provide a wonderful new set of data to educators. Different lesson plans could be offered to different populations of investors, and their test results could be analyzed to identify and enhance the most effective teaching materials.[12]

But note another very important effect of a licensing regime: it would serve as a warning signal. To all those investors about to embark on a career of managing their own money, the obligation to take lessons and to pass a test carries an *in terrorem* effect. Licenses act as implicit warnings: what you are about to do is dangerous. Driving, flying planes, owning guns. Conveying a similar cautionary message to investors would, irrespective of the improvement in financial literacy, be a worthwhile lesson to impart.

Moral Hazard, Waived

Finally, let us consider an argument in favor of licensing that may appeal to those who are wary of more governmental involvement in this sphere. Many fiscally conservative commentators oppose bailouts because of fears that they encourage morally hazardous behavior. If the government is going to clean up people's messes, the contention goes, people will have no incentive to avoid making those messes in future. Arguments such as these were made strenuously when we faced our economy-shattering mess in 2008, yet our Department of the Treasury, Federal Reserve, and Congress nevertheless dipped deep into the national treasure chest.[13]

If enough Americans make a mess of their defined contribution accounts, lawmakers may again have to decide whether to use public funds to rescue them. Now, consider those deliberations under our proposed licensing regime. Consider specifically the position of an investor who voluntarily chose to move his investments out of the standard defaults and took the lessons and test he needed to obtain his license to do so. That investor will have a very difficult time arguing that he ought to receive funds from the government for his fully informed and self-inflicted missteps. And his public officials will have a commensurately easier time declining to provide him with ex-post governmental assistance. A licensing regime could thus mitigate moral hazard and serve as a bulwark against future bailouts.

Structural Imbalances in Our Investment System

The new system of investing that America has adopted since the birth of the 401(k) dragoons lay investors into carry daunting new loads. But the investment tools and terrain we offer to those investors suffer from numerous structural imbalances, and the task is sure to challenge a great many individual investors. So, it would seem cheeky at best, and oblivious at worst, to address those problems merely by exhorting investors to pull up their socks by studying harder.

Preparing investors to succeed as best they can is a necessary prophylactic measure, but the system itself must also be improved. We should not only train investors to carry their load but also attempt to lighten their burden. How might we do so?

We can adopt two important measures. First, we can help individuals increase their bargaining power by pooling their economic strength. Second, we can police violations by their investing counterparties—like mutual fund advisers and 401(k) administrators—more aggressively.

Pooling Power

Individuality comes with a price. Not just some vague diminution in civic pride, but a real debit of hard dollars. Advertisements for mutual funds and IRAs may wax poetical about "independence," "control," and the rhetoric of empowerment, but they don't include a stanza about the accompanying price tag. A simple law of economics, however, dictates that sundry individuals possess far less bargaining power and enjoy far fewer economies of scale than does a group of those individuals working together.

As one example, consider the advice—routinely offered to individuals preparing for their retirement—to purchase a deferred annuity from a financial firm. A deferred annuity is a regular stream of payments that the buyer will receive from the time of her retirement until her death. Annuities are intended to ensure that their recipients are never left without any money. The alternative is for an investor to draw down her own savings until her death—but those savings, if mismanaged, might easily run out too soon.

So, for a sample annuity, a sixty-year-old male might pay a lump sum of $10,000 in exchange for monthly payments of $50 for the rest of his life. If he lives the expected 21.44 more years, he will receive 257 of those payments. And 257 payments of $50 amounts to $12,850, which is more than he paid originally. Of course, we would certainly expect his $10,000 to have increased over two decades, even if he had spent chunks of it regularly. But note how the annuity is a bet between the customer and the financial firm.

If the customer dies tomorrow, the firm wins by pocketing the $10,000 and not paying out anything. If the customer lives for forty years, the customer wins by receiving far more than the value of his original $10,000.

But note also what we have done here. An annuity works just like—a pension. So, in the past twenty-five years, we have eliminated many pensions, directed most individuals into accounts of their own, and then suggested that they buy something just like a pension on their own. The only difference, of course, is that the cost of buying these individualized pensions is far, far higher than the cost of buying them in bulk as part of a large group of employees. The whole rigmarole would be ironic if it were not so pernicious.

This phenomenon occurs throughout the landscape of individual investing and corrodes the economic clout of America's citizens. So, even the most brilliant, financially literate geniuses who invest individually in mutual funds are at an economic disadvantage: they must pay higher retail fund fees, their proportional burden is much greater for monitoring the performance or malfeasance of investment advisers, and their complaints can easily be dismissed by advisers and administrators without much consequence.

How can we increase the economic power of individuals in our current system?

Easy: just resurrect the pension. Hmm, no. Pensions have much to recommend them, but many drawbacks, too. Any financial instrument that defines a benefit decades in the future—be it a pension, Social Security, or a guaranteed retirement account[14]—risks promising more than it can pay. And our history is littered with many broken promises: private companies dropped their pensions, and their guarantor, the PBGC, is deep in the red; public pensions are underfunded by more than a trillion dollars; and Social Security is on a path to insolvency. Do those programs provide important benefits? Absolutely, they are vital to millions of Americans. But their resuscitation raises different questions. The policy debate over pensions has largely been overrun by the facts on the ground: employers, public and private, are marching double-time away from them. Any attempt to return to pensions now would surely be quixotic. We must find other ways to give investors more bargaining strength.

I propose that we allow individuals to invest their tax-advantaged savings through the Thrift Savings Plan (TSP). The TSP is the retirement plan that the federal government offers to its employees, and it resembles a very simple 401(k). The TSP menu includes only ten funds, five of which are broad-based index funds and five of which are target-date funds. The plan is modest, prudent, and incredibly cheap. The expense ratio of investing in the TSP is just 2.9 basis points, or

0.029 percent—far less than almost every other mutual fund or ETF in America. Yet the actual investing is done not by the federal government but by BlackRock, the well-known investment adviser. So, those 2.9 basis points are not going to buy some dreaded caricature of government work. The TSP achieves this compelling package through its economies of scale, with 4.6 million participants and more than $400 billion in assets.[15]

But if we open the plan to all, one might worry, wouldn't the TSP be flooded by people clamoring to participate? Perhaps, but surely that would be an indication of the proposal's success. Or perhaps not, as a distressing number of current TSP participants are actively withdrawing their savings to chase promises of better returns in private IRAs. Given the vast superiority of the TSP over those mythical returns, we should hope for enthusiastic participation. As Alicia Munnell, director of Boston College's Center for Retirement Research, warns: "Don't move out. You can't duplicate those fees anyplace else."[16]

An open TSP would provide a retirement plan for many who currently do not have access to one. Individuals who work at small businesses or who are self-employed may be unable to take advantage of a 401(k).[17] Though mutual funds and 401(k)s do have their drawbacks, in a world without pensions, they are a vital tool to which alarming numbers of Americans have no access. For employers, an open TSP would be a welcome boon. Small businesses would be freed from the regulatory and financial burden of offering their own 401(k) plans. Larger businesses, if they wished, could still provide their own plans with matching funds to compete more aggressively for talent in our labor pool.

Perhaps, though, the TSP would be unable to handle such an influx of new participants and money from the private sector. Of course, it could: if you come, they will build it. Recall that the cost of paying for this program, like all other 401(k)s plans, is levied on the participants. The whole appeal of the proposal, though, is that those costs can and would be far lower when the pool of participants is much larger than a single individual or even a large force of employees in a private corporation.

Certainly, the costs of handling private-sector employees might raise the expense ratio of the TSP above 2.9 basis points, and such an increase might aggrieve the federal employees who enjoy those low fees. We could solve that problem in one of two ways. We could either ignore the objection by concluding that a slightly more expensive TSP would still be a valuable governmental program, and federal employees have no vested right to an expense ratio of 2.9 basis points. Or we could establish a parallel TSP for just the new influx of private investors—leaving the current TSP untouched—and levy the higher fees on only the new investors. Again, a new, parallel TSP that is not quite as cheap as the current TSP could, thanks to its national scale, still be far cheaper than current mutual funds, 401(k) options, and multi-employer plans.

We can address an issue affecting broad swaths of the American citizenry using a public structure to aggregate those citizens into more effective and financially powerful groups. The private sector should certainly be able to do something similar to the TSP, but it hasn't. Investment advisers offer rates nothing like that of the TSP to individuals seeking IRAs. And lest we fear an expansion of governmental institutions, we can take some comfort from the support of a proposal to expand the TSP by Republican senator and recent presidential candidate Marco Rubio.[18]

Greater Enforcement

Should we revise the regulations governing mutual funds and 401(k) accounts? Probably. As we've seen in many of the foregoing chapters, a number of the rules in place are perplexing. And some of them are just silly.

For instance, we allow what in other contexts would be derided as kickbacks, so long as the practice is disclosed. But the disclosure can be farcical: fund prospectuses and SAIs now run to dozens or even a hundred pages in length, bloated with regurgitated boilerplate. They are often squirreled away on obscure websites visited by only a handful of investors and understood by fewer.

So, yes, we should probably tinker with many rules governing mutual funds in ways that we have discussed in earlier chapters. But that exercise is technical microsurgery enjoyed and appreciated by only the most devoted fund connoisseurs in legal practice, academia, and regulatory agencies. The average investor is more likely to appreciate—and to benefit from—not a revision to our rules but a greater effort to enforce them.

Our current enforcement efforts come in two dominant strains: misplaced private lawsuits and feeble public ones. Consider, as an example, the fiduciary duty that fund advisers owe to shareholders "with respect to the receipt of compensation for services" under the Investment Company Act of 1940. Our regime allows private plaintiffs, as well as public prosecutors, to bring claims of "excessive fees" against advisers.[19] Several law firms have obliged by filing a steady stream of those cases on behalf of large groups of fund shareholders. Though the settlements and recoveries from those lawsuits are largely confidential, one can assume they are remunerative to the law firms that continue to bring them. These cases have not, however, proved to be very salutary to mutual fund investors for the simple reason that they rarely target the worst offenders.

Law firms tend to bring cases against the biggest mutual fund families with the most investors because the large net asset values in those cases tend to produce larger settlements.[20] But large funds are not the chief perpetrators in charging the highest fees. Rather, small funds with fewer shareholders are among the very worst at charging the most outlandish fees.[21] And even though those kinds of fees can, in the aggregate, affect large numbers of fund investors, law firms have little financial incentive to sue the most egregious advisers. The costs of bringing those lawsuits simply outweigh the potential recoveries. What we need, instead, is a civic-minded plaintiff who could bring those cases without regard for the financial recovery.

As it happens, we have one: it's called the Securities and Exchange Commission. The SEC's purpose is to act in the public's interest, and it staffs an entire Division of Enforcement to bring lawsuits that will protect the public interest. In recent years, though, the SEC has been disappointing on mutual funds. In 2003, state attorneys general, not the SEC, began the investigations that uncovered the widespread abuses of market timing and late trading. And until very recently, the SEC had never brought an excessive fee case.[22]

This lacuna was not simply a matter of benign neglect. Courts noticed, regulators noticed, and, one presumes, so too did the advisers setting those fees. When the private lawsuit *Jones v. Harris* reached the Supreme Court in 2009, the justices asked whether the SEC had ever brought such a suit. The government's advocate offered an awkward and equivocal no.[23] And the implication was clear. How much of a problem could fund fees be if our constable on the beat had never bestirred itself to litigate them?

In 2010, the director of the SEC's Division of Enforcement, Robert Khuzami, attempted to rebut that presumption. He made headlines by testifying before Congress that he had established an initiative to investigate "the extent to which mutual fund advisers charge retail investors excessive fees."[24] Three years later, he left the SEC for a job with a private law firm without ever having brought a case for excessive fees.[25] Five years later, in 2015, the SEC announced a settlement in the first case arising out of this initiative.[26]

Perhaps the SEC's inaction did mean just what the justices implied: that there is no problem with fund fees. Such a conclusion contradicts the overwhelming weight of scholarly analysis and Morningstar tables revealing how some funds charge inexplicably higher fees for similar services. A suit by the SEC would not necessarily suggest that fees are a problem affecting all mutual funds or even a substantial portion of the industry. The SEC's suit could and should be brought against outlier advisers that charge the most outrageous fees.

Perhaps the SEC's inaction meant only that the legal standard for proving excessive fees is too cumbersome and unwinnable. After all, no plaintiff has ever prevailed under the *Gartenberg* standard. Possibly, but that position would be remarkably defeatist for a corps of the nation's elite attorneys, particularly given that the Supreme Court recently revised the legal standard with its ruling in *Jones v. Harris*. The SEC has unique abilities to test the new standard and should bring suit to determine the precise contours of the *Jones v. Harris* standard and to challenge truly stratospheric fees.

Unlike the private plaintiffs who have brought suit in the past quarter-century, the SEC can pick a defendant without worrying about the dollars it might win at trial. As a public enforcer, the SEC's lawsuit could benefit millions of fund investors by patrolling the upper bounds of fund fees. The mere presence of an active SEC could ensure greater compliance by financial firms that manage mutual funds.

The Stakes

The U.S. investment industry—and our reliance upon it for saving—is still growing rapidly, so mutual and other investment funds will remain our most important means of saving for the foreseeable future. The importance of mutual funds could spike more dramatically if Social Security were ever privatized. Most serious plans for privatizing Social Security involve moving trillions more dollars into private accounts modeled on 401(k)s. But we must be very sure the foundation of our financial system is solid before we build skyscrapers of personal savings upon it.

Even after digesting the buffet of unsavory financial antics discussed in this book, one might be tempted to conclude that the investment industry could not truly be a source of danger to our civitas. Our system of mutual funds and savings accounts safeguards assets that are simply too important and too heavily regulated.

We need cast our eyes back just a few years for a terrible rebuttal. No asset is more important or valuable to the average American family than its home. Yet the subprime debacle of the new millennium struck directly at the hearthstones of America. It pitted ordinary citizens against slick financial professionals, and the professionals won handily. Financial firms created a catastrophic mess, with many of the slickest absconding with treasure before the system collapsed. And throughout the arc of the fiscal tragedy, home mortgages and the financial firms were heavily regulated—just like mutual funds and their investment advisers.

Still, proposals to improve the way we save now will face the usual barrage of objections.

Surely the problems with mutual funds are just a few churlish quibbles about some isolated incidents. As we have seen throughout this book, some issues were isolated but important others are systemic.

Well, just a few bad apples, then! This tired defense to almost every accusation of wrongdoing tellingly ignores what even one bad apple does to the bunch.

Cassandra! History has traduced this sage daughter of Troy; Cassandra was right.

Objections that the issues here are too small quickly give way to objections that they are too large.

Perhaps there are problems, but we'll never be able to solve them—these complaints are just the rage of dreaming sheep. So, too, was despair about health insurance before the Affordable Care Act, about the cold war before Gorbachev tore down that wall, and about rebuilding Europe before the Marshall Plan. The Marshall Plan, incidentally, cost about $100 billion in today's dollars—just about the same amount we spend on mutual funds each year.[27]

The way we save now is almost certainly going to ensure we will not have enough in future. We must as individuals financially educate ourselves, and we must as a society combine our economic power if we are to safeguard America's commonwealth.

NOTES

Introduction

1. Charles D. Ellis, Alicia H. Munnell, & Andrew D. Eschtruth, *Falling Short: The Coming Retirement Crisis and What To Do About It*, at 1–3 (2014); see also Jeff Madrick, *The Rocky Road to Taking it Easy*, N.Y. Review of Books, Mar.5, 2015 (review of *Falling Short: The Coming Retirement Crisis and What To Do About It* by Charles D. Ellis, Alicia H. Munnell, & Andrew D. Eschtruth).

2. See *Employee Benefit Research Institute, Private-Sector Workers Participating in an Employment-Based Retirement Plan, by Plan Type, 1979–2011 (Among All Workers)*, at www.ebri.org/publications/benfaq/index.cfm?fa=retfaq14.

3. Social Security Administration, *Social Security Basic Facts*, Oct. 13, 2015, at www.ssa.gov/news/press/basicfact.html.

4. Pew Center on the States, *The Trillion Dollar Gap: Underfunded State Retirement Systems and the Road to Reform*, Feb. 2010, at www.pewtrusts.org/en/research-and-analysis/reports/2010/02/10/the-trillion-dollar-gap. See also Pew Center on the States, *The Widening Gap: The Great Recession's Impact on State Pension and Retiree Health Costs*, Apr. 2011, at www.pewtrusts.org/en/research-and-analysis/reports/2011/04/25/the-trillion-dollar-gap-grows-wider.

5. See *Employee Benefit Research Institute, Private-Sector Workers Participating in an Employment-Based Retirement Plan, by Plan Type, 1979–2011 (Among All Workers)*, at www.ebri.org/publications/benfaq/index.cfm?fa=retfaq14.

6. Investment Company Institute, *Trends in Mutual Fund Investing*, July 2015 (reporting total mutual fund assets of $16.28 trillion); see also their *2015 Fact Book*, at www.ici.org/pdf/2014_factbook.pdf [hereafter *2015 Fact Book*].

7. Thomas L. Friedman, *It's a 401(k) World*, N.Y. Times, May 1, 2013, at A25.

8. Ruth Helman, Craig Copeland, & Jack Van Derhei, *The 2015 Retirement Confidence Survey*, Apr. 2015, no. 413, Employee Benefit Research Institute, 13–14, at www.ebri.org/pdf/surveys/rcs/2015/EBRI_IB_413_Apr15_RCS-2015.pdf.

9. U.S. historical climate data for February 2011 in Wisconsin, at www.usclimatedata.com/climate/madison/wisconsin/united-states/uswi0411/2011/2.

10. ESPN game recap, at http://scores.espn.go.com/nfl/recap?gameId=310206009.

11. ESPN game recap, at http://scores.espn.go.com/nfl/recap?gameId=310123003.

12. See, *e.g.*, Kopps Frozen Custard, at www.kopps.com.

13. See, *e.g.*, Monica Davey & Steven Greenhouse, *Angry Demonstrations in Wisconsin as Cuts Loom*, N.Y. Times, Feb. 17, 2011, at A1.

14. See *id.*

15. A. G. Sulzberger, *For Wisconsin Lawmakers, a Hero's Homecoming*, N.Y. Times, March 13, 2011, at A25.

16. Crocker Stephenson, Cary Spivak, & Patrick Marley, *Justices' Feud Gets Physical*, Milwaukee Journal Sentinel, June 25, 2011, at www.jsonline.com/news/statepolitics/124546064. html.

17. Patrick Healy & Alexander Burns, *Walker Ends Run for Presidency as Funds Dry Up*, N.Y. Times, Sept. 22, 2015, at A1; Monica Davey & Richard A. OppelJr., *Wisconsin Budget Would Slash School and Municipal Aid*, N.Y. Times, Mar. 2, 2011, at A16.

18. Wisconsin General Assembly Bill 11, January 2011 Special Session, Feb. 15, 2011, 124, at http://docs.legis.wisconsin.gov/2011/related/proposals/jr1_ab11.pdf.

19. Roger Lowenstein, *The End of Pensions*, N.Y. Times Magazine, Oct. 30, 2005, at 56.

20. Pew Charitable Trusts, *State Credit Ratings from Standard & Poor's, 2001–2014, June 9, 2014*, at www.pewtrusts.org/en/research-and-analysis/blogs/stateline/2014/06/09/sp-ratings-2014; see also Susan Saulny, *Calls for Governor to Quit in Scandal*, N.Y. Times, Dec. 11, 2008, at A1.

21. Pew, *State Credit Ratings.*

22. Pew Charitable Trusts, *Illinois Moves Toward Evidence-based Rainy Day Fund*, Aug. 1, 2014, at www.pewtrusts.org/en/research-and-analysis/analysis/2014/07/illinois-moves-toward-evidence-based-rainy-day-fund. Note also that unrealistic discount rates of 7–8 percent used by state pension plans almost certainly understate the size of the problem significantly. See Robert Novy-Marx & Joshua D. Rauh, *The Liabilities and Risks of State-Sponsored Pension Plans*, 23(4) J. Econ. Perspectives 191 (2009).

23. Monica Davey, *Illinois Supreme Court Rejects Lawmakers' Pension Overhaul*, N.Y. Times, May 9, 2015, at A11.

24. Monique Garcia & Ray Long, *Pensions Up to Court, Rauner Says*, Chicago Tribune, Nov. 21, 2014, at 1.

25. Pew Center on the States, *The Trillion Dollar Gap.*

26. Pew Center on the States, *The Widening Gap*. See also Novy-Marx & Rauh, *Liabilities and Risks* (estimating a gap of more than $3 trillion).

27. Louis Lowenstein, *The Investor's Dilemma: How Mutual Funds Are Betraying Your Trust and What to Do About It* (2008).

28. Steven Greenhouse, *Wisconsin's Legacy for Unions*, N.Y. Times, Feb. 23, 2014, at B1.

29. Investment Company Institute, *2015 Fact Book.*

30. Pew, *Trillion Dollar Gap.*

31. See *id.*

32. Centers for Disease Control and Prevention, National Center for Health Statistics, Detailed Tables for the National Vital Statistics Report, Deaths: Final Data for 2013, at www.cdc.gov/nchs/data/nvsr/nvsr64/nvsr64_02.pdf.

33. Jane Austen, *Sense and Sensibility*, ed. Edward Copeland, at 12 (2006).

34. Reed Abelson, *Health Insurance Costs Rising Sharply This Year, Study Shows*, N.Y Times, Sept. 28, 2011, at A1.

35. Micheline Maynard, *United Air Wins Right to Default on Its Pensions*, N.Y Times, May 11, 2005, at A1.

36. For a discussion by U.S. Department of Labor on the benefits of defined benefits and defined contribution plans, see www.dol.gov/ebsa/publications/dbvsdc.htm.

37. Martin Dugard, *The Explorers: A Story of Fearless Outcasts, Blundering Geniuses, and Impossible Success*, at 238 (2014).

38. I.R.C. § 401(k) (2012).

39. NHTSA, National Center for Statistics and Analysis, *Traffic Safety Facts.*

40. See *id.*

41. Bob McTeer, *Who Got My Money*, N.Y. Times, Oct. 22, 2008, at http://economix.blogs.nytimes.com/2008/10/22/who-got-my-money/.

42. See, *e.g.*, Richard M. Phillips, *Mutual Fund Independent Directors: A Model for Corporate America?* Perspectives, Aug. 2003, at 2, 12.

43. Landon Thomas Jr., *Big Fine Over Trader's Mutual-Fund Moves*, N.Y Times, Sept. 4, 2003, at C1.

44. *Mutual Funds Under Investigation*, CNN Money, Sept. 4, 2003, broadcast, at http://money.cnn.com/2003/09/03/news/spitzer_hedgefund.

45. See Complaint, *State of New York v. Canary Capital Partners, LLC, et al.* (N.Y. 2003), at 3 [hereafter Canary Complaint], at www.ag.ny.gov/sites/default/files/press-releases/archived/canary_complaint.pdf.

46. Landon Thomas Jr., Charles V. Bagli, & Leslie Eaton, *A Son of the Ultrawealthy, Caught up in the Pursuit of Profit*, N.Y. Times, Sept. 7, 2003, at 37.

47. Canary Complaint, at 3.

48. See *id.*

49. See *id.*, at 30–32.

50. *Id.*, at 18.

51. See *id.*, at 30–31.

52. Patrick E. McCabe, *The Economics of the Mutual Fund Trading Scandal*, Board of Governors of the Federal Reserve System, Dec. 9, 2008, at www.federalreserve.gov/pubs/feds/2009/200906/200906pap.pdf.

53. Gretchen Morgenson, *Trials, Trials, Trials, and Then What?* N.Y. Times, Jan. 8, 2004, at C1.

54. Stephen Labaton, *S.E.C. Chief Vows to Act on Mutual Funds*, N.Y. Times, Nov. 8, 2003, at C1.

55. Ian McDonald & Tom Lauricella, *Mutual Funds' Pricing Flaw*, Wall Street Journal, Mar. 24, 2004, at C1.

56. Riva D. Atlas, *Mutual Fund Ex-Executive Is Sentenced to Prison*, N.Y. Times, Dec. 18, 2003, at C5.

57. Alliance Capital Management paid $250 million; MFS paid $225 million; Citigroup paid $208 million; AIG paid $126 million; Columbia Management Advisors paid $140 million; and Putnam Investment Management paid $154 million. (McCabe, *Economics of Mutual Fund*, table 2, at 50).

58. Michael Lewis, *The Big Short: Inside the Doomsday Machine* (2011).

59. Investment Company Institute, *2007 Fact Book*, 47th ed. (2007), 7, at www.ici.org/pdf/2007_factbook.pdf.

60. Alicia H. Munnell, *401(k)/IRA Holdings in 2013: An Update from the SCF*, Center for Retirement Research at Boston College, Sept. 2014, at http://crr.bc.edu/wp-content/uploads/2014/09/IB_14-151.pdf; Board of Governors, Federal Reserve System, *2013 Survey of Consumer Finances*, at www.federalreserve.gov/econresdata/scf/scfindex.htm. An individual may, of course, have more than one such account or multiple sources of retirement income.

61. Alyssa Brown, *In U.S., Average Retirement Age Up to 61*, Gallup, May 15, 2013, at www.gallup.com/poll/162560/average-retirement-age.aspx; CDC, *Deaths: Final Data for 2013*.

62. Sandra L. Colby & Jennifer M. Ortman, *The Baby Boomer Cohort in the United States: 2012 to 2060*, U.S. Census Office, May 2014.

63. Illinois State Constitution, Art. XIII, § 5.

64. See the PBGC's public description, at www.pbgc.gov/wr/find-an-insured-pension-plan/pbgc-protects-pensions.html.

65. PBGC, Annual Report, Fiscal Year 2015, Nov. 16, 2015, at 23, at http://www.pbgc.gov/documents/2015-annual-report.pdf.

66. *The Retirement Gamble*, Frontline, Apr. 23, 2013, broadcast (interview with Jack Bogle), at www.pbs.org/wgbh/pages/frontline/business-economy-financial-crisis/retirement-gamble/john-bogle-the-train-wreck-awaiting-american-retirement/.

67. Thomas Piketty, *Capital in the Twenty-First Century* (2014).

68. Investment Company Institute, *2015 Fact Book*, 25, 90–93; see also chap. 6 this volume.

69. 17 C.F.R. § 270.12b-1 (2010): "A registered, open-end management investment company may act as a distributor of securities of which it is the issuer: Provided, That any payments made by such company in connection with such distribution are made pursuant to a written plan describing all material aspects of the proposed financing of distribution."

70. Javier Gil-Bazo & Pablo Ruiz-Verdú, *The Relation Between Price and Performance in the Mutual Fund Industry*, 64 J. Fin. 2153 (2009); Javier Gil-Bazo & Pablo Ruiz-Verdú, *When Cheaper Is Better: Fee Determination in the Market for Equity Mutual Funds*, 67 J. Econ. Behav. & Org. 871 (2008).

71. See, *e.g.*, Richard H. Thaler & Cass Sunstein, *Nudge: Improving Decisions About Health, Wealth, and Happiness* (2009); David Swensen, *Unconventional Success* (2005), at 206, 336–37.

72. See *id*.

73. Richard Thaler, *Misbehaving: The Making of Behavioral Economics* (2015), at 50.

74. Daniel Kahneman, *Thinking, Fast and Slow* (2013).

Chapter 1

1. Jill E. Fisch & Tess Wilkinson-Ryan, *Why Do Retail Investors Make Costly Mistakes? An Experiment on Mutual Fund Choice*, 162 U. Penn. L. Rev. 605 (2014).

2. Investment Company Institute, *2015 Fact Book*, www.icifactbook.org.

3. See *id*.

4. Investment Company Act of 1940, § 3, 15 U.S.C. § 80a-3 (2000).

5. Investment Company Act of 1940, § 5(a)(1), 15 U.S.C. § 80a-5a1 (2000).

6. William Makepeace Thackeray, *Vanity Fair: A Novel Without a Hero*.

7. Charlotte Brontë, *Jane Eyre*.

8. Matthew Fink, *The Rise of Mutual Funds: An Insider's View* (2010).

9. Paul C. Cabot, *The Investment Trust*, Atlantic Monthly, Mar. 1929, quoted in Fink, *Rise of Mutual Funds*, 14.

10. Philip Larkin, "Toads." To shout "get stuffed" or "stuff [something]" is a colloquial imperative expressing disapprobation that has not yet traveled from British English to American English.

11. Mary Williams Walsh, *Pension Funds Wary as Bankrupt City Goes to Trial*, N.Y Times, Mar. 24, 2013, at www.nytimes.com/2013/03/25/business/economy/court-to-decide-on-pensions-in-stockton-calif-bankruptcy.html.

12. Joint Committee on Taxation, General Explanation of the Revenue Act of 1978, Mar. 12, 1979, 25, at https://archive.org/stream/generalexplanati03121979/generalexplanati0312 1979_djvu.txt.

13. *E.g.*, *Scott Tong, Father of Modern 401(k), Says It Fails Many Americans*, Marketplace, June 13, 2013, at www.marketplace.org/2013/06/13/sustainability/consumed/father-modern-401k-says-it-fails-many-americans.

14. See *id*.

15. Marshall E. Blume & Donald B. Keim, *Institutional Investors and Stock Market Liquidity: Trends and Relationships*, Aug. 21, 2012, at http://papers.ssrn.com/sol3/papers.cfm?abstract_id=2147757; see also Elisabeth de Fontenay, *Do the Securities Laws Matter? The Rise of the Leveraged Loan Market*, 39 J. Corp. L. 725, 741 (2014). According to de Fontenay, "Retail investors have been receding to varying degrees in all of the public markets, primarily because their participation is now funneled through intermediaries such as mutual funds and pension funds."

16. Investment Company Institute, *2015 Fact Book*, at www.icifactbook.org.

17. The precise figure, $2,501.63, is the sum of the closing prices of the thirty stocks of the Dow Jones Industrial Average as of Jan. 4, 2016.

18. E*Trade's commission and fee structure, at https://us.etrade.com/e/t/prospectestation/pricing?id=1206010000; TD Ameritrade's commission and fee structure, at www.tdamer-itrade.com/pricing.page.

19. TradeKing's commission and fee structure, at www.tradeking.com/rates.

20. Vanguard Total Stock Market Index Fund, 2014 five-page Summary Prospectus, at www.vanguard.com/pub/Pdf/sp85.pdf; see also its 58-page Statement of Additional Information, at https://personal.vanguard.com/pub/Pdf/sai040.pdf.

21. The specific price, as of Mar. 24, 2015, was $52.78; at https://personal.vanguard.com/us/funds/snapshot?FundId=0085&FundIntExt=INT.

22. Vanguard Statement of Additional Information, at https://personal.vanguard.com/pub/Pdf/sai040.pdf; see also Hussman Funds breakdown of brokerage fees page, at www.hussmanfunds.com/html/trancost.htm.

23. Anthony Trollope, *The Way We Live Now*.

24. See *id*.

25. Will Deener, *Index Investing vs. Active Investing: Which is Safer?* Dallas Morning News, Nov. 23, 2014, at www.dallasnews.com/business/columnists/will-deener/20141123-index-investing-vs.-active-investing-which-is-safer.ece.

26. *E.g., Buttonwood's Notebook, Reliably Unreliable*, The Economist, Dec. 12, 2014, at www.economist.com/blogs/buttonwood/2014/12/picking-funds.

27. Eugene F. Fama & Kenneth R. French, *Luck Versus Skill in the Cross Section of Mutual Fund Returns*, Social Science Research Network, Dec. 14, 2009, at http://ssrn.com/abstract=1356021.

28. Charles Stein, *Fama's Nobel Work Shows Active Managers Fated to Lose*, Bloomberg Business, Oct. 14, 2013, at www.bloomberg.com/news/2013-10-14/fama-s-nobel-work-shows-active-managers-fated-to-lose.html.

29. 17 C.F.R. § 270.22c-2.

30. SEC, guideline advisement, at www.sec.gov/answers/tplus3.htm.

31. FINRA, guideline advisement, at www.finra.org/industry/regulation-t-filings.

32. See Sections 5(a)(1) and 2(a)(32) of the Investment Company Act of 1940 for reference to mutual funds and the requirement that their securities be redeemable.

33. Board of Governors, Federal Reserve System, *Report on the Economic Well-Being of U.S. Households in 2013*, July 2014, at www.federalreserve.gov/econresdata/2013-report-economic-well-being-us-households-201407.pdf.

Chapter 2

1. *Janus Capital Group, Inc. v. First Derivative Traders*, 564 U.S. 135 (2011).

2. U.S. Supreme Court, oral argument of *Janus Capital Group, Inc. v. First Derivative Traders*, transcript, 8, at www.oyez.org/cases/2010-2019/2010/2010_09_525.

3. See *id.*, at 24.

4. Jonathan Swift, *The Examiner, No. XIII, November 2, 1710*, in *The Works of Jonathan Swift* (1824), 3:264–65.

5. Jill E. Fisch & Tess Wilkinson-Ryan, *Why Do Retail Investors Make Costly Mistakes? An Experiment on Mutual Fund Choice*, 162 U. Penn. L. Rev. 605 (2014).

6. CFP Board, at www.cfp.net/.

7. BlackRock, Inc., traded at $11.93 on October 1, 1999 and $369.25 on Feb. 2, 2015, at http://finance.yahoo.com/q/hp?s=BLK+Historical+Prices. The Goldman Sachs Group, Inc., traded at $85.31 on July 3, 2000 and $189.79 on Feb. 2, 2015, at http://finance.yahoo.com/q/hp?s=GS+Historical+Prices.

8. Fidelity Fund Group information, at www.fidelity.com/mutual-funds/overview.

9. Janus Fund Group information, at www.janus.com/retail/funds.

10. Putnam Investments, MFS Investment Management, and Fidelity Investments all maintain headquarters in Boston, Mass.

11. Matthew Fink, *The Rise of Mutual Funds: An Insider's View* (2010).

12. 15 U.S.C. 80a-10(a). Section 10(a) of the Investment Company Act of 1940 prohibits more than 60 percent of a fund's directors from being interested persons of the fund. See also Section 10(b)(2) of the Act, 15 U.S.C. 80a–10(b)(2), requiring, essentially, that independent trustees constitute a majority of a fund's board if the underwriter is an affiliate of the investment adviser; Section 15(f)(1) of the Act, 15 U.S.C. 80a–15(f)(1), providing a safe harbor for the sale of an investment adviser if independent trustees constitute at least 75 percent of a fund's board for at least three years after the assignment of the advisory contract.

13. Lyman Johnson, *A Fresh Look at Director "Independence": Mutual Fund Fee Litigation and Gartenberg at Twenty-Five,* 61 Vand. L. Rev. 497 (2008).

14. Anthony Trollope, *The Way We Live Now.*

15. James Sterngold, *On Board, at a Mutual Fund,* Wall Street Journal, Sept. 3, 2014, at www.wsj.com/articles/on-board-at-a-mutual-fund-1409757187.

16. Robert C. Pozen, *The Mutual Fund Business* (2002).

17. See the SEC's breakdown of what exactly an investment advisor is, at www.sec.gov/investor/pubs/invadvisers.htm.

18. *Janus Capital Group, Inc. v. First Derivative Traders,* 564 U.S. 135 (2011).

19. *In re Steadman Sec. Corp.,* 46 S.E.C. 896, 920 n.81 (1977).

20. See, *e.g.,* Alan R. Palmiter & Ahmed E. Taha, *Star Creation: The Incubation of Mutual Funds,* 62 Vand. L. Rev. 1485, 1488 (2009).

21. See *id.*

22. See *id.* Note, however, that Morningstar uses a fund's track record only when the fund possesses at least one outside investor.

23. John Morley, *The Separation of Funds and Managers: A Theory of Investment Fund Structure and Regulation,* 123 Yale L. J. 1228, 1252 (2014).

24. See Senate Report, 1970, U.S.C.C.A.N., 4897, 4907, interpreted by the 2nd Circuit Court of Appeals in *Gartenberg v. Merrill Lynch Asset Mgmt., Inc.,* 694 F.2d 923, 929 (2d Cir. 1982), to connote the Senate's awareness of "potentially incestuous" behavior.

25. "Nobel Laureate Paul Samuelson realized this more than forty years ago: 'I decided that there was only one place to make money in the mutual fund business—as there is only one place for a temperate man to be in a saloon, behind the bar and not in front of the bar. And I invested in . . . [a] management company.'" John P. Freeman, Stewart L. Brown, & Steve Pomerantz, *Mutual Fund Advisory Fees: New Evidence and a Fair Fiduciary Duty Test,* 61 Okla. L. Rev. 83 (2008).

26. Herman Melville, *Moby-Dick; or, The Whale.*

27. Investment Company Act of 1940 § 36(b), 15 U.S.C. § 80a-35 (2006).

28. U.S. Department of Treasury's educational circular regarding currency circulation, at www.treasury.gov/about/education/Pages/distribution.aspx.

29. As we shall see, distributors and other financial entities facilitate the sale of fund shares to investors, though these intermediaries do not typically take ownership of the shares in these transactions.

30. Kiplinger's Personal Finance Magazine, Mar. 2013, at 2–3.

31. Investment Company Institute, *2015 Fact Book,* at www.icifactbook.org; see SEC, Custody of Funds or Securities of Clients of Investment Advisers, release no. IA-2176, Sept. 24, 2003, at www.sec.gov/rules/final/ia-2176.htm.

32. Robert C. Pozen, *The Mutual Fund Business* (2002).

33. See *id.*

34. Prospectus and SAI of this family of funds, at www.jpmorganfunds.com/cm/Satellite?pagename=jpmfVanityWrapper&UserFriendlyURL=fdocuments.

35. Pozen, *Mutual Fund Business.*

36. SEC, Inspection Report on the Soft Dollar Practices of Broker-Dealers, Investment Advisers and Mutual Funds, Sept. 22, 1998, at www.sec.gov/news/studies/softdolr.htm.

37. Anita K. Krug, *Escaping Entity-Centrism in Financial Services Regulation,* 113 Colum. L. Rev. 2039 (2013).

38. *Janus Capital Group, Inc. v. First Derivative Traders*, 564 U.S. 135 (2011).
39. SEC, Inspection Report on the Soft Dollar Practices of Broker-Dealers, Investment Advisers and Mutual Funds, Sept. 22, 1998, at www.sec.gov/news/studies/softdolr. htm.

Chapter 3

1. See calculations for this figure in chap. 6.
2. John Galsworthy, *The Forsyte Saga* (1922).
3. See, *e.g.*, Javier Gil-Bazo & Pablo Ruiz-Verdú, *The Relation Between Price and Performance in the Mutual Fund Industry*, 64 J. Fin. 2153 (2009).
4. But not quite a full 100 percent increase because of fees.
5. Ron Lieber, *Investment Advice for Small Fry*, N.Y. Times, May 28, 2011, at B1.
6. Victor Fleischer, *Two and Twenty: Taxing Partnership Profits in Private Equity Funds*, 83 N.Y.U. L. Rev. 1, 3 (2008); see also Erik F. Gerding, *Volcker's Covered Funds Rule and Trans-Statutory Cross References: Securities Regulation in the Service of Banking Law*, Aug. 1, 2015, draft article, Social Science Research Network, at http://ssrn.com/abstract=2641545.
7. Nicholas Confessore, Christopher Drew, & Julie Creswell, *Buyout Profits Keep Flowing to Romney*, N.Y. Times, Dec. 19, 2011, at A1.
8. Peter Lattman, *A View Worth $60 Million*, N.Y. Times, Mar. 28, 2013, at B1.
9. See *id.*
10. Christian Ehm Sebastian Müller, & Martin Weber, *When Risk and Return Are Not Enough: The Role of Loss Aversion in Private Investors' Choice of Mutual Fund Fee Structures*, June 17, 2014, Social Science Research Network, at http://ssrn.com/abstract=2252646.
11. See the 2008 Bleacher Report recap of the ups and downs of the baseball careers of these two athletes, at http://bleacherreport.com/articles/81049-sammy-sosa-mark-mcgwire-changed-the-game-for-the-better.
12. John Morley, *The Separation of Funds and Managers: A Theory of Investment Fund Structure and Regulation*, 123 Yale L. J. 1228, 1257 (2014); see also Edwin J. Elton et al., *Incentive Fees and Mutual Funds*, 58 J. Fin. 779, 780–81 (2003).
13. See Joe Sharkey, *The Private Way Around the Checkpoints*, N.Y. Times, Nov. 9, 2010, at B5.
14. For a comprehensive breakdown of the SEC's definition of an accredited investor and, by elimination, a nonaccredited investor, see SEC, *Recommendation of the Investor Advisory Committee: Accredited Investor Definition*, Oct. 9, 2014, at www.sec.gov/spotlight/investor-advisory-committee-2012/investment-advisor-accredited-definition.pdf.
15. John Morley, *Collective Branding and the Origins of Investment Fund Regulation*, 6 Va. L. & Bus. Rev. 341 (2012); John Morley, *The Separation of Funds and Managers: A Theory of Investment Fund Structure and Regulation*, 123 Yale L. J. 1228, 1257 (2014). But see Steven M. Davidoff, *Paradigm Shift: Federal Securities Regulation in the New Millennium*, 2 Brook. J. Corp. Fin. & Com. L. 339 (2008).
16. See the SEC's Form N-1A, at www.sec.gov/about/forms/formn-1a.pdf; see also the SEC's explanation of the form, at www.sec.gov/investment/im-guidance-2014-08.pdf.
17. Kathleen C. Engel & Patricia A. McCoy, *A Tale of Three Markets: The Law & Economics of Predatory Lending*, 80 Tex. L. Rev. 1255 (2002)
18. See *id.*
19. See SEC, *Enhanced Disclosure and New Prospectus Delivery Option for Registered Open-End Management Investment Companies*, release no. IC-28584, Jan. 13, 2009, at www.sec.gov/rules/final/2009/33-8998.pdf.
20. 21 C.F.R. §§ 101.1–101.108 (2013).
21. See J.P. Morgan prospectus disclosure, at www.jpmorganfunds.com/cm/Satellite?pagename=jpmfVanityWrapper&UserFriendlyURL=otherresourcesld&cusip=4812A1845&fileName=PR-LCEABCS.pdf.

22. Anna Bernasek, *What a Difference a Percentage Point Can Make*, N.Y Times, Oct. 7, 2012, at B18.

23. See the Jan. 2, 2015, treasury rate: 2.69%, at www.treasury.gov/resource-center/data-chart-center/interest-rates/Pages/TextView.aspx?data=yieldYear&year=2015.

24. Alan Blinder, *After the Music Stopped: The Financial Crisis, the Response, and the Work Ahead* (2013), 74–75.

25. See the SEC's Form N-1A, at www.sec.gov/about/forms/formn-1a.pdf.

26. See *id.*

27. See, *e.g.*, Nell Minow, *Proxy Reform: The Case for Increased Shareholder Communication*, 17 J. Corp. L. 149 (1991); Nell Minow, *Shareholders, Stakeholders, and Boards of Directors*, 21 Stetson L. Rev. 197 (1991).

28. See the SEC's general information on access to mutual fund information, at www.sec.gov/answers/mfinfo.htm.

29. 17 C.F.R. § 210 (2005).

30. For a breakdown of the brokerage fees paid by the JP Morgan's U.S. Equity Fund of Funds, see part I, p. 47, at www.jpmorganfunds.com/cm/Satellite?pagename=jpmfVanityWrapper &UserFriendlyURL=otherresourcesld&cusip=4812C0506&fileName=SAI-USEQ.pdf.

Chapter 4

1. For Frank Easterbrook's *curriculum vitae*, see www.law.uchicago.edu/node/514/cv; for Richard Posner's, see www.law.uchicago.edu/node/79/cv.

2. For Frank Easterbrook's 7th Circuit biography, see www.fjc.gov/servlet/nGetInfo?jid=67 8&cid=999&ctype=na&instate=na; for Richard Posner's, see www.fjc.gov/servlet/nGetI nfo?jid=1922&cid=999&ctype=na&instate=na.

3. Richard Posner co-founded Lexecon, Inc.; see David Margolick, *The Law: At the Bar*, N.Y. Times, June 17, 1988, at www.nytimes.com/1988/06/17/us/the-law-at-the-bar.html.

4. See, *e.g.*, Robert Hiltonsmith, *The Retirement Savings Drain: The Hidden & Excessive Costs of 401(K)s*, Demos, at www.demos.org/sites/default/files/publications/TheRetirement SavingsDrain-Demos_0.pdf; Gregory Baer & Gary Gensler, *The Great Mutual Fund Trap: An Investment Recovery Plan* (2002); Louis Lowenstein, *The Investor's Dilemma: How Mutual Funds Are Betraying Your Trust and What To Do About It* (2008).

5. Anthony Trollope, *The Way We Live Now*.

6. Charles Dickens, *Bleak House*.

7. 17 C.F.R. § 270.12b-1 (2010).

8. *Jones v. Harris Associates, L.P.*, 04 C 8305 (N.D. Ill. 2007), at https://casetext.com/case/jones-v-harris-associates-lp-4.

9. See John Morley & Quinn Curtis, *An Empirical Study of Mutual Fund Excessive Fee Litigation: Do the Merits Matter?* 30 J. L. Econ. & Org. 275 (2014).

10. *Jones v. Harris Associates L.P.*, 527 F.3d 627, 629 (7th Cir. 2008).

11. See *id.*

12. See, *e.g.*, Richard A. Epstein, *The Neoclassical Economics of Consumer Contracts*, 92 Minn. L. Rev. 803 (2008).

13. See *id.*

14. Richard Posner, *The Economics of Justice* (1983).

15. Richard Posner, *Economic Analysis of Law*, 9th ed. (2014).

16. *Jones v. Harris Associates L.P.*, 527 F.3d 627 (7th Cir. 2008).

17. Federal Rule of Appellate Procedure 35(a).

18. See *id.*

19. *Jones v. Harris Associates L.P.*, 537 F.3d 728, 729 (7th Cir. 2008).

20. Indraneel Sur, *How Far Do Voices Carry: Dissents from Denial of Rehearing En Banc*, 2006 Wis. L. Rev. 1315 (2006).

21. *Jones v. Harris Associates L.P.*, 537 F.3d 728, 730 (7th Cir. 2008).

22. See *id.*

23. Andrew Ross Sorkin, *Too Big to Fail: The Inside Story of How Wall Street and Washington Fought to Save the Financial System—and Themselves* (2010); Henry M. PaulsonJr., *On the Brink: Inside the Race to Stop the Collapse of the Global Financial System* (2013); Timothy Geithner, *Stress Test: Reflections on Financial Crises* (2014).

24. See the SEC's investor bulletin on accredited investors, at www.investor.gov/news-alerts/ investor-bulletins/investor-bulletin-accredited-investors.

25. *Jones v. Harris Associates L.P.*, 537 F.3d 728, 732 (7th Cir. 2008).

26. *Jones v. Harris Associates L.P.*, 527 F.3d 627, 634 (7th Cir. 2008), vacated and remanded, 559 U.S. 335, 130 S. Ct. 1418, 176 L. Ed. 2d 265 (2010).

27. Epstein, *The Neoclassical Economics.*

28. See the SEC's investor bulletin on accredited investors, at www.investor.gov/news-alerts/ investor-bulletins/investor-bulletin-accredited-investors.

29. *Jones v. Harris Associates L.P.*, 537 F.3d 728, 731 (7th Cir. 2008).

30. John Morley & Quinn Curtis, *Taking Exit Rights Seriously: Why Governance and Fee Litigation Don't Work in Mutual Funds*, 120 Yale L. J. 84 (2010).

31. *Jones v. Harris Associates L.P.*, 527 F.3d 627, 634 (7th Cir. 2008), vacated and remanded, 559 U.S. 335, 130 S. Ct. 1418, 176 L. Ed. 2d 265 (2010).

32. In an interesting development, several highly sophisticated and wealthy institutional investors—such as CalPERS and university endowments—have been accused of not understanding the fees they pay to private equity firms that manage money on their behalf. See, *e.g.*, Dan Primack, *CalPERS Still Can't Get Out of Its Way on Private Equity*, Fortune, Sept. 4, 2015, at http://fortune.com/2015/09/04/calpers-still-cant-get-out-of-its-own-way-on-private-equity/; Victor Fleischer, *Stop Universities from Hoarding Money*, N.Y. Times, Aug. 19, 2015, at A23.

33. John P. Freeman & Stewart L. Brown, *Mutual Fund Advisory Fees: The Cost of Conflicts of Interest*, 26 J. Corp. L. 609, 629, & n.93; see also Ruth Simon, *How Funds Get Rich at Your Expense*, Money, Feb. 1995, at 130 (reporting that fund shareholders "pay nearly twice as much as institutional investors for money management").

34. Letter from Erik Sirri, chief economist, SEC, to John C. Bogle, chairman, Vanguard Group, March 23, 1999: "As to your suggestion that the SEC's Chief Economist do a revenue/ cost/profit study, I know I'd be interested, but I don't think the industry would oblige us"; quoted in John P. Freeman, Stewart L. Brown, & Steve Pomerantz, *Mutual Fund Advisory Fees: New Evidence and a Fair Fiduciary Test*, 61 Okla. L. Rev. 83 (2008).

35. John C. Coates & R. Glenn Hubbard, *Competition in the Mutual Fund Industry: Evidence and Implications for Policy*, 33 J. Corp. L. 151 (2007).

36. More Adam Smith, *Theory of Moral Sentiments* (1759) than Adam Smith, *The Wealth of Nations* (1776).

37. James J. Choi et al., *Why Does the Law of One Price Fail? An Experiment on Index Mutual Funds*, 23 Rev. Fin. Stud. 1405 (2010).

38. For a breakdown of U.S. index funds and their expense ratios, see http://money. usnews.com/money/personal-finance/mutual-funds/articles/2015/04/06/ great-index-funds-for-a-dirt-cheap-portfolio.

39. Javier Gil-Bazo & Pablo Ruiz-Verdú, *The Relation Between Price and Performance in the Mutual Fund Industry*, 64 J. Fin. 2153 (2009).

40. Burton G. Malkiel, *You're Paying Too Much for Investment Help*, Wall Street Journal, May 28, 2013, at www.wsj.com/articles/SB10001424127887323475304578502973521526236.

41. Gil-Bazo & Ruiz-Verdú, *The Relation Between Price and Performance.*

42. Jeff Sommer, *A Mutual Fund Master, Too Worried to Rest*, NY. Times, Aug. 12, 2012, at B1.

43. *Jones v. Harris Associates L.P.*, 537 F.3d 728, 733 (7th Cir. 2008).

44. See the Supreme Court's statistics on cases heard per year, at www.supremecourt.gov/faq. aspx#faqgi9.

45. *Jones v. Harris Associates L.P.*, 537 F.3d 728, 733 (7th Cir. 2008).

46. See *id.*; see also brief for John C. Bogle as *amicus curiae* in support of petitioners., *Jones v. Harris Associates L.P.*, June 2009, 556 U.S. 1104 (2009).

47. *Jones v. Harris Associates L.P.*, 559 U.S. 335 (2010).

48. *Jones v. Harris Associates L.P.*, Order No. 07-1624, (7th Cir. August 6, 2015).

49. 17 C.F.R. § 270.12b-1 (2010).

50. Karen Damato, *What Exactly Are 12b-1 Fees, Anyway?* Wall Street Journal, July 6, 2010, at C16.

51. See the ICI's Resource Center on 12b-1 Fees, at www.ici.org/rule12b1fees.

52. See *id.*

53. John P. Freeman, *The Mutual Fund Distribution Expense Mess*, 32 J. Corp. L. 739, 740 (2007).

54. Lori Walsh, *The Costs and Benefits to Fund Shareholders of 12b-1 Plans: An Examination of Fund Flows, Expenses, and Returns*, at www.sec.gov/rules/proposed/s70904/lwalsh042604.pdf.

55. FINRA, press release regarding this prosecution, at www.finra.org/newsroom/2004/fifteen-firms-pay-over-215-million-penalties-settle-sec-and-nasd-breakpoints-charges.

56. Damato, *What Exactly Are 12b-1 Fees.*

57. Kirsten Grind, *SEC Cranks Up Investigation into Fund Firms' Fees*, Wall Street Journal, July 17, 2015, at C1.

58. John Rekenthaler, *About that First Eagle Case*, Morningstar Rekenthaler Report, Sept. 29, 2015, at http://www.morningstar.com/advisor/t/109616718/about-that-first-eagle-case.htm; see also Securities and Exchange Commission, In the Matter of First Eagle Investment Management, LLC, Order Instituting Administrative and Cease-and-Desist Proceedings, no. 3-16823, Sept. 21, 2015.

59. *Jones v. Harris Associates L.P.*, 527 F.3d 627, 635 (7th Cir. 2008), vacated and remanded, 559 U.S. 335, 130 S. Ct. 1418, 176 L. Ed. 2d 265 (2010).

60. See ICI discussion of 12b-1 fee usage, at www.ici.org/rule12b1fees.

61. See ICI's *2015 Investment Company Fact Book*, 92, at https://www.ici.org/pdf/2015_fact-book.pdf; see also the SEC's 2010 release regarding 12b-1 fees and their impact on the industry, at https://www.sec.gov/rules/proposed/2010/33-9128.pdf.

62. Walsh, *The Costs and Benefits.*

63. FINRA, press release.

64. Chris Burritt, *Kellogg Shrinks Cereal Boxes to Add Store Shelf Space*, Bloomberg News, Jan. 26, 2009, at www.bloomberg.com/apps/news?pid=newsarchive&sid=aDXhSA.Cn3a0.

65. William A. Birdthistle, *Compensating Power: An Analysis of Rents and Rewards in the Mutual Fund Industry*, 80 Tul. L. Rev. 1401, 1463 (2006).

66. See the SEC's press release on this issue, at www.sec.gov/news/press/2004-177.htm; see also the corresponding enforcement order, at www.sec.gov/litigation/admin/33-8520.htm.

67. See Jason Zweig, *The Intelligent Investor: Why Funds Should Reward Investors*, Wall Street Journal, June 6, 2015, at B1.

68. Lorne Manly, *How Payola Went Corporate*, N.Y. Times, July 31, 2005, at Sunday Review, 1.

69. See the SEC's explanation of legal shelf space that must be disclosed, at www.sec.gov/news/press/2004-44.htm.

70. SEC, press release, at www.sec.gov/news/press/2004-177.htm; see also the corresponding enforcement order, at www.sec.gov/litigation/admin/33-8520.htm.

71. SEC, press release regarding Morgan Stanley's payment of $50 million to settle a pending SEC action, at www.sec.gov/news/press/2003-159.htm.

72. SEC, press release regarding Ameriprise Financial Services' payment of $30 million to settle SEC revenue sharing investigation, at www.sec.gov/news/press/2005-168.htm.

73. SEC, press release on the Citigroup settlement, at www.sec.gov/news/press/2005-39.htm.

74. SEC, press release on the PIMCO settlement, at www.sec.gov/news/press/2004-130.htm.

75. SEC, press release on the MFS shelf-space settlement, at www.sec.gov/news/press/2004-44.htm.

76. SEC, press release on the MFS market-timing settlement, at www.sec.gov/news/press/2004-14.htm.

77. SEC, press release on corrupted advising, at www.sec.gov/News/PressRelease/Detail/PressRelease/1365171484512.

78. Nathaniel Popper, *JPMorgan to Pay $307 Million for Steering Clients to Own Funds*, N.Y. Times, Dec. 19, 2015, at B3.

79. James B. Stewart, *He Was a JPMorgan Chase Whistle-Blower. Then Came the Blowback*, N.Y. Times, Dec. 11, 2015, at B1.

80. MFS Fund's SAI, at http://mfs.onlineprospectus.net/mfs/MFS_OTC/index.html?open=Statement%20of%20Additional%20Information.

81. See *id.*

82. Leslie P. Norton, *When Fund Companies Pay to Play, So Do You*, Barron's, Apr. 14, 2014, at 30.

83. Gil-Bazo & Ruiz-Verdu, *The Relation between Price and Performance*; Coates & Hubbard, *Competition in the Mutual Fund Industry*; and Burton G. Malkiel, *You're Paying Too Much for Investment Help*, Wall Street Journal, May 29, 2013, at A15.

Chapter 5

1. See, *e.g.*, the movie *Up in the Air* (2009), in which George Clooney, as Ryan Bingham, says: "Our business expense allots forty dollars each for dinner. I plan on grabbing as many miles as I can. . . . I don't spend a nickel, if I can help it, unless it somehow profits my mileage account."

2. John C. Bogle, *The End of 'Soft Dollars?*, 65 Fin. Analysts J. 48 (2009).

3. See *id.*

4. Letter of David Jones & Eric Roiter to Jonathan Katz, SEC Concept Release Comments, release no. IC-26313, March 2, 2004, at www.sec.gov/rules/concept/s72903/fidelity03022004.htm.

5. Robert C. Pozen, *The Mutual Fund Business* (2002).

6. Investment Company Institute, *2015 Fact Book*, at www.icifactbook.org.

7. Vanguard Index Funds Statement of Additional Information, B-43, at https://personal.vanguard.com/pub/Pdf/sai040.pdf.

8. SEC, Inspection Report on the Soft Dollar Practices of Broker-Dealers, Investment Advisers and Mutual Funds, Sept. 22, 1998, at www.sec.gov/news/studies/softdolr.htm.

9. Michael Lewis, *Flash Boys* (2014).

10. SEC, Inspection Report on the Soft Dollar Practices.

11. Michael Lewis, *Liar's Poker* (2010).

12. FINRA, press release regarding charges of favorable coverage in the "Toys R Us" IPO, at www.finra.org/Newsroom/NewsReleases/2014/P602059; see also SEC, fact sheet on Global Analyst Research Settlements, at www.sec.gov/news/speech/factsheet.htm.

13. Sebastian Mallaby, *More Money Than God: Hedge Funds and the Making of a New Elite* (2011).

14. Gretchen Morgenson, *Is Insider Trading Part of the Fabric?* N.Y. Times, May 20, 2012, at B1.

15. SEC, advisory interpretation of Rule 28(e), at www.sec.gov/rules/interp/2006/34-54165.pdf.

16. For an excellent discussion of fiduciary duties in the context of mutual funds, see Deborah A. DeMott & Mark L. Ascher, Brief for *Amici Curiae* in Support of Petitioners, *Jones et al. v. Harris Associates*, 559 U.S. 335 (2010).

17. SEC, interpretation of this concept, at www.sec.gov/rules/interp/2006/34-54165.pdf; see also SEC, Inspection Report on the Soft Dollar Practices.

18. Disclosure by Investment Advisers Regarding Soft Dollar Practices, Investment Advisers Act, release no. 1469, Feb. 14, 1995 ("Adviser Soft Dollar Release"), 9, at www.sec.gov/rules/final/adopt2.txt.

19. SEC, advisory interpretation of Rule 28(e).
20. SEC, advisory information on the term "best execution," at www.sec.gov/divisions/investment/advoverview.htm.
21. Jonathan Burton, *Pay the Freight*, MarketWatch, Mar. 17, 2004, at www.marketwatch.com/story/soft-dollar-deals-abuse-investors-fund-exec-charges.
22. Lewis, *Flash Boys*.
23. Anthony Trollope, *The Way We Live Now*.
24. SEC, press release announcing charges against a New York-based brokerage firm for a soft-dollar scheme, at www.sec.gov/News/PressRelease/Detail/PressRelease/1370540557746.
25. SEC, Inspection Report on the Soft Dollar Practices.
26. Ian McDonald, *Soft Dollars and 12b-1 Fees: Ideas Whose Time Has Gone*, Wall Street Journal, Mar. 22, 2004, at www.wsj.com/articles/SB107989517277561101.
27. Harold Bradley, Senior VP of American Century Investment Management, written testimony in a hearing regarding the mutual fund industry, 10, at http://financialservices.house.gov/media/pdf/031203hb.pdf.
28. SEC, Inspection Report on the Soft Dollar Practices.
29. Whitney Tilson, *The Disgrace of Soft Dollars*, The Motley Fool, Mar. 19, 2004.
30. Bruce D. Johnsen, *The SEC's 2006 Soft Dollar Guidance: Law & Economics*, 30 Cardozo L. Rev. 1545 (2009).
31. *Bayer v. Beran*, 49 N.Y.S.2d 2 (Sup. Ct. 1944).
32. SEC, Inspection Report on the Soft Dollar Practices.
33. Reuters, *Move by S.E.C. on "Soft" Dollars*, N.Y. Times, Sept. 22, 2005, at C3.
34. SEC, order instituting cease and desist proceedings against J.S. Oliver, at www.sec.gov/litigation/admin/2013/33-9446.pdf.
35. Ari Weinberg, *Finding Transparency in Soft Dollars*, Forbes, May 20, 2004, at www.forbes.com/2004/05/20/cx_aw_0520softdollars.html.
36. Investment Company Institute, *2015 Fact Book*.
37. Investment Counsel Association of America, response to the Investment Company Institute's proposal to eliminate soft dollars, at www.investmentadviser.org/eweb/docs/Publications_News/PressReleases/PressArc/press_030304.pdf.

Chapter 6

1. *Consolidated Fourth Amended Complaint, Bauer-Ramazani v. TIAA-CREF*, No. 1:09-cv-190 (D. Vt. Oct. 12, 2012).
2. Lauren Ingeno, *Class Action Against TIAA-CREF*, Inside Higher Ed., July 12, 2013, at www.insidehighered.com/news/2013/07/12/class-thousands-professors-suing-retirement-provider.
3. Kurt Orzeck, *College Profs Seek Final OK of $19.5M Retirement Row Deal*, Law360, Aug. 19, 2014, at www.law360.com/articles/568985/college-profs-seek-final-ok-of-19-5m-retirement-row-deal.
4. Ingeno, *Class Action Against TIAA-CREF*.
5. Orzeck, *College Profs Seek Final OK*.
6. John C. Bogle, Address to the Philadelphia Federal Reserve Policy Forum on Innovation and Regulation in the Financial Markets, 2007, at www.vanguard.com/bogle_site/sp20071130.html.
7. Investment Company Institute, *2015 Fact Book*, 92, at www.icifactbook.org.
8. See *id.*, at 10.
9. Robert C. Pozen, *The Mutual Fund Business* (2002).
10. Stock prices can be easily gathered from reputable sources; see, *e.g.*, http://markets.wsj.com/; http://finance.yahoo.com/; www.bloomberg.com/markets/world; www.google.com/finance.

11. David Gelles & Conor Dougherty, *Americans' Retirement Funds Increasingly Contain Tech Start-Up Stocks*, N.Y. Times, Mar. 23, 2015, at B1.

12. David Gelles & Michael J. De La Merced, *Rich Start-Ups Go Back for Another Helping*, N.Y. Times, Apr. 14, 2014, at B1.

13. Evelyn M. Rusli & Peter Eavis, *A Festive Atmosphere at Facebook*, N.Y. Times, May 18, 2012, at B1.

14. Andrew Ross Sorkin, *Goldman Deal with Facebook Hits U.S. Snag*, N.Y. Times, Jan. 18, 2011, at A1.

15. Alex Wilmerding, *Term Sheets & Valuations—A Line by Line Look at the Intricacies of Term Sheets & Valuations* (2006).

16. Though real estate holdings are also highly illiquid, mutual funds very rarely make such investments.

17. Henry M. PaulsonJr., *On the Brink: Inside the Race to Stop the Collapse of the Global Financial System* (2013).

18. SEC, press release announcing SEC charges against UBS Global Asset Management, at www.sec.gov/News/PressRelease/Detail/PressRelease/1365171488750; see also SEC, order against UBSGAM, at www.sec.gov/litigation/admin/2012/ia-3356.pdf.

19. SEC, order instituting administrative and cease-and-desist proceedings against UBS Global Asset Management, at www.sec.gov/litigation/admin/2012/ia-3356.pdf.

20. Michael Lewis, *The Big Short: Inside the Doomsday Machine* (2011).

21. SEC, proceedings against UBS Global Asset Management.

22. Paulson, *On the Brink*; Timothy Geithner, *Stress Test: Reflections on Financial Crises* (2014).

23. SEC, In the Matter of Mission Corporation, at www.sec.gov/litigation/opinions/1943/ic-472.pdf.

24. See *id.*

25. See *id.*, at 1140.

26. See *id.*, at 1141.

27. SEC, explanation of Section 2(a)(41)(b), definition of the term "value," at www.sec.gov/divisions/investment/icvaluation.htm.

28. See *id.*

29. SEC, charges against UBS Global Asset Management.

30. SEC, proceedings against UBS Global Asset Management.

31. Paul D. Ellenbogen, *The Larger Implications of the Morgan Keegan Case for Fund Directors and other Fiduciaries*, Morningstar, Nov.–Dec. 2013, at http://corporate.morningstar.com/us/documents/15%28c%29/Ellenbogen-PCRMSI-Morgan-Keegan-Case.pdf.

32. Lewis, *The Big Short*; Andrew Sorkin, *Too Big to Fail: The Inside Story of How Wall Street and Washington Fought to Save the Financial System—and Themselves* (2010).

33. SEC, proceedings against UBS Global Asset Management.

34. See *id.*

35. Parnassus Investments et al., Initial Decision Release No. 131, Administrative Proceeding, File no. 3-9317, 1998 SEC LEXIS 1877, Sept. 3, 1998, at www.sec.gov/litigation/aljdec/id131rgm.txt.

36. *Food Lion, Inc. v. Capital Cities/ABC, Inc.*, 194 F.3d 505, 510 (4th Cir. 1999).

37. Parnassus Investments et al., Initial Decision Release No. 131.

38. SEC, order instituting administrative cease-and-desist proceedings against Morgan Asset Management, at www.sec.gov/litigation/admin/2010/33-9116.pdf.

39. SEC, press release announcing charges against Morgan Keegan and two employees relating to subprime mortgages, at www.sec.gov/news/press/2010/2010-53.htm.

40. SEC, proceedings against Morgan Asset Management.

41. See *id.*, at 4.

42. See *id.*, at 5.

43. See *id.*, at 4.

44. See *id.*

45. See *id.*, at 5.

46. See *id.*

47. See *id.*, at 9.

48. See *id.*

49. See *id.*, at 7.

50. Gretchen Morgenson, *The Debt Crisis, Where It's Least Expected*, N.Y. Times, Dec. 30, 2007, at A31.

51. SEC, press release on the $200M settlement and individual charges, at www.sec.gov/News/PressRelease/Detail/PressRelease/1365171486708.

52. SEC, press release on additional charges against individuals for failures to properly value the assets of a fund, at www.sec.gov/News/PressRelease/Detail/PressRelease/1365171486708.

53. Brandon Garrett, *Too Big to Jail: How Prosecutors Compromise with Corporations* (2014).

54. For a comparison of the Savings and Loan Crisis and the Mortgage Crisis, see Gretchen Morgenson & Louise Story, *A Financial Crisis with Little Guilt*, N.Y. Times, Apr. 14, 2011, at A1, with *Two Financial Crises Compared: The Savings and Loan Debacle and the Mortgage Mess*, N.Y. Times, Apr. 13, 2011, at www.nytimes.com/interactive/2011/04/14/business/20110414-prosecute.html.

55. David A. Kaplan, *Tyco's 'Piggy,' Out of Prison and Living Small*, N.Y. Times, Mar. 2, 2015, at A1.

56. Caryl Churchill, *Serious Money: A City Comedy* (1990).

57. Jed S. Rakoff, *The Financial Crisis: Why Have No High-Level Executives Been Prosecuted?* N.Y. Review of Books, Jan. 9, 2014, at www.nybooks.com/articles/2014/01/09/financial-crisis-why-no-executive-prosecutions/.

58. SEC, order instituting public administrative proceeding and cease-and-desist proceedings against nine individual former fund board members, at www.sec.gov/litigation/admin/2012/ic-30300.pdf.

59. SEC, Charges Eight Mutual Fund Directors for Failure to Properly Oversee Asset Valuation, press release, Dec. 10, 2012, at www.sec.gov/News/PressRelease/Detail/PressRelease/1365171486708.

60. SEC, proceedings against nine individual former fund board members.

61. Andrew Tanzer, *Two Morgan Keegan Funds Crash and Burn*, Kiplinger, Dec. 6, 2007, at www.kiplinger.com/article/investing/T041-C009-S001-two-morgan-keegan-funds-crash-and-burn.html.

62. Paul D. Ellenbogen, *The Larger Implications of the Morgan Keegan Case for Fund Directors and other Fiduciaries*, Morningstar, Nov–Dec 2013, at http://corporate.morningstar.com/us/documents/15%28c%29/Ellenbogen-PCRMSI-Morgan-Keegan-Case.pdf.

63. Tanzer, *Two Morgan Keegan Funds Crash.*

64. Ellenbogen, *The Larger Implications.*

65. SEC, guidance on proper valuation, at www.sec.gov/divisions/investment/icvaluation.htm.

66. See *id.*

67. See *id.*

Chapter 7

1. Robin Sidel & Kate Kelly, *Bear Stearns: A Year Later: From Fabled to Forgotten: Bear's Name, and Culture, Fade Away After J.P. Morgan's Fire Sale Deal*, Wall Street Journal, Mar. 14, 2009, at B1.

2. SEC, press release regarding the settlement of fraud charges against Bear Stearns for late trading and market timing violations, at www.sec.gov/news/press/2006-38.htm.

3. See *id.*

4. Charles Dickens, *Martin Chuzzlewit.*

5. Eric Zitzewitz, *How Widespread Is Late Trading in Mutual Funds?* Stanford Graduate School of Business Research Paper No. 1817, Sept. 2003, at www.dartmouth.edu/~ericz/latetrading.pdf.

6. 17 C.F.R. § 270.22c-1 (2005).

7. Investment Company Act of 1940, §§ 2(a)(41), 22(c)(1); 17 C.F.R. §§ 270.2a-4, 270.22c-1.

8. Certainly any changes in the pricing of securities occurring at the level of microseconds might also be beyond the power of simple processors today and may account for why ETFs permit redemptions-in-kind rather than in cash.

9. SEC, press release on forward pricing, at www.sec.gov/rules/proposed/ic-26288.htm.

10. SEC, explanation of how NAV is calculated, at www.sec.gov/answers/nav.htm.

11. Depository Trust & Clearing Corporation, explanation of the Fund/SERV system, at www.dtcc.com/investment-product-services/wealth-management-services/fund-serv.aspx.

12. See *id.*

13. In the Matter of Bear, Stearns & Co., Inc., Order Instituting Administrative and Cease-and-Desist Proceedings, Release No. 33-8668, Mar. 16, 2006, at www.sec.gov/litigation/admin/33-8668.pdf.

14. See *id.*

15. SEC, settlement of fraud charges against Bear Stearns.

16. SEC, order associated with Bear Stearns press release (n.417), at www.sec.gov/litigation/admin/33-8668.pdf.

17. New York State Attorney General, press release, Sept. 3, 2003, at www.ag.ny.gov/press-release/state-investigation-reveals-mutual-fund-fraud.

18. SEC, order associated with Bear Stearns.

19. Peter Elkind, *The Secrets of Eddie Stern: If You Think You Know How Bad the Mutual Fund Scandal Is, You're Wrong. It's Worse,* Fortune, Apr. 19, 2004, at http://archive.fortune.com/magazines/fortune/fortune_archive/2004/04/19/367348/index.htm.

20. SEC, opinion and description of sticky assets in regard to settlement of charges with mutual fund complexes, press release, at www.sec.gov/news/press/2004-143.htm.

21. See the complaint alleging this *quid pro quo,* at www.ag.ny.gov/sites/default/files/press-releases/archived/canary_complaint.pdf.

22. Elkind, *The Secrets of Eddie Stern.*

23. Complaint alleging *quid pro quo,* 6.

24. Elkind, *The Secrets of Eddie Stern.*

25. Complaint alleging *quid pro quo.*

26. See *id.*

27. See the late trading of Federated, detailed in Tom Lauricella, *Hostilities, Disclosures in Mutual-Fund Cases – Federated Investors Acknowledges Its Workers Allowed 15 Instances of Late Trading by a Hedge Fund,* Wall Street Journal, Nov. 26, 2003, at C1; see additional actions of Geek Securities, at www.sec.gov/litigation/litreleases/lr18738.htm.

28. Elkind, *The Secrets of Eddie Stern.*

Chapter 8

1. Randy Diamond, *One-Time Powerhouse Strong Financial Down to a Staff of 1,* 40 Pensions & Investments 4 (Aug. 6, 2012).

2. Carrie Antlfinger, *Richard Strong: Driven, Detail-Oriented, Volatile,* Journal Times, Nov. 12, 2003, at http://journaltimes.com/news/state-and-regional/richard-strong-driven-detail-oriented-volatile/article_398bde69-73a0-528d-b069-d9891cd724e2.html.

3. Tamar Frankel & Lawrence Cunningham, *The Mysterious Ways of Mutual Funds: Market Timing,* 25 Ann. Rev. Banking & Fin. L. 235 (2006).

4. Office of New York State Attorney General, press release, Sept. 3, 2003, at www.ag.ny.gov/press-release/state-investigation-reveals-mutual-fund-fraud.

5. Federal Reserve, statistics on investing, at www.federalreserve.gov/releases/z1/Current/z1.pdf.

6. 17 C.F.R. § 270.22c-1 (2005).

7. Ari Weinberg, *Eliot Spitzer Finds His Canary*, Forbes, Sept. 3, 2003, at www.forbes.com/2003/09/03/cx_aw_0903spitzer.html.

8. NASDAQ, definition of stale pricing, at www.nasdaq.com/investing/glossary/s/stale-price-arbitrage.

9. Japan Exchange Group, FAQ's for the Tokyo Stock Exchange, in English, at www.jpx.co.jp/english/faq/others_general.html#others-01.

10. David Sanger & Matt Wald, *Radioactive Releases in Japan Could Last Months, Experts Say*, N.Y. Times, Mar. 14, 2011, at A1.

11. Investment Company Institute, *Introduction to Fair Valuation*, at www.ici.org/pdf/05_fair_valuation_intro.pdf.

12. 17 C.F.R. § 270.2a-7 (2005).

13. Eric Zitzewitz, *Who Cares About Shareholders? Arbitrage-Proofing Mutual Funds*, 19 J. L. Econ. & Org. 245 (2002).

14. Christine Benz & Jason Stipp, *Do Foreign Stocks Really Diversify?* Morningstar, May 2015, at www.morningstar.com/cover/videocenter.aspx?id=697324.

15. SEC, analysis of the costs and losses associated with various types of market timing, at www.sec.gov/rules/final/33-8408.htm.

16. Ty Bernicke, *The Real Cost of Owning a Mutual Fund*, Forbes, Apr. 4, 2011, at www.forbes.com/2011/04/04/real-cost-mutual-fund-taxes-fees-retirement-bernicke.html.

17. Sebastian Mallaby, *More Money Than God: Hedge Funds and the Making of a New Elite* (2010).

18. Patrick E. McCabe, *The Economics of the Mutual Fund Trading Scandal*, report of Board of Governors of the Federal Reserve System, Dec. 9, 2008, at www.federalreserve.gov/pubs/feds/2009/200906/200906pap.pdf.

19. SEC, costs and losses associated with market timing.

20. Mallaby, *More Money Than God.*

21. SEC, costs and losses associated with market timing.

22. Disclosure Regarding Market-timing and Selective Disclosure of Portfolio Holdings, Investment Company Act, release no. 26,418, 69 Fed. Reg. 22,300, 22,301-05 (Apr. 23, 2004).

23. 17 C.F.R. § 240.10b5-1 (2008); see also SEC, release on anti-market-timing clauses in prospectuses of Evergreen Investment Management Company and Affiliates, at www.sec.gov/news/press/2007/2007-186.htm, and American Enterprise Financial Corporation, at www.sec.gov/news/press/2005-169.htm.

24. Randall Smith, *Of Good Timing and Bad Timing and Prof. Zitzewitz*, Wall Street Journal, Dec. 9, 2003, at C1.

25. SEC, opinion and description of sticky assets regarding the settlement of charges with mutual fund complexes, press release, at www.sec.gov/news/press/2004-143.htm.

26. Peter Elkind, *The Secrets of Eddie Stern: If You Think You Know How Bad the Mutual Fund Scandal Is, You're Wrong. It's Worse*, Fortune, Apr. 19, 2004, at http://archive.fortune.com/magazines/fortune/fortune_archive/2004/04/19/367348/index.htm.

27. SEC, explanation of late trading as it relates to market timing, as well as its effect on other investors, at www.sec.gov/answers/latetrading.htm.

28. Stephen Labaton, *A Push to Fix the Fix on Wall Street*, N.Y. Times, Dec. 17, 2006, Section 4 (Sunday Review), at 4.

29. SEC, press release detailing Putnam agreeing to pay settlement to resolve SEC Enforcement Action, at www.sec.gov/news/press/2004-49.htm.

30. SEC, cease-and-desist proceedings against Strong Capital Management, at www.sec.gov/litigation/admin/34-49741.htm.

31. SEC, press release regarding Richard Strong's ban from the mutual fund industry, at www. sec.gov/news/press/2004-69.htm.

Chapter 9

1. *Superman III*, distributed by Warner Bros., 1983.
2. · Selective Disclosure and Insider Trading, Investment Company Act, release no. 24,599, 65 Fed. Reg. 51,716, 51,716 (Aug. 24, 2000).
3. 17 C.F.R. § 274.11A.
4. SEC, Form N-1A, at www.sec.gov/about/forms/formn-1a.pdf.
5. David M. Bovi, *Rule 10b-5 Liability for Front-Running: Adding A New Dimension to the "Money Game,"* 7 St. Thomas L. Rev. 103 (1994).
6. Sebastian Mallaby, *More Money Than God: Hedge Funds and the Making of a New Elite* (2010).
7. · Floyd Norris, *Pile of Pennies Is Adding up to a Scandal in Mutual Funds*, N.Y. Times, Nov. 1, 2003, at C1.
8. Executive Office of the President, *The Effects of Conflicted Investment Advice on Retirement Savings*, Feb. 2015, at www.whitehouse.gov/sites/default/files/docs/cea_coi_report_final.pdf.
9. *Office Space*, distributed by 20th Century Fox, 1999.
10. SEC, press release on selective disclosure and insider trading, at www.sec.gov/rules/final/ 33-7881.htm.
11. Orin S. Kramer, *Hidden Issues in Mutual Fund Governance*, Columbia Law School Online, at www.law.columbia.edu/center_program/corp_gov/corp_govwrit.
12. SEC, selective disclosure and insider trading, executive summary.
13. SEC, selective disclosure and insider trading, final ruling.
14. More precisely, Regulation FD applies to closed-end funds (a species of investment that we have not discussed in this book) but not to open-end funds (which have been our focus throughout this book); see www.sec.gov/rules/final/33-7881.htm.
15. John C. CoffeeJr., *The Mutual Funds Scandals: What Should the SEC Do?* Columbia Law School Online, at www.law.columbia.edu/center_program/corp_gov/corp_govwrit.
16. See *id.*
17. SEC, recommendations regarding market timing and selective disclosure of portfolio holdings, at www.sec.gov/rules/final/33-8408.htm.
18. Peter Elkind, *The Secrets of Eddie Stern: If You Think You Know How Bad the Mutual Fund Scandal Is, You're Wrong. It's Worse*, Fortune, Apr. 19, 2004, at http://archive.fortune.com/ magazines/fortune/fortune_archive/2004/04/19/367348/index.htm.

Chapter 10

1. Frontline, 401(k)s: The New Retirement Plan, For Better or Worse, PBS broadcast, report on the 401(k) account, at www.pbs.org/wgbh/pages/frontline/retirement/world/401k. html.
2. Paul Katzeff, *Getting Started In 401(k) Investing* (2000).
3. U.S. Department of Labor, *Pension Plan Bulletin*, Sept. 2014, at www.dol.gov/ebsa/pdf/ 2011pensionplanbulletin.pdf; see also Federal Reserve, statistics on 401(k) investing, at www.federalreserve.gov/releases/z1/Current/z1.pdf.
4. Jennifer S. Taub, *Able But Not Willing: The Failure of Mutual Fund Advisers to Advocate for Shareholders' Rights*, 34 J. Corp. L. 843; see also Lucian A. Bebchuk, *The Myth of the Shareholder Franchise*, 93 Va. L. Rev. 675 (2007).

5. Rick Baert, *DC Plans Snag a Bigger Piece of the Pie*, 41 Pensions & Investments 1 (Feb. 4, 2013); see also Russell Investments, *Seven Attributes of an Excellent Defined Contribution Plan*, Feb. 2012, at 2 (average defined contribution plan offers 22 investment options).

6. Deloitte Consulting LLC, *Annual 401(k) Benchmarking Survey*, 2011, at 49, fig.7.2.

7. Josh Cohen & Ben Jones, *Seven Attributes of an Excellent Defined Contribution Plan*, Russell Investments Newsletter, at https://www.asppa.org/Resources/Publications/Plan-Consultant-Online/PC-Mag-Article/ArticleID/5144; but see John Rekenthaler, *Are 401(k) Funds Second-Rate?* Morningstar Rekenthaler Report, July 20, 2014, at www.morningstar.com/advisor/t/94740162/are-401-k-funds-second-rate.htm.

8. Complaint, *Bilewicz v. FMR LLC*, at http://blog.fraplantools.com/wp-content/uploads/2013/09/Bilewicz-v.-FMR-LLC-13-10636-Doc.-34-Proposed-Amended-Complaint.pdf.

9. See *id.*

10. Elisabeth Bumiller, *Public Lives: A Cautious Rise to a Top Name in Fashion*, N.Y. Times, Mar. 12, 1999, at www.nytimes.com/1999/03/12/nyregion/public-lives-a-cautious-rise-to-a-top-name-in-fashion.html.

11. Tom Ashbrook, *As Employment Growth Slows, Where are American Jobs?* On Point, at http://onpoint.wbur.org/2015/04/07/job-growth-unemployment-wage-growth.

12. Investment Company Institute, *2015 Fact Book*, at www.icifactbook.org.

13. GAO, *Individual Retirement Accounts: IRS Could Bolster Enforcement on Multimillion Dollar Accounts But More from Congress Is Needed*, Oct. 2014, at www.gao.gov/assets/670/666595.pdf.

14. Anne Tucker, *The Citizen Shareholder: Modernizing the Agency Paradigm to Reflect How and Why a Majority of Americans Invest in the Market*, 35 Seattle L. Rev. 1299 (2012).

15. 15 U.S.C. §§ 80b-1, et seq. (2006).

16. Financial Industry Regulatory Authority states that it is "dedicated to investor protection and market integrity through effective and efficient regulation of the securities industry"; at https://www.finra.org/about.

17. *Donovan v. Bierwirth*, 680 F.2d 263, 272 (2d Cir. 1982).

18. *Meinhard v. Salmon*, 249 N.Y. 458, 464, 164 N.E. 545 (1928).

19. FINRA, explanation of the suitability rule, at www.finra.org/investors/suitability-what-investors-need-know.

20. Tara Siegel Bernard, *U.S. Plans Stiffer Rules Protecting Retiree Cash*, N.Y. Times, Apr. 15, 2015, at B1.

21. Arthur B. Laby, *Fiduciary Obligations of Broker-Dealers and Investment Advisers*, 55 Villanova L. Rev. 701 (2010).

22. Tara Siegel Bernard, *Seeking to Toughen the Rules for Brokers*, N.Y. Times, Nov. 2, 2013, at B1.

23. Executive Office of the President, *The Effects of Conflicted Investment Advice on Retirement Savings*, Feb. 2015, at www.whitehouse.gov/sites/default/files/docs/cea_coi_report_final.pdf.

24. Justin Baer & Andrew Ackerman, *SEC Head: Raise the Bar for Advisers*, Wall Street Journal, Mar. 18, 2015, at C5.

25. Bernard, *U.S. Plans Stiffer Rules.*

26. Sebastian Mallaby, *More Money Than God: Hedge Funds and the Making of a New Elite* (2010).

27. 29 U.S.C. Ch. 18 (2012).

28. ERISA § 404(a)(1)(B), 29 U.S.C. § 1104 (2012).

29. Ron Lieber, *Revealing Hidden Costs of Your 401(k)*, N.Y. Times, June 10, 2011, at B1.

30. Richard H. Thaler & Cass Sunstein, *Nudge: Improving Decisions About Health, Wealth, and Happiness* (2009).

31. *Superman III*, distributed by Warner Bros., 1983.

32. Thaler & Sunstein, *Nudge.*

33. *Braden v. Wal-Mart Stores, Inc.*, 588 F.3d 585, 589 (8th Cir. 2009).

34. *Jones v. Harris Associates L.P.*, 527 F.3d 627, 629 (7th Cir. 2008), vacated and remanded, 559 U.S. 335, 130 S. Ct. 1418, 176 L. Ed. 2d 265 (2010); see Stephen Choi & Marcel Kahan, *The Market Penalty for Mutual Fund Scandals*, 87 B. U. L. Rev 1021 (2007).

35. Ian Ayres & Quinn Curtis, *Beyond Diversification: The Pervasive Problem of Excessive Fees and "Dominated Funds" in 401(k) Plans*, 124 Yale L. J. 1476 (2015).
36. See *id.*, at 1481.
37. W. Scott Simon, *A Closer Look at the Braden v. Wal-Mart Case*, Morningstar, Feb. 2, 2012, at www.morningstar.com/advisor/t/51507864/a-closer-look-at-the-braden-v-wal-mart-case.htm.
38. Mercer Bullard, *The Social Costs of Choice, Free Market Ideology and the Empirical Consequences of the 401(k) Plan Large Menu Defense*, 20 Conn. Ins. L.J. 335 (2014).
39. Sheena S. Iyengar & Wei Jiang, *The Psychological Costs of Ever Increasing Choice: A Fallback to the Sure Bet*, Working Paper, Columbia University, April 2005, at http://cbdr.cmu.edu/seminar/Iyengar.pdf.
40. Jane Meacham, *Fidelity Settles 401(k) Suit with Employees for $12 Million*, Thompson Information Services, at http://smarthr.blogs.thompson.com/2014/08/15/fidelity-settles-401k-suit-with-employees-for-12-million/.

Chapter 11

1. Andrew Ross Sorkin, *Too Big to Fail: The Inside Story of How Wall Street and Washington Fought to Save the Financial System—and Themselves* (2010); Timothy Geithner, *Stress Test: Reflections on Financial Crises* (2014); Henry Paulson, *On the Brink: Inside the Race to Stop the Collapse of the Global Financial System* (2013); Bethany McLean & Joe Nocera, *All the Devils Are Here: The Hidden History of the Financial Crisis* (2010).
2. Gregory Zuckerman, *The Greatest Trade Ever: The Behind-the-Scenes Story of How John Paulson Defied Wall Street and Made Financial History* (2010).
3. Michael Lewis, *The Big Short: Inside the Doomsday Machine* (2011).
4. See, *e.g.*, Investment Company Institute, *The Differences Between Mutual Funds and Hedge Funds*, Apr. 2007, at www.ici.org/files/faqs_hedge.
5. Tim Gray, *Target-Date Funds Can Pose Complexities*, N.Y. Times, Jan. 11, 2015, at B11.
6. Abe Ashton, *Is the 'Rule of 100' Broken?* Money, Jan. 13, 2015, at http://time.com/money/content-from/impact-partnership/s101283_0/Is-the-Rule-of-100-Broken/?ntv_a=o4sBA2SEBASVILA.
7. Investment Company Institute, *2015 Fact Book*, at www.icifactbook.org; see also SEC, release and proposed rule regarding target-date retirement fund names and marketing, at www.sec.gov/rules/proposed/2010/33-9126.pdf.
8. Brad M. Barber & Terrance Odean, *Trading is Hazardous to Your Wealth: The Common Stock Investment Performance of Individual Investors*, 2 LV J. Fin. 773 (April 2000); David Segal, *Day Traders 2.0: Wired, Angry and Loving It*, N.Y. Times, Mar. 28, 2010, at B1.
9. Investment Company Institute, *2015 Fact Book*; see also Morningstar's 2014 report on target-date funds and their relevant statistics, at http://corporate.morningstar.com/us/documents/MethodologyDocuments/MethodologyPapers/2014-Target-Date-Series-Research-Paper.pdf.
10. Vanguard, Target Retirement 2055 Fund information, at https://personal.vanguard.com/us/funds/snapshot?FundId=1487&FundIntExt=INT.
11. SEC, target-date retirement fund names and marketing.
12. SEC, breakdown of target-date funds, at www.sec.gov/investor/alerts/tdf.htm; as stated, "Often a target date fund invests in other mutual funds, and fees may be charged by both the target date fund and the other funds."
13. See Vanguard fund's breakdown and prospectus documents, at ttps://personal.vanguard.com/us/funds/snapshot?FundId=1487&FundIntExt=INT.
14. See *id.*
15. Department of Labor, press release about the virtues of target-date funds as QDIA, at www.dol.gov/ebsa/newsroom/fstargetdatefunddisclosures.html.

16. Vanguard, research report on the effects of the Department of Labor's endorsement of target-date funds as QDIAs, at https://advisors.vanguard.com/iwe/pdf/CRRNTDF. pdf.

17. Ron Lieber, *Target-Date Funds Not Equally Safe*, N.Y. Times, June 16, 2012, at B1.

18. Fran Hawthorne, *In Target-Date Funds, Hidden Homework*, N.Y. Times, Oct. 15, 2009, at F8.

19. See *id.*

20. Social Security Administration, Actuarial life table, 2011, at www.ssa.gov/oact/STATS/ table4c6.html.

21. Tom Idzorek, *Ibbotson's Reaction to the Joint SEC DOL Target-Date Fund Hearing*, Morningstar, at http://corporate.morningstar.com/us/documents/MediaMentions/IbbotsonSEC_ DOJ_Target-DateHearingCommentary.pdf.

22. David Grim, deputy director of investment management, SEC, speech and remarks about the solicitation of commentary regarding standardized glide paths, at www.sec.gov/ News/Speech/Detail/Speech/1370541453144.

23. Investment Company Institute, *2009 Fact Book*, at www.ici.org/pdf/2009_factbook.pdf.

24. Vanguard, study of target-date funds and their implications, at https://personal.vanguard. com/pdf/icrtdf.pdf.

25. GMO, *The Road Less Traveled: Minimizing Shortfall and Dynamically Allocating in DC Plans*, white paper, at www.gmo.com/docs/default-source/research-and-commentary/strate-gies/asset-allocation/the-road-less-traveled-minimizing-shortfall-and-dynamically-allocating-in-dc-plans.pdf?sfvrsn=0.

26. Nassim Nicholas Taleb, *The Black Swan: The Impact of the Highly Improbable* (2007).

27. Ronco Manual, 4, at www.ronco.com/manuals/3000-compact-black-rotisserie-oven.pdf.

Chapter 12

1. Richard A. Ferri, *The ETF Book: All You Need to Know About Exchange-Traded Funds* (2009).

2. Robert C. Pozen, *The Mutual Fund Business* (2002).

3. Interview with John C. Bogle by IndexUniverse.com, Sept. 2011, at www.etf.com/sec-tions/features/9947-bogle-etf-trading-has-no-social-value.html.

4. Ian Salisbury, *ETFs Make Inroads with 401(k) Investors*, Wall Street Journal, Jan. 13, 2010, at C15.

5. David J. Abner, *The ETF Handbook: How to Value and Trade Exchange Traded Funds* (2010).

6. Gary L. Gastineau, *The Exchange-Traded Funds Manual* (2010).

7. SPDR S&P 500 ETF Trust Prospectus, at www.spdrs.com/library-content/public/ SPDR_500%20TRUST_PROSPECTUS.pdf.

8. Gastineau, *Exchange-Traded Funds Manual*.

9. Sebastian Mallaby, *More Money Than God: Hedge Funds and the Making of a New Elite* (2011).

10. Michael Lewis, *Flash Boys* (2014).

11. SEC, notice of an application for exemptive release and response regarding tracking error in the ETF context, at www.sec.gov/rules/ic/2014/ic-31300.pdf.

12. Investment Company Institute, *2015 Fact Book*, at www.icifactbook.org.

13. Interview with Jack Bogle, Morningstar, Oct. 2010, at www.morningstar.com/cover/vid-eoCenter.aspx?id=355645.

14. Mark Hulbert, *Are ETFs Really Cheaper Than Open-End Index Funds?* Wall Street Journal, Mar. 29, 2014, at B7.

15. Lawrence Carrel, *ETFs for the Long Run: What They Are, How They Work* (2008).

16. For a list of the biggest U.S. ETFs as of May 2015, see www.etf.com/sections/top-10-biggest-etfs/big-outflows-yank-gld-top-10-etf-list.

17. Landon Thomas, Jr., *BlackRock's New Breed of Exchange-Traded Fund Prizes Stability Over Swagger*, N.Y. Times, Mar. 19, 2015, at B1.

18. See *id.*

19. Tim Gray, *Guru Funds, Mimicking the Smart Money*, N.Y. Times, Jan. 12, 2014, at B11.
20. Conrad De Aenlle, *Active E.T.F.'s, Still Trying to Make Waves*, N.Y. Times, Oct. 6, 2013, at B23.
21. Andrew Ross Sorkin, *Volatility, Thy Name is E.T.F.*, N.Y. Times, Oct. 11, 2011, at B1.
22. SEC, application for exemptive release and response regarding tracking error.
23. Daisy Maxey, *SEC Rejects Precidian Over ETF Plan Again*, Wall Street Journal, July 28, 2015, at C3.
24. De Aenlle, *Active E.T.F.'s*.
25. Deborah Fuhr, *Tracking the Phenomenal Growth of the ETF Market*, Pensions & Investments, Oct. 28, 2013, at www.pionline.com/article/20131028/PRINT/310289985/tracking-the-phenomenal-growth-of-the-etf-market.

Chapter 13

1. See, *e.g.*, Valuation of Debt Instruments and Computation of Current Price by Certain Open-End Investment Companies (Money Market Funds), 48 Fed. Reg. 32,555, July 18, 1983, adopting reforms that permitted money market funds to move from floating to fixed NAVs.
2. Investment Company Institute, *2015 Fact Book*, at www.icifactbook.org.
3. David Zaring, *Administration by Treasury*, 95 Minn. L. Rev. 187 (2010).
4. Investment Company Institute, *2015 Fact Book*.
5. But see Eric A. Posner & E. Glen Weyl, *An FDA for Financial Innovation: Applying the Insurable Interest Doctrine to Twenty-First-Century Financial Markets*, 107 Nw. U. L. Rev. 1307 (2013).
6. Henry M. Paulson Jr., *On the Brink*, at 228–37 (2010): "I feared the start of a run on the $3.5 trillion industry"; see also Andrew Ross Sorkin, *Too Big to Fail: The Inside Story of How Wall Street and Washington Fought to Save the Financial System—and Themselves*, at 409 (2009), describing Timothy Geithner as "most anxious about the latest shocking development," the breaking of the buck in the Reserve Primary Fund.
7. Jerry W. Markham, *A Financial History of the United States*, at 6 (2011).
8. R. Alton Gilbert, *Requiem for Regulation Q: What It Did and Why It Passed Away*, 68 Fed. Res. Bank St. Louis Rev. 22 (1986).
9. 17 C.F.R. § 270.2a-7 (2005).
10. In 1994, the Community Bankers U.S. Government Fund—an institutional fund—became the first money market fund to break the buck, falling to ninety-six cents per share. See David Evans, *Unsafe Havens*, Bloomberg Markets, broadcast, Oct. 2007, at bloomberg.com/apps/news?pid=nw&pname=mm_ 1007_story2.html.
11. Sorkin, *Too Big to Fail*.
12. Jeffrey N. Gordon & Christopher M. Gandia, *Money Market Funds Run Risk: Will Floating Net Asset Value Fix the Problem?*, 2014 Colum. Bus. L. Rev. 313 (2014).
13. The Reserve, press release, Sept. 16, 2008: "[T]he NAV of the Primary Fund, effective as of 4:00PM, is $0.97 per share," at https://fraser.stlouisfed.org/scribd/?title_id=5092&filepath=/docs/historical/fct/reservefund_ pressrelease_ 20080916.pdf#scribd-open.
14. According to Sam Mamudi and Jonathan Burton, "The size and speed of the withdrawals was stunning. At 3 p.m. on Tuesday, Primary Fund's assets stood at $23 billion, a $40 billion hit from the $62.6 billion in the fund on Friday," in *Money Market Breaks the Buck, Freezes Redemptions*, MarketWatch, Sept. 17, 2008, at www.marketwatch.com/story/money-market-fund-breaks-the-buck-freezes-redemptions.
15. *S.E.C. Plan to Distribute Money Fund Is Accepted*, N.Y. Times, Nov. 25, 2009, at B3: "The estimated $3.5 billion remaining assets of the Reserve Primary Fund should be distributed on a prorated basis to shareholders, a federal judge ruled on Wednesday in response to lawsuits filed after the fund's value dropped below $1 a share in September 2008. . . . In

a ruling that largely accepts a distribution plan proposed by the Securities and Exchange Commission, the judge said that regulators and the fund's trustees estimated that investors would recover 99 cents a share if remaining assets were distributed pro rata."

16. U.S. Department of the Treasury, *Treasury Announces Guaranty Program for Money Market Funds*, press release announcing the authorization of "the assets of the Exchange Stabilization Fund for up to $50 billion to guarantee" money market funds, Sept. 19, 2008, at www.ustreas.gov/press/releases/hp1147.htm.

17. Money Market Fund Reform, Investment Company Act release no. 29,132, Feb. 23, 2010.

18. Some commentators had complained about the rating agencies long before the 2008 crisis. See, *e.g.*, Frank Partnoy, *The Siskel & Ebert of Financial Markets?: Two Thumbs Down for the Credit Rating Agencies*,77 Wash. U. L.Q. 619 (1999).

Chapter 14

1. Barbara Black, *Behavioral Economics and Investor Protection: Reasonable Investors, Efficient Markets*, 44 Loy. U. Chi. L.J. 1493 (2013).

2. Natalya Shnitser, *Funding Discipline for U.S. Public Pension Plans: An Empirical Analysis of Institutional Design*, 100 Iowa L. Rev. 663 (2015).

3. Howell E. Jackson, *To What Extent Should Individual Investors Rely on the Mechanisms of Market Efficiency: A Preliminary Investigation of Dispersion in Investor Returns*, 28 J. Corp. L. 671, 683–86 (2003).

4. John C. Bogle, *The Battle for the Soul of Capitalism*, at 191–214 (2005).

5. See, *e.g.*, Leo Lionni, *Frederick* (1967).

6. Henry T. C. Hu, *Illiteracy & Intervention: Wholesale Derivatives, Retail Mutual Funds, and the Matter of Asset Class*, 84 Geo. L.J. 2319 (1996).

7. Cf. Dirk Zetzsche, *The Need for Regulating Income Trusts: A Bubble Theory*, 63 U. T. Fac. L. Rev. 45 (2005).

8. James A. Fanto, *We're All Capitalists Now: The Importance, Nature, Provision & Regulation of Investor Education*, 49 Case W. Res. L. Rev. 105 (1998).

9. Richard H. Thaler, *Financial Literacy, Beyond the Classroom*, N.Y. Times, Oct. 6, 2013, at B16.

10. See *id.*

11. See *id.*

12. Justin Wolfers, *A Better Government, One Tweak at a Time*, N.Y. Times, Sept. 27, 2015, at B6; Wolfers advocates for the government's greater use of A/B testing to "keep what works, and discard what doesn't."

13. Andrew Ross Sorkin, *Too Big to Fail* (2009).

14. Teresa Ghilarducci & Hamilton E. James, *A Smarter Plan to Make Retirement Savings Last*, N.Y. Times, Jan. 2, 2016, at A15.

15. Thrift Savings Plan, Financial Statements, Dec. 31, 2013, at www.tsp.gov/PDF/forms-pubs/financial-stmt.pdf.

16. John Hechinger, *Brokers Lure Soldiers out of Low-Fee Federal Retirement Plan*, Bloomberg Business, Aug. 11, 2014, at www.bloomberg.com/news/articles/2014-08-12/brokers-lure-soldiers-out-of-low-fee-federal-retirement-plan.

17. Employees of small businesses and the self-employed can, however, invest in a Simplified Employee Pension Individual Retirement Arrangement (SEP-IRA), which is a variation of the more common IRA option. See Internal Revenue Service, *Who Can Participate in a SEP or SARSEP Plan?*, Oct. 28, 2015, at www.irs.gov/Retirement-Plans/Plan-Participant,-Employee/Who-Can-Participate-in-a-SEP-or-SARSEP-Plan.

18. Josh Hicks, *Rubio, Retirement Benefits and a Thrift Savings Plan for All Americans*, Washington Post, May 14, 2014, at www.washingtonpost.com/news/federal-eye/wp/2014/05/14/rubio-retirement-benefits-and-a-thrift-savings-plan-for-all-americans/.

19. Donald C. Langevoort, *Private Litigation to Enforce Fiduciary Duties in Mutual Funds: Derivative Suits, Disinterested Directors and the Ideology of Investor Sovereignty*, 83 Wash. U. L. Q. 1017 (2005).

20. John Morley & Quinn Curtis, *An Empirical Study of Mutual Fund Excessive Fee Litigation: Do the Merits Matter?*, 30 J. L. Econ. & Org. 275 (2014).

21. See *id.*

22. H. Norman Knickle, *The Mutual Fund's Section 15(c) Process: Jones v. Harris, The SEC, and Fiduciary Duties of Directors*, 31 Rev. Banking & Fin. L. 265 (2011).

23. U.S. Supreme Court, oral argument of *Jones et al. v. Harris Associates*, transcript, 20–22, at www.supremecourt.gov/oral_arguments/argument_transcripts/08-586.pdf.

24. According to Robert Khuzami, director, SEC Division of Enforcement, "These analytics are expected to result in examinations and investigations of investment advisers and their boards of directors concerning duties under the Investment Company Act," testimony, 2010, at www.sec.gov/news/testimony/2010/ts092210rk.htm.

25. According to Morley & Curtis, *An Empirical Study of Mutual Fund Excessive Fee Litigation*, "The SEC has never brought an excessive fee suit."

26. SEC, *Charges Investment Adviser with Improperly Using Mutual Fund Assets to Pay Distribution Fees*, press release, Sept. 21, 2015, www.sec.gov/news/pressrelease/2015-198.html.

27. Peter Coy, *Afghanistan Has Cost the U.S. More Than the Marshall Plan*, Bloomberg Business, July 31, 2014, at www.bloomberg.com/bw/articles/2014-07-31/afghanistan-has-cost-the-u-dot-s-dot-more-than-the-marshall-plan.

SELECTED BIBLIOGRAPHY

Blinder, Alan. *After the Music Stopped: The Financial Crisis, the Response, and the Work Ahead* (2013).

Bogle, John. *The Battle for the Soul of Capitalism* (2005).

Bogle, John. *Common Sense on Mutual Funds* (2009).

Bogle, John. *Don't Count on It!: Reflections on Investment Illusions, Capitalism, "Mutual" Funds, Indexing, Entrepreneurship, Idealism, and Heroes* (2010).

Ellis, Charles, Alicia Munnell, & Andrew Eschtruth. *Falling Short: The Coming Retirement Crisis and What to Do About It* (2014).

Fink, Matthew. *The Rise of Mutual Funds: An Insider's View* (2008).

Garrett, Brandon. *Too Big to Jail: How Prosecutors Compromise with Corporations* (2014).

Geithner, Timothy. *Stress Test: Reflections on Financial Crises* (2014).

Investment Company Institute. *2015 Fact Book: A Review of Trends and Activities in the U.S. Investment Company Industry*, 55th ed. (2015).

Kahneman, Daniel. *Thinking, Fast and Slow* (2013).

Lanchester, John. *I.O.U.: Why Everyone Owes Everyone and No One Can Pay* (2010).

Lewis, Michael. *The Big Short: Inside the Doomsday Machine* (2011).

Lewis, Michael. *Flash Boys* (2014).

Lewis, Michael. *Liar's Poker* (2010).

Lowenstein, Louis. *The Investor's Dilemma: How Mutual Funds Are Betraying Your Trust and What To Do About It* (2008).

Lowenstein, Roger. *Origins of the Crash: The Great Bubble and Its Undoing* (2004).

Lowenstein, Roger. *When Genius Failed: The Rise and Fall of Long-Term Capital Management* (2001).

Mallaby, Sebastian. *More Money Than God: Hedge Funds and the Making of a New Elite* (2011).

McLean, Bethany, & Peter Elkind. *The Smartest Guys in the Room: The Amazing Rise and Scandalous Fall of Enron* (2003).

McLean, Bethany, & Joe Nocera. *All the Devils Are Here: The Hidden History of the Financial Crisis* (2010).

Olen, Helaine. *Pound Foolish: Exposing the Dark Side of the Personal Finance Industry* (2012).

Paulson Jr., Henry M. *On the Brink: Inside the Race to Stop the Collapse of the Global Financial System* (2013).

Pew Center on the States. *The Trillion Dollar Gap: Underfunded State Retirement Systems and the Road to Reform* (2010).

Pew Center on the States. *The Widening Gap: The Great Recession's Impact on State Pension and Retiree Health Costs* (2011).

Piketty, Thomas. *Capital in the Twenty-First Century* (2014).

Posner, Richard. *Economic Analysis of Law*, 9th ed. (2014).

Posner, Richard. *The Economics of Justice* (1983).

Pozen, Robert C. *The Mutual Fund Business* (2002).

Sorkin, Andrew Ross. *Too Big to Fail: The Inside Story of How Wall Street and Washington Fought to Save the Financial System—and Themselves* (2010).

Swensen, David. *Unconventional Success: A Fundamental Approach to Personal Investment* (2005).

Thaler, Richard H. *Misbehaving: The Making of Behavioral Economics* (2015).

Thaler, Richard H., & Cass Sunstein. *Nudge: Improving Decisions about Health, Wealth, and Happiness* (2009).

Zukerman, Gregory. *The Greatest Trade Ever: The Behind-the-Scenes Story of How John Paulson Defied Wall Street and Made Financial History* (2010).

INDEX